Political Discourse Analysis

Political Discourse Analysis

Legitimisation Strategies in Crisis and Conflict

EDITED BY ROBERT BUTLER

EDINBURGH
University Press

Edinburgh University Press is one of the leading university presses in the UK. We publish academic books and journals in our selected subject areas across the humanities and social sciences, combining cutting-edge scholarship with high editorial and production values to produce academic works of lasting importance. For more information visit our website: edinburghuniversitypress.com

© editorial matter and organisation Robert Butler, 2024, 2025
© the chapters their several authors, 2024, 2025

Edinburgh University Press Ltd
13 Infirmary Street
Edinburgh EH1 1LT

First published in hardback by Edinburgh University Press 2024

Typeset in 9 on 12pt Noto Serif
by Cheshire Typesetting Ltd, Cuddington, Cheshire

A CIP record for this book is available from the British Library

ISBN 978-1-3995-2318-9 (hardback)
ISBN 978-1-3995-2319-6 (paperback)
ISBN 978-1-3995-2320-2 (webready PDF)
ISBN 978-1-3995-2321-9 (epub)

The right of Robert Butler to be identified as the editor of this work has been asserted in accordance with the Copyright, Designs and Patents Act 1988, and the Copyright and Related Rights Regulations 2003 (SI No. 2498).

Contents

List of figures and tables vii
Notes on contributors ix
Preface xii
Acknowledgements xv

Introduction: Legitimisation strategies for a de-legitimised political world 1
Robert Butler

PART I The role of legitimisation in institutional contexts

1 Education and political socialisation in contemporary China: From institutional discourse to teaching materials 25
   Chiara Bertulessi

2 Smoothing processes in United Nations discourse on violence against women: A diachronic perspective 42
   Célia Atzeni

3 Who calls whom a populist? A pragmatic analysis of the uses of *populism(s)* and *populist(s)* in French and Spanish parliamentary debates 60
   Nadezda Shchinova

4 The Brexit saga: Stancetaking, control and identity in political discourse 78
   Juana I. Marín-Arrese

PART II Legitimisation and new media

5 Political discourse and the new media: New architectures of communication 103
   Mariya Chankova

6 Meaning-making in Trump's anti-Biden political campaign commercials: Multimodal perspective 123
   Tetiana Krysanova

PART III Legitimisation strategies and conceptualisation

7 A critical analysis of figurative language in the political discourse of conflict in Africa 147
   Issa Kanté

8 The CARD metaphor 'play the X card' as a social practice and its pragmatic functions 167
   Yuuki Tomoshige

9 Metaphors and political arguments in environmental debates: 'Our house is still on fire' 187
   Anaïs Augé

   Concluding remarks: Towards Legitimisation Studies in contemporary crises 204
   Robert Butler and Anaïs Augé

   Index 215

Figures and tables

Figures

2.1	Correspondence analysis of the corpus	47
2.2	Progression charts of 'will', 'must' and 'should' in press releases (left) and reports (right)	49
3.1	The distribution of *populis** in the French dataset	65
3.2	The distribution of *populis** in the Spanish dataset	65
6.1	*Break In* (00.00.05)	133
6.2	*Break In* (00.00.13)	136
6.3	*Cards* (00.00.20)	137
6.4	*Break In* (00.00.21)	138
6.5	*Break In* (00.00.24)	138
7.1	(Non-)metaphoric and metonymic uses of some key concepts	152
7.2	Bar plot of lexical foregrounding and backgrounding in the corpus	162

Tables

1.1	Xi Jinping Corpus details	32
2.1	Summary of the contents of the corpus	45
2.2	Lists of the ten most frequent verbs used with 'must', 'should' and 'will' ordered by frequency	50
4.1	Epistemic and effective stance: Categories and expressions	91
4.2	Epistemic and effective stance in speeches: May vs Johnson vs Conservatives (N and ratio per thousand words) (Chi^2 = 23.6065; p-value < 0.00001)	93
4.3	Categories of epistemic stance in speeches: May vs Johnson vs Conservatives (N and ratio per ten thousand words)	94
4.4	Categories of effective stance in speeches: May vs Johnson vs Conservatives (N and ratio per ten thousand words)	95

7.1	Metaphoric and metonymic uses of *Homeland, State, Country* and *Nation*	153
8.1	Nouns and adjectives in the slot (COCA)	174
8.2	Nouns in the slot (COCA)	175
8.3	Nouns and adjectives in the slot of 'play the X card' (COCA)	183

Notes on contributors

Célia Atzeni, a graduate of ENS Paris Saclay, holds the agrégation d'anglais and currently serves as a Temporary Teaching and Research Assistant at Université Paris 1 Panthéon Sorbonne. Her PhD thesis in English linguistics focuses on the diachronic analysis of the United Nations' discourse on violence against women. Her research interests include the analysis of specialised discourses, terminology, gender issues, and diachronic variations in English and in French.

Anaïs Augé is a research fellow and a lecturer at the University of Louvain, in the Institute of Political Sciences and Institute of Language and Communication. She is also an associate researcher at the University of Bangor. She is the author of a monograph entitled *Metaphor and Argumentation in Climate Crisis Discourse* published by Routledge (2023), and she is the co-editor of the *International Journal of Language and Culture* published by John Benjamins.

Chiara Bertulessi is a Postdoctoral Researcher in Chinese Studies at the University of Milan. She holds a PhD from the same university, obtained with a thesis in critical Chinese lexicography, and is the author of a monograph analysing the *Modern Chinese Dictionary* (现代汉语词典) from this scholarly perspective. Her research and publications revolve around the study of the interconnections between discourses, politics and ideology in contemporary China, especially with regard to political discourse, lexicology and terminology.

Robert Butler is Senior Lecturer in the Arts and Languages Faculty at the University of Lorraine (Nancy) and is a member of the Interdisciplinarity in English Studies research group. His research interests include discourse, cognition and multimodality, primarily in the political sphere. His published work focuses on force dynamics and gesture in political management strategies. He was a member of the national *CAPES* (competitive teacher training) examination board in France from 2013 to 2016.

Mariya Chankova, DPhil in English Linguistics from the RWTH Aachen, is Senior Assistant Professor of English and French at the South-West University – Blagoevgrad, Bulgaria. She is currently pursuing a post-doctorate project on strategic interaction, and is a researcher on an interdisciplinary project investigating attitudes towards plagiarism of Bulgarian scholars and science policy-makers.

Issa Kanté is a lecturer in English and contrastive linguistics at the University of La Reunion, member of the research team DIRE (*Déplacements, Identités, Regards, Écritures*). Adopting a cognitive and functional approach, his main research areas are the syntax and semantic interface, contrastive linguistics and Critical Discourse Studies – focusing particularly on (geo)political and academic discourses. His main research themes include *that/que*-clause complementation, lexical modality, metonymy and metaphor, political and linguistic ideologies, foregrounding and backgrounding constructions.

Tetiana Krysanova is Professor of Linguistics at Lesya Ukrainka Volyn National University, Ukraine. She obtained her DSc (Philology) in 2020 for her thesis in meaning-making in film. Her research interests are centred on discourse and multimodal studies, emotive linguistics and cognitive pragmatics. She is the author of more than ninety articles and the co-author of two monographs: *Text – Image – Music: Crossing the Borders* (2021) and *Ukraine – Canada: Modern Scientific Studies* (2018).

Juana Isabel Marín-Arrese is Emeritus Professor in the Department of English Studies at the Universidad Complutense de Madrid. Her recent research focuses on stance, epistemicity and the expression of inter/subjectivity in discourse. Recent publications include international journals (*Journal of Pragmatics*, 2021; *Culture, Language and Representation*, 2021, 2019), chapters in collective volumes (Mouton de Gruyter, 2022; John Benjamins, 2021, 2020, 2018; Routledge, 2020; Vernon Press, 2020; Peter Lang, 2023) and edited volumes (Mouton de Gruyter, 2022; *Journal of Pragmatics*, 2022; Peter Lang, 2023).

Andreas Musolff graduated from Düsseldorf University, worked at a School for Disabled Children and taught at universities in Germany, the Netherlands and the United Kingdom. He is currently Professor of Intercultural Communication at the University of East Anglia (Norwich, UK). His research interests focus on the Study of Political Discourse, Metaphor Analysis and Intercultural Linguistics. His book publications include the monographs *National Conceptualisations of the Body Politic* (2021), *Political*

Metaphor Analysis: Discourse and Scenarios (2016) and *Metaphor, Nation and the Holocaust* (2010); he has co-edited eleven volumes, the most recent ones being *Pandemic and Crisis Discourse: Communicating COVID-19 and Public Health Strategy* (2022) and *Migration and Media: Discourses about Identities in Crisis* (2019).

Nadezda Shchinova is a PhD student in the Institute of Language and Communication at the UCLouvain (Belgium). As part of her PhD thesis she investigates (online) political and media discourses about *populism* in Belgium, France and Spain.

Yuuki Tomoshige is an assistant professor in the School of International Studies at Kwansei Gakuin University in Nishinomiya, Hyogo, Japan. Much of his work revolves around how metaphors create political reality and their functions and effects in US presidential speeches, drawing on cognitive linguistics and critical metaphor analysis. His research interests include construction grammar, Critical Discourse Studies (political discourse analysis), and related fields.

Preface

Andreas Musolff

In an era of publicly proclaimed *permacrisis, post-truth*,[1] and politicians 'dancing with doxa' (Finlayson 2018) regardless of the sometimes disastrous consequences, analysing (de-)legitimisation strategies in crisis is urgently needed to understand and mitigate conflicts in public discourse. However, as the following quotations from an earlier era show (albeit the second one is a twenty-first-century fictional version of the thoughts of a sixteenth-century politician), the problem of how to provide political actions, actors and institutions with legitimacy in a de-legitimised world is by no means a new one:

> . . . the people in general were so ignorant of their duty, as that not one perhaps of ten thousand knew what right any man had to command him, or what necessity there was of King or Commonwealth (Hobbes 1990: 4)

> Where the word of the king is, there is power and who may say to him, what doest thou?
> (Thomas Cromwell quoting Ecclesiastes 8:4, in Mantel 2012: 38)

For Hobbes, the erosion of political legitimacy lay at the root of the Civil War in Britain, as told in *Behemoth*, and its only chance of rescue lay for him in a renewed 'covenant' among all citizens to submit together to sovereign authority, as explicated in *Leviathan* (Hobbes 1996: 117–21). For Hilary Mantel's fictional Thomas Cromwell, speaking as Henry VIII's Secretary in a conversation with Bishop Stephen Gardiner about 'true obedience' of subjects to their King, the biblical reference serves as a safe repartee to Gardiner's accusation that he, Cromwell, favoured a view that the sovereign's authority 'flowed' from the subjects' consensus to obedience, rather than exclusively and directly from God (Mantel

---

[1] See Flood (2016); Angermüller (2022); Spicer (2022).

2012: 38–9). Both the historical Hobbes's notion of covenant and the fictional Cromwell's idea of obedience imply a linkage of ('hard') power-based political and spiritual authority with the *creation of legitimacy in discourse*, as opposed to the pre-modern reliance on divine authority. Without discursive confirmation by the subjects, hard power may be able to force people to pay lip service to state 'authority', but such oppression-based authority is, from an enlightened perspective, unsustainable if no further attempts at legitimation are made to back it up during social and/or political crises.

This dependence of state authority on legitimising discourse is as relevant today as it was in the sixteenth and seventeenth centuries, as the studies in this volume show, covering as they do the transfer of ideology from party-political texts to educational genres in China, the discursive smoothing in United Nations (UN) discourse on violence against women, allegations of *populism* in French and Spanish parliamentary debates, stance-taking as a means of gaining 'epistemic control' in British 'Brexit' discourse, social actor construction in social media in Bulgaria, multimodality in US political advertising and the role of metaphors in glorification ideology, persuasion-targeting idioms and in arguments about climate change in further international settings. In all these cases, legitimacy in a crisis context is (re-)created or destroyed through its reconstruction as an implication of narrative-cum-argumentative scenarios that confer discursive authority on the speaker. Disconcerting and traumatic crisis experiences are thus transformed and streamlined into coherent, seemingly commonsensical stories and identity-confirming conclusions that reassure the recipients that their experience can be both explained and overcome practically, if only they put their trust in the speaker's version of what is legitimate or not.

As the current boom in conspiracy narratives or 'theories' concerning alleged origins of present-day crises such as 'hot' wars and inflation, pandemic and climate change, mass migration and fragmentation of collectives show, the demand for coherence- and identity-building scenarios is, if anything, growing, and so is the necessity of their critical analysis and reflection, which is being answered to some extent by a growing number of publications (Uscinski 2018; Butter and Knight 2020; Demata, Zorzi and Zottola 2022). But the question of how political and ethical legitimacy is established, maintained, defended and attacked goes beyond the focus on conspiracy stories and, crucially, involves an interdisciplinary methodology that combines critical discourse analysis with sociological, psychological, historical and epistemological approaches. This volume provides a fascinating outlook on the contours of such a research programme.

References

Angermüller, J. (2022). Beyond discourse theory in the conspirational mode? The critical issue of truth in the age of post-truth. In: Demata, M., Zorzi, V. and Zottola, A., eds, *Conspiracy Theory Discourses*. Amsterdam: John Benjamins, pp. 489–94.

Butter, M. and Knight, P., eds. (2020). *The Routledge Handbook of Conspiracy Theories*. London: Routledge.

Demata, M., Zorzi, V. and Zottola, A., eds. (2022). *Conspiracy Theory Discourses*. Amsterdam: John Benjamins.

Finlayson, A. (2018). 'Dancing with doxa': A 'rhetorical political analysis' of David Cameron's sense of Britishness. In: Kranert, M. and Horan, G., eds. *Doing Politics: Discursivity, Performativity and Mediation in Political Discourse*. Amsterdam: John Benjamins, pp. 59–77.

Flood, A. (2016). 'Post-truth' named word of the year by Oxford Dictionaries. *The Guardian*, 15 November. Available from: https://www.theguardian.com/books/2016/nov/15/post-truth-named-word-of-the-year-by-oxford-dictionaries [accessed 20 March 2023].

Hobbes, T. (1990). *Behemoth. Or The Long Parliament*. Ed. F. Tönnies. Chicago and London: The University of Chicago Press.

Hobbes, T. (1996). *Leviathan*. Ed. R. Tuck. Cambridge: Cambridge University Press.

Mantel, H. (2012). *Bring up the Bodies*. London: 4th Estate.

Spicer, A. (2022). If 'permacrisis' is the word of 2022, what does 2023 have in store for our mental health? *The Guardian*, 30 December. Available from: https://www.theguardian.com/commentisfree/2022/dec/30/permacrisis-word-of-2022-2023-mental-health [accessed 20 March 2023].

Uscinski, J. E., ed. (2018). *Conspiracy Theories & the People Who Believe Them*. Oxford: Oxford University Press.

Acknowledgements

I am very grateful to Edinburgh University Press for publishing this volume and to the editors there for their valuable assistance in guiding this book along the route to publication. I would like to thank all the peer reviewers for the time they have invested throughout the different stages of reviewing of this book. My words of thanks extend to the authors for their support and their significant contributions which make up the present volume. In particular, I would like to thank Professor Andreas Musolff for his valuable words of support and encouragement, and Dr Anaïs Augé for her assistance and advice during the drafting and rereading stages.

The following authors would like to acknowledge funding they received: Chapter 3 by Nadezda Shchinova: this research is funded by the Fédération Wallonie-Bruxelles (FWB) through the Actions de Recherche Concertées (ARC) fellowship. Chapter 4 by Juana I. Marín-Arrese: this research has received support from the research project Stance and Subjectivity in Discourse: Towards an Integrated Framework for the Analysis of Epistemicity, Effectivity, Evaluation and Inter/Subjectivity from a Critical Discourse Perspective (STANCEDISC), ref. PGC2018-095798-B-I00, funded by the Ministerio de Ciencia, Innovación y Universidades (Spanish Ministry of Science, Innovation and Universities). Chapter 9 by Anaïs Augé: funded by Le Fonds Spécial de Recherche (FSR) within the Institute of Political Sciences Louvain-Europe (ISPOLE).

INTRODUCTION

Legitimisation strategies for a de-legitimised political world

Robert Butler

1 Politics in crisis and conflict

In recent years politics has entered a state of crisis (Wodak 2011; Ekström and Firmstone 2017a; Huang and Holmgreen 2020). In many countries, this political crisis is associated with competition from populist waves (Wodak 2015). In the European political context, the 'tensions and disruptions' (Ekström and Firmstone 2017a: 4–5) which have contributed to this crisis not only encompass the rise of populism, but also include disenfranchisement due to globalisation and austerity linked to economic crises and refugee crises. This state of crisis is particularly salient in the case of the interactional relationships between politicians, the public and the media (Ekström and Firmstone 2017a). Moreover, major global challenges have also had a bearing on the political crisis. In the face of a growing crisis of legitimacy and credibility, politicians and regimes have been forced to adapt their discursive strategies in response to growing and pressing challenges such as climate crisis discourse (Augé 2023) and government responses to the COVID-19 crisis (Musolff 2022).

Effective discourse requires not only the politician's presence in the media, but also the ability of politicians to demonstrate what makes their message and their political creed unique (Ben Hamed and Mayaffre 2015). Despite these crises, the professional training of politicians to deal with the media in the face of the gap between what the public expects and what politicians actually deliver has long been identified (Fairclough 1995). Using the media to express an original political identity has already resulted in challenges to 'conventional orders of political communication', as witnessed by the success of populist parties in France, Greece, the United Kingdom (UK) and Sweden in 2014 (Ekström and Firmstone 2017b: 329). Yet, as Mudde and Kaltwasser (2017: 18–19) suggest, it can be argued that populism 'is essentially anti-political' because actors 'seek to create anti-political utopias' in which dissent does not exist.

The need for political actors to adapt their discursive strategies to address the growing state of crisis has led to a growing reliance on new forms of discourse. These include political discourse of a fictionalised nature, where the boundaries become blurred between fact and fiction on the one hand, and entertainment and information on the other (Wodak 2011). Growing public dissatisfaction with politics has resulted in a vicious circle in which people prefer fiction, but as 'the real world of politics can never compete with its idealized version, the fiction necessarily reinforces this dissatisfaction' (Wodak 2011: 206). In addition, as Coulomb-Gully and Esquenazi (2012: 7) claim, storytelling and scripting techniques have given rise to a new political reality which has made the boundaries between genres less stable. New genres like 'infotainment' (a mix of information and entertainment) may also blur the line in audience reception between fact and fiction (Ferré 2016).

Crucially, politicians and the media rely on each other for the dissemination of their programmes, manifestos, policies and other information, as any void can give rise to speculation and rumours (Wodak 2011: 19–21). Recently there has been a rise in the use of 'fake news' in the counter-attack against unprecedented challenges such as climate crisis (Al-Rawi et al. 2021) and interpretations of what counts as 'truth' in the 'post-truth' era (Montgomery 2017; McIntyre 2018). New forms of media may facilitate a powerful alternative voice for communication in political discourse (Montgomery 2017), while providing a new platform for populist movements (Mazzoleni and Bracciale 2018). Political discourse thus finds itself in the midst of a multitude of global socio-economic, health and environmental crises, combined with the manipulative potential of new media genres. Political actors may search for approval for their actions and policies, including maintaining power, being socially accepted or remaining popular (Reyes 2011: 782). Seeking approval is the means by which those in power, or seeking power, become or remain legitimate. Obtaining approval may, however, entail the use of manipulation as a means of control (van Dijk 2006). It now appears that politicians have discovered new ways to disguise the gap between public expectations and political outcomes.

Consequently, understanding how politics has reached a state of crisis requires, firstly, an account of how political discourse has evolved to the present day within Critical Discourse Studies (CDS), and secondly, how the concept of legitimacy in political science has given rise to legitimisation. This introductory chapter situates the concept of legitimisation within political discourse and in relation to the related concept of legitimacy. A summary of current research on crisis and conflict will be provided before defining the concepts of crisis and conflict more clearly in relation to the present approach. The Introduction will then proceed to outline the analysis of legitimisation in crisis and conflict as an area of research which requires further attention. Finally, the chapters will be presented in this book in relation to how they broach the challenge for political actors to legitimise their discourse in times of crisis.

Introduction

2 Situating legitimacy and legitimisation in political discourse analysis

In order to provide a working definition of legitimisation, this introductory chapter will first of all consider the definitions given to the concept of legitimacy by key scholars from a historical perspective and in relation to authority and power. This will enable the link between the study of legitimacy in political science and research on the process of legitimisation in CDS to be pinpointed. Consideration will then be given to how legitimisation fits within political discourse as one of three key 'strategic functions' (Chilton 2004: 45).

2.1 Legitimacy within political philosophy

As a concept in political philosophy, legitimacy – along with power – is a component of political authority. Power is 'the ability to get things done', while 'legitimacy is the quality of ascribed entitlement to exercise that power' (Birch 1993: 32). Max Weber defines power as how 'one actor within a social relationship will be in a position to carry out his own will despite resistance' (Weber 1964: 152). Political power may extend to a state's monopoly of 'the use of force' (Weber 1964: 156). Coercion is typically available to back up political authority even if it is rarely used (Birch 1993: 32), although it can be a source of compliance (Held 1996: 195).

Defining legitimacy, however, requires a greater understanding of the historical and cultural values of what constitutes entitlement. For example, legitimacy can be achieved through traditional forms of authority: individuals may comply because of tradition or conformity (Weber 1964; van Leeuwen 2007: 108–9).

In liberal democracies, the legitimacy to govern is achieved not only through the consent of the people (Held 1996: 81) but also through the 'conformity to established rules' and a system of values with 'shared beliefs' (Beetham 2013: 19). Locke refers to the organisation of society based on consent, where individuals 'make themselves members of some politic society' (Locke 2021 [1690]: sect. 2.15), with 'freedom from absolute, arbitrary power' and enslavement (Locke 2021 [1690]: sect. 2.23). As Weber (1964: 324) argues, the legitimacy to govern requires the people's consent in exchange for the public's 'obedience to commands' with at least some degree of 'voluntary submission' to those who represent them. Legitimacy based on legal and rational authority is rooted in a normative interpretation of what is considered correct at the present time, or will be correct at some future time (Held 1996: 195). The legality of rules gives 'those elevated to authority' the right 'to issue commands' in accordance with those rules (Weber 1964: 328).

However, legitimacy may not necessarily be achieved through normative, legal-rational means. Individuals may instead be apathetic, prepared to conform to authority because it is in their interests to acquiesce, or instrumentally accept their circumstances in order to secure a different long-term outcome (Held 1996: 195). In such circumstances, individuals appear not to challenge the status quo. Yet, as Habermas (1976) argues, legal-rational political systems in the twentieth century faced a crisis of legitimacy emanating from the demands which faced state-managed capitalism, and the threats posed by totalitarianism and fascism. Charismatic forms of legitimacy exposed the fragile nature of legal-rational legitimacy (McCormick 2007: 30–1). According to Weber (1964: 359), charismatic individuals possess certain exceptional qualities within a society, but the authority of these leaders is only considered legitimate where they are able to recognise the duties to be undertaken which they have been called upon to perform. The leader's power is therefore legitimised through the status of role model (van Leeuwen 2007: 107–8).

Recently, challenges to the political status quo have turned out to reflect a growing challenge to democracy and 'a wider malaise' (Ekström and Firmstone 2017a: 5). Political scepticism, the threat or fear of coercion and the rise of new types of leaders provide a compelling need to examine not only how political regimes can retain legitimacy in the face of political crisis, but also what discursive strategies may be used by leaders to legitimise their power. In an era of mediatised political discourse (Ekström and Firmstone 2017b) and media proliferation, new opportunities have emerged for securing legitimacy. Consider the instrumental use of online media during Donald Trump's 2020 election campaign to de-legitimise his opponent, Joe Biden (Krysanova, Chapter 6) or the dissemination of popular messages through social media (Chankova, Chapter 5). How charismatic leaders rise to power is important to understand in times of political crisis, and also how the discourse they use can perpetuate, exacerbate or alleviate a crisis.

The crisis of legitimacy may be a response to coercive measures – a form of resignation that circumstances will not change whatever one does – or it may be the result of the expression of competing social interests which cannot gain sufficient momentum to be heard and acted upon. Attributing one single definition of legitimacy fails to take account of the diversity of political systems and values which exist in the contemporary world. Nonetheless, certain traits which can be highlighted here include the rightfulness to govern (Beetham and Lord 1998; Beetham 2013: x–xi) which is conferred upon leaders by the governed, and where the people within a political system accept the conditions of being governed, consciously or otherwise.

2.2 Legitimisation within political discourse

The aim of this volume is to focus on one specific function of political discourse (namely legitimisation) among the three 'strategic functions' proposed by Chilton (2004: 45). Indeed, political speakers must 'manage their interests' (Chilton 2004: 45) through the use of strategies. These fall into one of three 'strategic functions', which can be interrelated: coercion, representation and misrepresentation, and legitimisation and de-legitimisation (Chilton 2004: 45-6). The notions of coercive power, the representation of the people and the legitimisation of power in the sphere of political science can thus be translated into discursive processes in the linguistic sphere. Coercion is not a purely linguistic strategy, as it is dependent upon power structures and mechanisms such as sanctions at the institutional level, in addition to structural factors such as speaker status (Chilton 2004: 45-6). Yet coercion remains an important factor in how consent may be forced upon individuals.

Furthermore, representation and misrepresentation constitute political control linked to the dissemination of information, including censorship (Chilton 2004: 46). Official sources of information, such as official documents and institutions, constitute reliable sources of shared knowledge (van Dijk 2011), while specialised or technical discourse can be recontextualised by journalists in the shape of 'popularizing discourse' linked to 'general, common knowledge, occasionally enriched by a few technical terms' (van Dijk 2014: 135). The legitimising dimension of official sources contributes to the representation of discourse and political discourse in particular.

Crucially, political actors may need to legitimise their actions and policies through discourse in order to retain power or normalise certain ideologies (Reyes 2011; Abuelwafa 2021). Legitimisation is a 'process by which speakers accredit or license a type of social behaviour' through the argumentation process to 'explain our social actions, ideas, thoughts, [or] declarations' (Reyes 2011: 782). In other words, legitimisation and de-legitimisation strategies involve establishing 'the right to be obeyed' – otherwise known as legitimacy (Chilton 2004: 46). In legitimising strategies there is no presupposition that an act is not right or that the action is being denied (Chilton 2004: 208). Drawing on Austin (1962), Chilton (2004: 208) argues that legitimisation involves an action which is intended, with positive intentions and circumstances in which the act is permissible. Legitimisation techniques incorporate 'arguments about voters' wants, general ideological principles, charismatic leadership projection, boasting about performance and positive self-presentation' (Chilton 2004: 46). Conversely, de-legitimisation involves negatively identifying 'others' in society, with 'difference and boundaries' highlighted and speech acts including 'blaming, accusing, [and] insulting' (Chilton 2004: 46).

Legitimisation fits within the evolution of Critical Discourse Studies (henceforth CDS); the latter has already been well documented, notably by van Dijk (1997).[1] Although the use of political language can be traced back to

---

[1] CDS is also referred to as Critical Discourse Analysis (CDA), especially in earlier studies in the discipline.

Aristotle (2010) and the language of rhetoric, van Dijk (1997: 25–7) explains that Critical Discourse Studies only emerged in its relatively modern form in the 1960s, when a number of disciplines in the humanities and social sciences also developed, along with the theory of speech acts (Austin 1962; Searle 1969). Of particular note is the influence of ethnography, at a time when the conventions of how to interact in a social setting became of greater interest to researchers (van Dijk 1997: 25). Added to advances in technology and a growing interest in the social and psychological dimensions of conversation is the convergence in critical research into the 'contemporary struggle around the neo-liberal new global order' in the face of 'the massive destruction of human communities and natural resources' (Fairclough 2001: 215). Analysing the potential for the manipulation of vulnerable groups in society through discourse forms a key component of CDS (van Dijk 2006).

Recent approaches in CDS include the Discourse-Historical Approach (Reisigl and Wodak 2009) and its applications (cf. Bertulessi, Chapter 1; Atzeni, Chapter 2), the social-semiotic approach (van Leeuwen 2007, 2008) and its applications (cf. Krysanova, Chapter 6), the Discourse-Society-Cognition model proposed by van Dijk (2006, 2011) and its use in relation to crisis (cf. Kanté, Chapter 7), and Proximisation Theory (Cap 2008, 2013, 2014, 2017). One significant area of focus within CDS is the analysis of political metaphors. Through the combination of cognitive, pragmatic and discourse analysis, political metaphors have been analysed in Critical Metaphor Analysis (CMA) (Charteris-Black 2011, 2014) and the analysis of metaphor scenarios in discourse (Musolff 2016). Political Linguistics has become a heterogeneous domain of 'political setting', while the notion of Political Discourse Analysis contains connotations of ideological motivations (Okulska and Cap 2010a: 3). What remains clear is that approaches in CDS are inevitably interdisciplinary because their focus centres around problems (Unger et al. 2016).

3 Situating crisis and conflict in political discourse analysis: current research

Both conflict and crisis are significant objects of current research in political discourse. This makes it important not only to assign a clear definition of crisis to discourse, but also to overcome the difficulty in identifying a specific definition of discourse in relation to research on crisis (Huang 2020: 5). It also highlights the question of the ways in which crisis and conflict may be considered to be two interrelated dimensions of the same problem.

3.1 Crisis

The concept of crisis is rooted in classical Greek, according to Koselleck (2006: 358–9), where the notions of choosing and quarrelling in politics

Introduction

extended to the notion of reaching a decision at a point 'which would tip the scales' (Koselleck 2006: 358). The historical 'tendency towards imprecision and vagueness' in the use of the term 'crisis' may form part of a broader phenomenon of crisis which cannot yet be measured in its entirety (Koselleck 2006: 399). Furthermore, the concept 'once had the power to pose unavoidable, harsh and non-negotiable alternatives' but has, in more recent times, 'been transformed to fit the uncertainties of whatever might be favored at a given moment' (Koselleck 2006: 399). The ambiguity of the notion points to a risk that crisis can be adapted too loosely to whichever political scenario happens to be presented through discourse. Indeed, Huang (2020: 3) reiterates the claim made by Coombs and Holladay (2010) that the multiple causes, effects and characteristics of crises mean that the concept does not have any one specific definition. Of possibly greatest significance is that since 1780 'crisis' has come to signify 'a new sense of time' and a new 'epoch' or era, but it has also come to represent a chronic situation or a 'recurring event' (Koselleck 2006: 358).

A number of studies have analysed discourse in contexts of crisis (Huang and Holmgreen 2020) or in terms of political crisis (Patrona and Thornborrow 2017; Krzyżanowski 2019). For instance, in their analysis of the European Parliament elections which took place in May 2014, Patrona and Thornborrow (2017) argue that economic and political crises in Europe were framed in terms of what was at stake nationally, by apportioning blame and responsibility on the one hand, and attempts to legitimise or de-legitimise the aims of the European Union (EU) on the other. Their study points to varying levels of salience of the notion of crisis according to the country. For example, there was little salience of the notion of crisis in Italy, while in the United Kingdom the EU was portrayed as being a distant institution, and the notion of any crisis in France was downplayed (Patrona and Thornborrow 2017: 84–6). More recently, a study by Krzyżanowski (2019) analyses the media representation of the debates surrounding the United Kingdom's 2016 referendum ('Brexit') on leaving the European Union in four EU countries with very different profiles in relation to membership and demographics: Austria, Germany, Poland and Sweden. (Krzyżanowski 2019: 487) concludes that the referendum was portrayed as a significant crisis for EU member states (both in the present and in the future) and the media drew on the recontextualisation of previous socio-economic and political crises.

3.2 Conflict

Conflict, however, has been defined differently (Scharlaj 2020; Chiluwa 2021a). Specifically, Chiluwa's definition of conflict incorporates 'violent conflicts' which 'include verbal aggression and hate speech, as well as physical confrontation between (political) groups or states over values' and claims to power, in addition to the notions of war and physical hostility

(2021a: 4). Scharlaj (2020) focuses on the interplay between aggression and argumentation, and cooperation and conflict, notably in the Russia–Ukraine conflict from 2014 onwards and in other areas of conflict.

Extensive research has already been carried out into the use of language in contexts of conflict (Evans et al. 2019; Chiluwa 2021b; Chun 2022). While Chiluwa (2021a: 2–3) affirms that 'the knowledge of the world should not be treated as objective truth', conflict can even give rise to polarisation in relation to both social and political conflicts, and symbolic and cultural conflicts (Filardo-Llamas et al. 2021). The approach adopted by Filardo-Llamas et al. (2021) makes it possible to account for both conflicts visible on the surface, and deeper, polarised levels of conflict linked to conceptions of reality or beliefs: in other words, how discourse is represented by conflict, and how conflict can be created as a result of discourses (Filardo-Llamas et al. 2021). Chun (2022) considers not only how language may serve as a vehicle for conflict, but also how it may be used tactically to limit the scope for conflict. He argues that linguistics can be mobilised to promote a greater level of fairness in discourse and society (Chun 2022).

The de-legitimising impact during political conflict has also received attention. Berrocal (2020), for example, conducts a qualitative analysis of the aggressive language of populism in a study of a series of ten political interviews with the President of the Czech Republic between December 2017 and February 2018. Specifically, Berrocal identifies forms of insults with 'negative attributions'; insults which make negative reference; condescension; and 'pointed criticism' (Berrocal 2020: 292–7).

Conflict has also been the focus of a number of other studies, including the mediatisation of conflict. Nahajec (2019) contends that negation in televised interviews contributes to conflict at the local level in turn-taking and interview management (as opposed to resolving conflict), and also has repercussions on the conflict of ideas and even the wider risk of tension and conflict. Debates, televised political interviews and parliamentary questions are the three communicative genres analysed by Bull and Simon-Vandenbergen (2019). In some cases, a politician can use the question form to attack the 'face' of another politician in the interview (Bull and Simon-Vandenbergen 2019: 266). Specifically, they conclude that questions 'present a threat to a politician's positive face', and can 'threaten their freedom of action' when negative face has to be defended (Bull and Simon-Vandenbergen 2019: 266).[2] More broadly, research has already been conducted into cross-cultural issues regarding political interviewing in the more traditional broadcast media (Ekström and Patrona 2011). One of the key challenges identified by Ekström and Patrona's (2011) approach focuses on improving the accountability of political actors in broadcast talk.

---

[2] Bull and Simon-Vandenbergen (2019: 248) define 'face' as generally meaning 'prestige, honour or reputation'.

3.3 Interrelationships between crisis and conflict

Crisis and conflict in this volume are interrelated in a number of ways. Firstly, political crisis can be seen in public disillusionment and the political inability to deal satisfactorily with pressing global challenges. Although interaction between political actors may normally entail conflict through discourse, in contexts of crisis this interaction becomes exacerbated by the need to act urgently and in the face of major threats to stability. Secondly, the contexts in which political conflict may occur have become increasingly urgent and uncertain, in terms of political interaction through new forms of media, unprecedented global crises and proliferating forms of disorder, all of which require new approaches in CDS.

The role of social and digital media, such as online political advertisements and weblogs, has also been the focus of attention in crisis and conflict (Okulska and Cap 2010b; Kopytowska 2013; Unger et al. 2016). It has been shown how genre styles proliferate through genre mediatisation, hybridity and multimodality, thereby demonstrating that some of the problems of political genres apply to communicative genres in general (Cap and Okulska 2013a). Kopytowska (2013: 401) claims that blogs provide a lot of insight into 'political deliberation', where there is some 'fluidity' between the blogger's ability to use self-promotion and his or her ability to create polemics through proximisation and interactivity. The problem is that political genres are heterogeneous and require adequation with methodological approaches: 'Researching political genres is, without exaggeration, a continual struggle to maintain analytic consistency, in the face of all the possible evolutions a given genre is capable of' (Cap and Okulska 2013b: 8).

Crisis and conflict have also been analysed through conceptual approaches. For example, Musolff (2022) analyses the use of metaphors relating to WAR and COMPETITION which result in exaggerated claims of success by the British and American governments in the fight against COVID-19 on the one hand, and the satirical debunking of those claims by the media, on the other. In one case, the British prime minister at the time 'did not escape sarcastic debunking' while trying to 'reassure the British public that the pandemic could be beaten' at both the national and personal levels (Musolff 2022: 81). As Musolff contends, not only may exaggerated claims of victory by speakers become hollow, but also 'they undermine their personal standing and may scare and panic audiences' (2022: 84). Charteris-Black (2021) explores the coercive moral power of metaphor and metonymy in debates around the COVID-19 pandemic. He analyses how metaphors are used and subsequently contested by society. Moreover, Ullmann (2020) applies Critical Metaphor Analysis and methods in corpus linguistics in a study of political speeches at the time of the Arab revolutions which began in 2011. In the context of revolution, the source domains considered favourably in the West include those linked to BIRTH, SPRING, WATER or PREGNANCY, while these notions were portrayed differently by certain Arab leaders (Ullmann

2020: 163). Specifically, the metaphor REVOLUTION IS A CHILD is used for positive impact in American discourse, including the notion of 'new futures' and the birth of new democracies, but for negative impact in other discourses mainly in Egypt and Syria, where the images conveyed focus on abortion, stillbirth and incubators (Ullmann 2020: 151).

Finally, crisis and conflict have been analysed through the lens of protest and disorder. Unger et al. (2016: 288) state that the most popular images of protests are those which become recontextualised and reproduced the most, and therefore 'constitute the global discourse on protest movements'. Unger et al. (2016: 287) also explain that the 'relationships between protest movements across the globe are not unlike those between linguistic communities, whereby global languages (particularly English) often dominate'. These relationships mirror the global economic structures, with many social media giants being located in Western countries like the United States of America (USA) (Unger et al. 2016: 289). Additionally, Hart and Kelsey (2018) explore civil disorder in contemporary and more historical examples in media discourse and argue that strikes, protests and riots form a significant component in politics. In their linguistic and multimodal approach to the language of disorder, they claim that the 'mainstream media, for reasons of political economy, tend to marginalise, delegitimise and undermine riots, strikes and protests' and instead portray them as 'illegitimate acts of non-conformity or criminality that constitute a "threat" to civil society' (Hart and Kelsey 2018: 1). Their CDS-based approach investigates the structural and political factors which bring about civil disorder (as opposed to the destructive outcomes) and enables 'micro-level' semiotic factors to be analysed within the broader framework of social identities, norms, inequalities and 'power relations' (Hart and Kelsey 2018: 3). For example, Kotzur (2020) analyses metaphors in the protests against the Stuttgart 21 railway project (which aims to provide a through station for long-distance trains and faster links): these metaphors may be used by protesters to fuel existing tensions and to remove credibility from their opponents. The study therefore seems to point to the de-legitimisation of the scheme's proponents rather than the legitimisation of the protesters' own case against the project.

4 The approach to crisis and conflict in this volume

In a globalised and mediatised political environment where crisis entails catastrophe largely due to human activity, and conflict involves verbal and sometimes physical acts of aggression, political actors are faced with crisis, conflict and challenges to their reputation. This book follows the approach to the language of crisis adopted by Huang (2020), who highlights three main constitutive elements of a crisis: threat, uncertainty and urgency. Firstly, there is a threat if 'something of great value to an agent is at risk if no intervention takes place' (Huang 2020: 3). Secondly, uncertainty is defined by the

Introduction 11

extent to which the agent may be vulnerable in the face of the 'unknown or hard-to-predict consequences' and outcomes of a given crisis (Huang 2020: 3). Thirdly, urgency applies if the time available for intervention to curtail or avert the threat is limited (Huang 2020: 3). Huang retains risk and uncertainty as the principal features of a crisis, and states that the response to the dangers posed by one can be enhanced by the efficiency of leadership and 'communication among social groups and individuals' (Huang 2020: 3). Huang's (2020) approach to crisis in political discourse is reinforced by Koselleck's interpretation of the evolution of the term: 'Conceptualized as chronic, "crisis" can indicate a state of greater or lesser permanence, as in a longer or shorter transition towards something better or worse or towards something altogether different' (Koselleck 2006: 358). Threat may be linked to a worse outcome; uncertainty may coincide with a completely different outcome; urgency may be brought on by a situation where permanence is not guaranteed or is actively compromised.

Crisis is therefore defined as a situation in which one or more of the parameters of threat, uncertainty and urgency might cause profound changes to the social, political, economic or environmental situation facing a people against their will or their interests. One may then question how the concept of conflict can fit into an analysis of crisis and discourse. According to Sørensen and Johansen (2016: 88), examples of (non-violent) conflicts include civil and political rights movements, minority rights, animal rights, (nuclear) disarmament, protecting the environment, and independence movements. They argue that there is a 'prevailing negative view of conflict' in studies of conflict resolution due to 'the field's focus on violent conflict and the subsequent sidelining of nonviolent resistance to oppression and violence' (Sørensen and Johansen 2016: 83). It has also been acknowledged that 'conflict can be both desirable and necessary for human and societal development' (Sørensen and Johansen 2016: 84). In these contexts, conflict can be seen as the discursive representation of a crisis in which the problems of threat, uncertainty and urgency can be identified and analysed in relation to the interaction between different social and political actors.[3]

Any analysis of political discourse cannot avoid taking the powerful influence of the media into account. According to Patrona and Thornborrow (2017: 59–60), the media make 'concrete choices' in their use of 'language and image':

---

[3] This definition of conflict enables us to focus on the non-violent dimension of conflict and show how it fits into contexts of crisis, while not refuting or forgetting the violent nature by which conflict can manifest itself in some crises. A slightly different interpretation of conflict is put forward by Chiluwa (2021a). Conflict is assimilated to war rather than 'interpersonal differences, misunderstanding or grievances between individuals', and conflict is situated as a form of hostility or aggression between broad layers of society such as ethnic conflicts, inter-state conflicts or global-level conflicts, all of which are susceptible to 'economic and political struggle' (Chiluwa 2021a: 4).

the media both *frame* and *construct* events and actions as 'crisis', simultaneously realising the news values of negativity, prominence, impact, novelty and *superlativeness* (the maximised or intensified aspect of an event), while also allowing for the discursive construction of *consonance* (a fit with stereotypes that people hold about the events and people portrayed in them), and *personalisation* (the personal or human interest aspect of an event).

(Patrona and Thornborrow 2017: 59–60)

In other words, the media play on stereotypical views held by the public, exaggerate certain features of the news event, and deliberately appeal to curiosity through negative undertones. These observations reinforce the three tenets of a crisis situation: the revelation of a threat seeks to scare the public into taking notice and preparing for action, while urgency can play into the hands of event intensification, and uncertainty appeals to human nature and curiosity. They also bring into question whether the media's representation of conflict makes it an observer of, or a participant in, a crisis situation.

This volume contends that conflict is the manifestation of a crisis of any given level of intensity, whose notion can extend from violent interaction and military conflict to non-violent interaction in discourse and debates. This incorporates those conflicts which pit opposing groups against one another but not necessarily involving physically violent interaction, such as hate speech. Legitimisation in crisis and conflict is, however, a little-researched area. What remains to be analysed in great detail is the legitimisation and de-legitimisation of political discourse in contexts of crisis and conflict.

5 The approach to legitimisation in crisis and conflict in this volume

The present volume addresses the key issue of the role of legitimisation in political discourse and asks: what strategies are available for politicians and political institutions to legitimise their own actions and stances in the face of crisis situations? Does the legitimisation of one's own actions inevitably result in the de-legitimising of those of other political actors and further conflict? Conversely, does the de-legitimisation of other political actors' actions serve to legitimise one's own conduct? Do legitimisation strategies alleviate, perpetuate or exacerbate conflict and crisis situations? The approach used here draws primarily on elements of the frameworks of legitimisation proposed by van Leeuwen (2007, 2008) and Reyes (2011), in addition to Cap (2021) and Nguyen and Williams (2020). It shows how certain ideologies become normalised through the authority of political actors (Abuelwafa 2021).

Introduction

5.1 The framework for legitimisation and de-legitimisation

Firstly, it has been claimed that 'legitimizing one position automatically implies the (de)legitimizing of alternative positions' (Reyes 2011: 804); in other words, legitimisation and de-legitimisation are considered to be two sides of the same coin. This book argues that this situation sets political actors by default on a collision course with conflict, but that it is not always in the speaker's interests for one side of the coin to be as salient as the other. For example, how can one account for situations where de-legitimisation and ensuing conflict are not the objective of smoothing discourses (Atzeni, Chapter 2) which aim to avoid conflict; or where speakers de-legitimise their opponents but do not have more legitimate alternatives to offer to a given debate or crisis; or the case of political actors who distort the truth?

This volume explores the different contexts in which legitimisation occurs and the cognitive-social processes which underpin legitimisation in political discourse. As van Leeuwen (2007, 2008) explains, legitimisation is invariably linked to a context, and his typology of legitimisation consists of four principal ways in which discourse can be legitimised, or legitimated: authorisation, rationalisation, moral evaluation and mythopoesis (namely tales containing a moral message). Similarly, Reyes (2011) identifies five categories: emotions (especially fear), 'a hypothetical future', rationality, 'voices of expertise' and altruism. Applying legitimisation and de-legitimisation methods to contexts of crisis makes it possible to explain the mediatised nature of crises through linguistics. In addition, cognitive approaches help us to discern areas of impending crisis which may be revealed through discourse, where, for example, speakers may not explicitly mention crisis but may be implicitly implying crisis scenarios through language.

5.1.1 Authorisation

Within this category proposed by van Leeuwen (2007, 2008), legitimisation is constructed discursively through custom, authority or recommendation. The sub-category of custom shadows Weber's (1964) classification of traditional authority, where tradition is based more on how things have always been carried out (as opposed to coercion) and conformity refers to authority based on the normative replication of the actions of others (van Leeuwen 2008: 108–9).

Authority is split into personal and impersonal authority (van Leeuwen 2008: 106–9). Personal authority is invested in a given individual who is assigned a status and no justification is needed for their orders or commands (van Leeuwen 2008: 106). On the contrary, impersonal authority is not linked to commands given by a figure in power, but because of laws or rules (van Leeuwen 2008: 108).

Finally, van Leeuwen (2008: 107–9) claims that experts and role models form part of the sub-category of recommendation. The expert's authority may be legitimised through his or her ability to provide expertise in a given field, especially to support politicians' actions (Reyes 2011: 786). The role model serves as an example for members of society to follow, such as famous celebrities or peers within a social group.

5.1.2 Rationalisation

Legitimisation which is 'founded on some kind of truth' as opposed to 'whether the action is morally justified or not, [or] whether it is purposeful or effective' is referred to as theoretical rationalisation (van Leeuwen 2008: 115–16). Conversely, instrumental rationalisation involves a focus either on the goal to be achieved by action, or the means by which some action is to be achieved (van Leeuwen (2008: 113–15). Within rationalisation, the notion of 'hypothetical futures' will also be incorporated, in which a future threat is presented in the present time, based on fact or reason (Reyes 2011: 786). Also included in the current approach is the notion of 'privileged futures' based on a speaker's modalisations of the future through the use of facts and evidence (Cap 2021).

5.1.3 Moral evaluation

Moral evaluation is a legitimation strategy in which evaluative judgements are made 'without further justification' (van Leeuwen 2008: 109). The veracity of the values ascribed to conduct or a situation is therefore not questioned or scrutinised. Moral evaluation involves either 'evaluation', 'abstraction' or 'comparison' (van Leeuwen 2008: 109–13). Legitimisation through evaluation relies on mainly adjectival descriptions; abstraction uses terminology of a more abstract and vague nature than the concrete terms to which a notion may refer; comparison occurs through the use of positive or negative analogies assigned to a particular conduct (van Leeuwen 2008: 110–13). Negative evaluation also exposes opponents to de-legitimisation.

5.1.4 Mythopoesis

Legitimisation may also entail some threat of future consequences through reference to a story or scenario. Mythopoesis, or *'moral tales'*, is a form of storytelling where 'protagonists are rewarded for engaging in legitimate social practices or restoring the legitimate order' (van Leeuwen 2008: 117, original italics). While such stories may serve to promote positive behaviour, mythopoesis may also be used in the form of a threat of undesired consequences: 'Cautionary tales, on the other hand, convey what will happen if you do not conform to the norms of social practices. Their protagonists engage in deviant activities that lead to unhappy endings' (van Leeuwen 2008: 118). Such cautionary and moral tales may therefore have a de-legitimising effect on opponents or rival ideologies. Similarly, Cap (2021) refers to 'oppositional futures' based on a speaker's fears, or the fear the speaker wishes to instil in others.

5.1.5 Altruism

This category is adopted from Reyes (2011), as this form of legitimisation covers actions which the speaker deems beneficial to the other, even if in reality they may not be beneficial. The category is not included within 'authorisation', because what can be legitimised by people in authority (including experts) may not be in the best interests of others, just as an altruistic position may not be backed up by genuine concern in the psyche of the speaker. Indeed, the typology proposed by Reyes applies to scenarios where 'discourses are presented as truth' (2011: 804).

5.1.6 Extreme emotional elicitation

The appeal to the emotions of recipients is considered a form of legitimisation by some researchers (Reyes 2011: 785–6; Nguyen and Williams 2020). Recent research points to 'moral outrage porn', where morality is used 'for gratification on the part of its users', and the news is not for 'seeking moral truth' but 'using our morality reactions for pleasure' (Nguyen and Williams 2020: 159). In such cases, the information or ideas transmitted may be patently false or factually misleading. Although certain emotions like fear are considered especially relevant to legitimisation (Reyes 2011: 785–6), this volume contends that they can be manifested either in the patient or experiencer, or in the processes linked to actors or agents which may induce the emotion, rather than the manifestation of the emotion itself in the patient. In addition, some expressed emotions may be the result of messages transmitted principally but not exclusively through moral evaluation or mythopoesis. The present approach nonetheless takes account of cases where extreme forms of emotion are ostensibly generated by the producer of the discourse rather than in the recipient's manifestation of it.

5.2 Related approaches to legitimisation

Reyes (2011) states that legitimisation strategies can be used alone or in combination with other strategies, while van Leeuwen (2007, 2008) acknowledges that more than one type of legitimisation may be at work at any given time. However, rationalisation and moral evaluation are two forms of legitimisation which tend to repel one another (van Leeuwen 2007). In order to legitimate actions in the present time, a political actor needs to address potential future consequences (typically using linguistic constructions with 'if'). This is what is referred to as a 'hypothetical future' by Reyes (2011: 786). The hypothetical future may, however, be salient through mythopoesis and a cautionary or moral tale on the one hand, or through rationalisation on the other hand, depending on how the 'future' is construed and warranted in relation to a crisis scenario.

In the legitimisation process, Cap (2008, 2010, 2014) has developed a spatial-temporal-axiological model (STA) employed by political actors, known as Proximisation Theory. The STA thus makes it possible for a controversial policy to be justified at a given time and in a given situation. It is based on Chilton's (2004) theory of 'spatial proximisation' and complements this with temporal and axiological elements. Although Proximisation Theory was initially intended for issues of legitimisation in state-level discourse, the theory is also 'applicable in the vast area of public discourses, including such heterogeneous domains as preventive medicine, cyber-threat or policies to contain climate change' (Cap 2014: 16–17).

5.3 This volume's contributions to Legitimisation Studies

Within the framework explored above, this book adopts the position that legitimisation, as an affirmative course of action conducted by the self, may result in the de-legitimisation of the status or actions of another. It therefore posits the case that de-legitimisation serves not only to discredit the other, but also to legitimise the actions of the self. Legitimisation becomes necessary when conflict or crisis arises. The contention is that the more a conflict is polarised, or the more a crisis is marked by one or more factors of threat, urgency or uncertainty, the greater the need for a legitimisation strategy. The political actor in need of greater credibility is already on the receiving end of de-legitimisation, due to the weakness of either their ideas, their ideology, their policies, their actions or their reputation. This means that legitimisation is situated in an ongoing process which is preceded by a perception (or predicament) of de-legitimisation, and in order to legitimise one's position, there will be, intentionally or unintentionally, a corresponding de-legitimisation of the other. It is argued that not only does a greater scale of crisis lead to a greater need for legitimisation, but also the potential for overt de-legitimisation strategies becomes much greater, as does the risk of greater conflict through discourse. It also contended that the de-legitimisation strategies which appear to discredit opponents more transparently or overtly have two key features. Firstly, they help to give credibility to the agent using the strategy; secondly, they reveal a latent cognitive awareness of one or more dimensions of a crisis scenario which the political actor is attempting to pre-empt or overcome. Legitimising and de-legitimising are therefore present, but not necessarily in equal proportions at the discursive interface. In other words, giving one's opinion does not automatically and discursively invalidate another's differing opinion, even though recipients may be able to discern differences in the validity of opinions in context.

6 Chapter summary

Part I explores how political regimes may impose or reproduce a set of values through the management of genres. It examines how institutional factors can influence the legitimisation process through discursive stabilising techniques. This means that the institutional apparatus of democratic

Introduction

and non-democratic regimes can stabilise power through the authority of conformity, tradition or the rule of law on the one hand, and means or goal-oriented rationalisation on the other. It may also resort to moral evaluation strategies to impose 'the way things are'. Through these techniques of management or control, legitimisation can be achieved. It also investigates the destabilising threat posed by de-legitimisation.

In Chapter 1, Chiara Bertulessi applies the Discourse-Historical Approach (DHA) to investigate how the education system in China seeks control over education while maintaining the dominant ideology of those in power. Education has had a moralising function in Chinese schooling, and Bertulessi explains that educational policies in China are continually adapted in order to respond to evolving social, economic and political needs. A stringent form of control is an essential tool for the legitimisation of political power and maintaining the dominant ideology.

Chapter 2, by Célia Atzeni, examines the concept of 'discursive smoothing' in international discourse, where controversial topics require consensus in the way the United Nations manages and represents them. Through a diachronic approach linked to corpus linguistics, Atzeni argues that this discourse seeks consensus which is less likely to be challenged by political actors (leaders, states and so on). The legitimisation process at the international level involves removing elements of heterogeneity, difficulty, conflict or polarised positions from discourse, especially since 2010.

In Chapter 3, Nadezda Shchinova analyses de-legitimisation strategies involving the use of accusations of 'populism' in the French and Spanish parliaments. She analyses the power of moral evaluation to discredit opponents from the perspective of pragmatics and shows how the notion of crisis can be made salient through the use of a discursive technique. Shchinova's comparative study quantitatively and qualitatively analyses the occurrences of the term *populis** (*populism* and its derivatives) using two datasets of parliamentary debates from 2019 in the French National Assembly and the Spanish Congress of Deputies.

In Chapter 4, Juana I. Marín-Arrese applies the macro-categories of epistemic and effective stances to a CDS-based analysis of the key players in the Brexit debate, and the need for political actors to legitimise their knowledge about the process of Brexit. Marín-Arrese demonstrates how the need for legitimate control of conceptions of reality (in terms of epistemic stances) and the need for control of relations at the level of reality (through the use of effective stances) are both different at the discursive level. This approach makes it possible to expose the strategic functions not only of (de-)legitimisation, but also of coercion involved in the Brexit debate.

Part II shows how new forms of media (especially digital media and social platforms) have resulted in the proliferation of media genres and new challenges for politicians in the management of political discourse. This proliferation may come into conflict with the stabilising forces of authority and rationalisation, and have the potential to reinvigorate the superficiality of moral evaluation and the manipulative potency of mythopoesis through the dissemination of cautionary tales. The contributors analyse how these new media formats have had an impact on the delivery of the message and the management of communication in relation to different types of authority – especially personal authority and role model authority. The authors also address how these new outlets for the superficiality of legitimisation through moral evaluation and labels can lead to the de-legitimisation of political opponents.

Chapter 5, by Mariya Chankova, explores political discourse practices across new forms of media and examines how the traditional paradigm of communication may have changed. She shows how the liberalisation of communicative media has resulted in political actors having more tools available to reach their public, more freedom in the content they disseminate and less exposure to scrutiny. Chankova draws on examples from the online social media platform Facebook, and argues that the proliferation of new media calls into question the accountability and legitimisation techniques of political actors.

A multimodal approach is employed by Tetiana Krysanova in Chapter 6. The author argues that politicians may be construed as filmmakers and the electorate as viewers as a means of using intersubjective interaction to construct 'meaning-in-context'. Focusing on Donald Trump's 2020 election campaign commercials, Krysanova examines the use of video commercials in political campaigns and meaning-making through the use of multisemiotic resources and an integrated cognitive-pragmatic and cognitive-semiotic approach. Such discourse may be used for both legitimising purposes, but also to de-legitimise the political opponent, in this case Joe Biden. In Trump's anti-Biden discourse, Biden is presented as a threat to the USA through the elicitation of emotions, mainly fear.

Part III focuses on the cognitive dimension of rhetorical devices, and the chapters highlight the relevance of cognitive linguistic methods in CDS and the manipulative potential of rhetorical devices not only to legitimise political actors but also to de-legitimise their opponents. The authors show how rhetorical techniques form part of the personal authority of leaders and other political actors who impose their will because they want to or say so, and how such rhetoric may interact with the authority of experts and rationalisation processes. The chapters focus primarily on Critical Metaphor Analysis with regard to political survival in unstable regimes, the CARD metaphor and the climate crisis.

In Chapter 7, Issa Kanté explores the rhetorical techniques used for glorifying ideology as a means of backgrounding the real causes and catastrophes of military conflicts, while obfuscating accountability and failure. Kanté analyses metaphor and metonymy associated with war rhetoric and presents a corpus-based study of fifteen political speeches from six African countries facing conflict (including ethnic rebellions, military coups and terrorism). These legitimising approaches may also inadvertently expose the underlying personal fragility of certain political leaders.

Yuuki Tomoshige analyses how legitimising and de-legitimising strategies may be employed through the use of the CARD metaphor in Chapter 8. This metaphor normally presupposes social class, but may also be used to persuade the recipient to adopt a given position. While legitimisation may be used by those of a socially 'low' status to make people sympathetic to their cause, de-legitimisation involves criticising another social actor by targeting their social position, their gender and their race. Consequently, people of different levels of perceived social status are able to legitimise their influence or ability to yield sympathy through the use of 'playing the X card'.

Finally, in Chapter 9, Anaïs Augé demonstrates how political arguments undergo a metaphorical depiction to promote a particular viewpoint on the environmental crisis. She explores the argumentative function of quoted metaphors in political debates on climate change in attempts by politicians and climate activists to strive for expert authority. Augé argues that figurative conceptualisations can depict a complex issue on the one hand, while opponents may be able to highlight the inaccuracy of the figurative conceptualisations on the other hand, thus leading to de-legitimisation.

References

Abuelwafa, M. A. (2021). Legitimation and manipulation in political speeches: A corpus-based study. *Procedia Computer Science*, 189, pp. 11–18. doi: 10.1016/j.procs.2021.05.066.

Al-Rawi, A., O'Keefe, D., Kane, O. and Bizimana, A.-J. (2021). Twitter's fake news discourses around climate change and global warming. *Frontiers in Communication*, 6 (November), pp. 1–9. doi: 10.3389/fcomm.2021.729818.

Aristotle. (2010). *Rhetoric*. New York: Cosimo Classics.

Augé, A. (2023). *Metaphor and Argumentation in Climate Crisis Discourse*. New York: Routledge.

Austin, J. (1962). *How to Do Things with Words*. Oxford: Clarendon Press.

Beetham, D. (2013). *The Legitimation of Power*. 2nd edn. Basingstoke: Palgrave Macmillan.

Beetham, D. and Lord, C. (1998). Legitimacy and the European Union. In: Nentwich, M. and Weale, A., eds, *Political Theory and the European Union: Legitimacy, Constitutional Choice and Citizenship*. London: Routledge, pp. 15–33.

Ben Hamed, M. and Mayaffre, D. (2015). Les thèmes du discours. Du concept à la méthode. *Mots. Les Langages du politique*, 108, pp. 5–13. Available from: http://journals.openedition.org/mots/21975 [accessed 13 June 2023].

Berrocal, M. (2020). Language aggression as an inherent part of populist discourse. In: Scharlaj, M., ed., *Language and Power in Discourses of Conflict*. Berlin: Peter Lang, pp. 285–302.

Birch, A. H. (1993). *The Concepts and Theories of Modern Democracy*. London: Routledge.

Bull, P. and Simon-Vandenbergen, A.-M. (2019). Conflict in political discourse: Conflict as congenital to political discourse. In: Evans, M., Jeffries, L. and O'Driscoll, J., eds, *The Routledge Handbook of Language in Conflict*. London: Routledge, pp. 246–70.

Cap, P. (2008). Towards the proximization model of the analysis of legitimization in political discourse. *Journal of Pragmatics*, 40 (1), pp. 17–40.

Cap, P. (2010). Axiological aspects of proximization. *Journal of Pragmatics*, 42 (2), pp. 392–407.
Cap, P. (2013). *Proximization: The Pragmatics of Symbolic Distance Crossing*. Amsterdam: John Benjamins.
Cap, P. (2014). Applying cognitive pragmatics to Critical Discourse Studies: A proximization analysis of three public space discourses. *Journal of Pragmatics*, 70 (1), pp. 16–30.
Cap, P. (2017). Studying ideological worldviews in political Discourse Space: Critical-cognitive advances in the analysis of conflict and coercion. *Journal of Pragmatics*, 108 (January), pp. 17–27. doi: 10.1016/j.pragma.2016.11.008.
Cap, P. (2021). Alternative futures in political discourse. *Discourse & Society*, 32 (3), pp. 328–45. doi: 10.1177/0957926520977218.
Cap, P. and Okulska, U., eds. (2013a). *Analysing Genres in Political Communication: Theory and Practice*. Amsterdam: John Benjamins.
Cap, P. and Okulska, U. (2013b). Analyzing genres in political communication: An introduction. In: Cap, P. and Okulska, U., eds, *Analysing Genres in Political Communication: Theory and Practice*. Amsterdam: John Benjamins, pp. 1–26.
Charteris-Black, J. (2011). *Polticians and Rhetoric: The Persuasive Power of Metaphor*. Basingstoke: Palgrave Macmillan.
Charteris-Black, J. (2014). *Analysing Political Speeches: Rhetoric, Discourse and Metaphor*. Basingstoke: Palgrave Macmillan.
Charteris-Black, J. (2021). *Metaphors of Coronavirus: Invisible Enemy or Zombie Apocalypse?* Cham: Springer Nature.
Chilton, P. (2004). *Analysing Political Discourse: Theory and Practice*. London: Routledge.
Chiluwa, I. (2021a). Introduction: discourse, conflict and conflict resolution. In: Chiluwa, I., ed., *Discourse and Conflict: Analysing Text and Talk of Conflict, Hate and Peace-building*. London: Palgrave Macmillan, pp. 1–15.
Chiluwa, I., ed. (2021b). *Discourse and Conflict: Analysing Text and Talk of Conflict, Hate and Peace-building*. London: Palgrave Macmillan.
Chun, C., ed. (2022). *Applied Linguistics and Politics*. London and New York: Bloomsbury Academic.
Coombs, W. T. and Holladay, S. J., eds. (2010). *The Handbook of Crisis Communication*. Chichester: Blackwell.
Coulomb-Gully, M. and Esquenazi, J.-P. (2012). Fiction et politique: doubles jeux. *Mots. Les Langages du Politique*, 99, pp. 5–11. Available from: http://journals.openedition.org/mots/20680 [accessed 13 June 2023].
Ekström, M. and Firmstone, J. (2017a). Introduction: a discourse analytical approach to researching mediated political communication. In: Ekström, M. and Firmstone, J., eds, *The Mediated Politics of Europe: A Comparative Study of Discourse*. Cham: Palgrave Macmillan, pp. 3–35.
Ekström, M. and Firmstone, J. (2017b). Conclusion: Tensions and disruptions in mediated politics. In: Ekström, M. and Firmstone, J., eds, *The Mediated Politics of Europe: A Comparative Study of Discourse*. Cham: Palgrave Macmillan, pp. 319–38.
Ekström, M. and Patrona, M., eds. (2011). *Talking Politics in Broadcast Media: Cross-Cultural Perspectives on Political Interviewing, Journalism and Accountability*. Amsterdam: John Benjamins.
Evans, M., Jeffries, L. and O'Driscoll, J., eds. (2019). *The Routledge Handbook of Language in Conflict*. London: Routledge.

Fairclough, N. (1995). *Media Discourse*. London: Edward Arnold.
Fairclough, N. (2001). *Language and Power*. 2nd edn. London: Longman.
Ferré, G. (2016). Between fact and fiction: Semantic fields and image content in crime infotainment programs. *Multimodal Communication*, 5 (2), pp. 127–41. doi: 10.1515/mc-2016-0018.
Filardo-Llamas, L., Morales-López, E. and Floyd, A., eds. (2021). *Discursive Approaches to Socio-Political Polarization and Conflict*. London: Routledge.
Habermas, J. (1976). *Legitimation Crisis*. London: Heinemann.
Hart, C. and Kelsey, D., eds. (2018) *Discourses of Disorder: Riots, Strikes and Protests in the Media*. Edinburgh: Edinburgh University Press.
Held, D. (1996). *Models of Democracy*. 2nd edn. Stanford, CA: Stanford University Press.
Huang, M. (2020). Introduction: constructing and communicating crisis discourse from cognitive, discursive and sociocultural perspectives. In: Huang, M. and Holmgreen, L.-L., eds, *The Language of Crisis: Metaphors, Frames and Discourses*. Amsterdam: John Benjamins, pp. 1–19.
Huang, M. and Holmgreen, L.-L., eds. (2020). *The Language of Crisis: Metaphors, Frames and Discourses*. Amsterdam: John Benjamins.
Kopytowska, M. (2013). Blogging as the mediatization of politics and a new form of social interaction: A case study of 'proximization dynamics' in Polish and British political blogs. In: Cap, P. and Okulska, U., eds, *Analyzing Genres in Political Communication: Theory and Practice*. Amsterdam: John Benjamins, pp. 379–421.
Koselleck, R. (2006). Crisis. *Journal of the History of Ideas*, 67 (2), pp. 357–400.
Kotzur, G. (2020). Metaphors for protest: The persuasive power of cross-domain mappings on demonstration posters against Stuttgart 21. In: Huang, M. and Holmgreen, L.-L., eds, *The Language of Crisis: Metaphors, Frames and Discourses*. Amsterdam: John Benjamins, pp. 169–96.
Krzyżanowski, M. (2019). Brexit and the imaginary of 'crisis': A discourse-conceptual analysis of European news media. *Critical Discourse Studies*, 16 (4), pp. 465–90. doi: 10.1080/17405904.2019.1592001.
Locke, J. (2021) [1690]. *Second Treatise of Government*. Available from: https://www.gutenberg.org/files/7370/7370-h/7370-h.htm [accessed 23 February 2023].
Mazzoleni, G. and Bracciale, R. (2018). Socially mediated populism: The communicative strategies of political leaders on Facebook. *Palgrave Communications*, 50 (4), pp. 1–10. doi: 10.1057/s41599-018-0104-x.
McCormick, J. P. (2007). *Weber, Habermas, and Transformations of the European State: Constitutional, Social and Supranational Democracy*. Cambridge: Cambridge University Press.
McIntyre, L. (2018). *Post-Truth*. Cambridge, MA: MIT Press.
Montgomery, M. (2017). Post-truth politics? Authenticity, populism and the electoral discourses of Donald Trump. *Journal of Language and Politics*, 16 (4), pp. 619–39. doi: 10.1075/jlp.17023.mon.
Mudde C. and Kaltwasser C. R. (2017). *Populism: A Very Short Introduction*. Oxford: Oxford University Press.
Musolff, A. (2016). *Political Metaphor Analysis: Discourse and Scenarios*. London: Bloomsbury Academic.
Musolff, A. (2022). 'World-beating' pandemic responses: Ironical, sarcastic, and satirical use of war and competition metaphors in the context of COVID-19 pandemic. *Metaphor and Symbol*, 37 (2), pp. 76–87. doi: 10.1080/10926488.2021.1932505.

Nahajec, L. (2019). Projecting your 'opponent's' views: Linguistic negation and the potential for conflict. In: Evans, M., Jeffries, L. and O'Driscoll, J., eds, *The Routledge Handbook of Language in Conflict*. London: Routledge, pp. 64–82.

Nguyen, C. T. and Williams, B. (2020). Moral outrage porn. *Journal of Ethics and Social Philosophy*, 18 (2), pp. 147–72. doi: 10.26556/jesp.v18i2.990.

Okulska, U. and Cap, P. (2010a). Analysis of political discourse: Landmarks, challenges and prospects. In: Okulska, U. and Cap, P., eds, *Perspectives in Political Discourse*. Amsterdam: John Benjamins, pp. 3–20.

Okulska, U. and Cap, P., eds. (2010b). *Perspectives in Political Discourse*. Amsterdam: John Benjamins.

Patrona, M. and Thornborrow, J. (2017). Mediated constructions of crisis. In: Ekström, M. and Firmstone, J., eds, *The Mediated Politics of Europe: A Comparative Study of Discourse*. Cham: Palgrave Macmillan, pp. 59–88.

Reisigl, M. and Wodak, R. (2009). The Discourse-Historical Approach (DHA). In: Wodak, R. and Meyer, R., eds, *Methods of Critical Discourse Analysis*. 2nd ed. London: Sage, pp. 87–121.

Reyes, A. (2011). Strategies of legitimization in political discourse: From words to actions. *Discourse & Society*, 22 (6), pp. 781–807. doi: 10.1177/0957926511419927.

Scharlaj, M, ed. (2020). *Language and Power in Discourses of Conflict*. Berlin: Peter Lang.

Searle, J. (1969). *Speech Acts*. Cambridge: Cambridge University Press.

Sørensen, M. J. and Johansen, J. (2016). Nonviolent conflict escalation. *Conflict Resolution Quarterly*, 34 (1). doi: 10.1002/crq.21173.

Ullmann, S. (2020). 'Today, the long Arab winter has begun to thaw': A corpus-assisted discourse study of conceptual metaphors in political speeches about the Arab revolutions. In: Huang, M. and Holmgreen, L.-L., eds, *The Language of Crisis: Metaphors, Frames and Discourses*. Amsterdam: John Benjamins, pp. 137–68.

Unger, J. W., Wodak, R. and KhosraviNik, M. (2016) Critical Discourse Studies and social media data. In: Silverman, D., ed., *Qualitative Research*. 4th edn. London: Sage, pp. 277–93.

van Dijk, T. A. (1997). The study of discourse. In: van Dijk, T. A., ed., *Discourse as Structure and Process: Discourse Studies: A Multidisciplinary Introduction*. London: Sage.

van Dijk, T. A. (2006). Discourse and manipulation. *Discourse & Society*, 17 (3), pp. 359–83. doi: 10.1177/0957926506060250.

van Dijk, T. A. (2011). Discourse, knowledge, power and politics: Towards critical epistemic discourse analysis. In: Hart, C., ed., *Critical Discourse Studies in Context and Cognition*. Amsterdam: John Benjamins, pp. 27–63.

van Dijk, T. A. (2014). *Discourse and Knowledge: A Sociocognitive Approach*. Cambridge: Cambridge University Press.

van Leeuwen, T. (2007). Legitimation in discourse and communication. *Discourse & Communication*, 1 (1), pp. 91–112. doi: 10.1177/1750481307071986.

van Leeuwen, T. (2008). *Discourse and Practice: New Tools for Critical Discourse Analysis*. Oxford: Oxford University Press.

Weber, M. (1964) [1922]. *The Theory of Social and Economic Organization*. 2nd edn. Translated by A. M. Henderson and T. Parsons. New York: Free Press.

Wodak, R. (2011). *The Discourse of Politics in Action: Politics as Usual*. Basingstoke: Palgrave Macmillan.

Wodak, R. (2015). *The Politics of Fear: What Right-Wing Populist Discourses Mean*. London: Sage.

Part I

The role of legitimisation in institutional contexts

CHAPTER 1

Education and political socialisation in contemporary China: From institutional discourse to teaching materials

Chiara Bertulessi

1 Introduction

Education is often regarded as one of the domains of social life to which, especially in the context of nation-states, political elites have assigned the task of cultivating people to become 'good citizens'. Such conceptualisation of the role of education within society is inevitably linked to the connection between educational policies, political objectives and the states' ideologies. As observed by Lall (2009: 1), 'Governments have long used education and the school curriculum amongst other vehicles for disseminating political ideologies with a view to transforming societies and subjecting them to more effective state control.'

Throughout history and in different societies, education has thus assumed considerable significance as part of the visions and interests of political elites, who have placed emphasis on 'the role of education – and particularly schooling – as a tool for shaping and sustaining political systems' (Lall 2009: 1). Education, as a means to socialise people (or citizens) into sets of values and norms considered acceptable by the dominant elites, has therefore frequently assumed a crucial importance in the political agendas of governments, including laying, or preserving, the foundations of political legitimisations and fostering political and social stability (Lall and Vickers 2009).

When investigating processes of political socialisation, the study of official political discourse on the topic of education can offer valuable insights into how those who govern in different socio-political systems and historical contexts construct and disseminate specific discourses regarding the functions and tasks assigned to education within society, and in relation to objectives of a political and ideological nature. This also acquires an even greater relevance with regard to the ways education and its tasks are framed in relation to the need for governments to foster adherence and loyalty on the part of citizens, notably at times of (potential) crisis or conflict, or to avoid such scenarios. The ways, the extent, and how this is manifested at the level of political discourse vary depending on the specific features of the sociopolitical and historical context under scrutiny.

This chapter centres on the People's Republic of China (PRC), exploring the relationship between education and political socialisation from a discursive perspective. It explores how the interconnections between education, politics and the Party-State[1] ideology are manifested and circulated in contemporary China through different instantiations of the official discourse of the Communist Party of China (CPC) on the subject. This study is guided by two interrelated research questions: (1) How is the relationship between education, politics and the Party-State ideology framed in the official discourse of the Xi Jinping Era, as represented from the selected sources? (2) What are the keywords and fixed formulations of the official discourse on education, which recur through different texts, genres and domains of this discourse? What kind of discursive frames do these activate?

To address these questions, the contribution first analyses the discourse constructed by a corpus of texts meant to encapsulate Xi Jinping's vision on education between 2012 and 2022; second, the educational dimension is considered, with examples provided from a textbook designed to teach the leader's thought to children. The chapter is structured as follows: section 2 provides some background regarding the emphasis that the political leadership of the PRC has placed, and continues to place, on education, in relation to its political and ideological objectives; section 3 clarifies the theoretical and methodological framework informing the study and outlines the data and method of the analysis; sections 4 and 5 centre on the case study, providing examples from the analysis of the selected sources, regarded as representative of the dominant discourse and views of China's current political leader on education. Section 6 sets out the concluding remarks of the chapter.

2 Education, politics and discourse in the PRC

In the PRC, as part of the CPC's agenda, education and politics have long been interconnected. Over the decades, educational policies and practices have been adapted to serve evolving social, economic and political needs, with extensive and strict control being maintained on educational practices, contents and materials (Doughty 1978; Pepper 1996; Vickers 2009a, 2009b; Vickers and Zeng 2017). As stressed by Vickers and Zeng (2017), as 'Party ideology has evolved during the post-Mao era, so have curricula, textbooks and the pedagogical practices advocated (if not always adopted) for classroom use.' The strong connection between education and politics is

---

[1] The term 'Party-State' is frequently employed when referring to China's political system which, as a one-party system, is dominated by the CPC; this term highlights the intertwining between the CPC and the State.

also manifested and reinforced at the discursive level. Cao (2014) and Lams (2018) have discussed the persistence of specific discursive strategies in the official political discourse, dominated by the CPC, in China. Together with 'consensus building' and 'a drive for unity', Cao has identified a persistent focus on education, which has continued to be conceived as 'the principal mechanism through which the discursive consensus is promoted, transmitted, sustained and reproduced, both within the CCP membership and wider public' (Cao 2014: 7). In this respect, education, in its wider sense, is carried out through a 'range of institutional instruments', such as 'training courses organised by CCP Party schools, publicity campaigns through state-run media, and incorporating consensus into the education curriculum in schools and universities' (Cao 2014: 7–8; Vickers and Zeng 2017). With regard to political socialisation, the PRC political leadership has, especially since the 1980s, employed different terms (moral, ideological-political, patriotic education, and so on) to identify a range of educational practices and subjects which, despite differences in terminology, have all been interwoven, equally serving the common purpose 'to socialize people (including students) into the norms, values and ideologies deemed acceptable to and prescribed by the CPC-led state' (Law 2013: 608; Xu 2021).

These observations maintain their validity in the so-called Xi Jinping Era. As discussed in this chapter, given the relevance it acquires within society and politics, education has featured as one of the main concerns within the CPC agenda and, specifically, within Xi's official discourse since he came to power in 2012. For instance, as part of his Report to the 19th Congress of the CPC in 2017, Xi stressed the importance of making China an 'educational powerhouse',[2] presenting this as one of the most important tasks of the so-called 'Great rejuvenation of the Chinese nation'.[3] The formulation 'educational powerhouse' has since acquired a growing centrality in the Chinese official political and media discourse on the subject; see, for example, Cao (2018). In discussing the CPC contemporary vision on education and the discourse it constructs and circulates on this crucial subject, particular significance should also be attributed to the fact that, in July 2020, Xi's thoughts on education were collected by the Ministry of Education (MOE n.d.) in a book, presented as a tool to promote the study and implementation of the leader's views on the subject in different institutional, work and educational settings (MOE 2020).[4] Moreover, a special column on the topic is hosted on the MOE official website, on which the analysis presented in section 4 of this chapter is based (MOE n.d.).

---

[2] 教育强国 in Chinese. Using the search tool Factiva Global Headlines and selecting Xinhua and the People's Daily as sources, it is possible to observe how this wording has become widely used in this official medium since 2017, especially in 2019.
[3] 中华民族伟大复兴.
[4] In 2022 an English translation of the book was published (Xinhua 2022; Compilation and Translation Team 2022).

In terms of educational policies, in 2019 (the year marking the 70th anniversary of the founding of the PRC) important institutional documents were published, among which features the Plan for a new 'modernisation of China's education' to be carried out by 2035, issued by the CPC Central Committee and the State Council (CPCCC & SC 2019). Besides addressing critical issues including the universalisation of education, equity and access, quality, innovation, and training for teachers, among others, the Plan presents the guiding principles of such a process. One significant feature is the prominent position assigned to the political thought of China's top leader, as exemplified by the formulation 'Xi Jinping Thought on Socialism with Chinese Characteristics for a New Era'[5] (hereafter 'Xi Jinping Thought'). Moreover, the document calls for the need to integrate this thought into the educational system and, specifically, into classes and teaching materials. In this context, in the summer of 2021 the Ministry of Education announced the publication of a new set of textbooks designed to teach Xi Jinping Thought to the Chinese youth at different levels of schooling (section 5), which have been described as crucial tools for ideological-political education and the integration of the leader's official thought into teaching materials (CPCCC & SC 2019; MOE 2021a).

Those touched upon in this section constitute just some of the many examples testifying to both the crucial role that China's contemporary political leadership assigns to education, as well as the will to systematise the official and dominant vision regarding the principles which should guide educational practices at all levels of society, and the functions it should fulfil.

3 Framework and study design

The theoretical and methodological framework adopted for this study shares common ground with Critical Discourse Analysis (CDA) (Fairclough 1989, 1995; Wodak 2001; Reisigl and Wodak 2009) and especially with the Discourse-Historical Approach (DHA) (Reisigl and Wodak 2009). Three elements of the DHA appear to be particularly useful for what is addressed in this chapter. These include, firstly, its definition of discourse as a 'cluster of context-dependent semiotic practices that are situated within specific fields of social action' (Reisigl and Wodak 2009: 89); secondly, the importance that this approach attributes to context. According to Reisigl and Wodak (2009: 93), the meaning of 'context' involves four different levels, ranging from the 'the text-internal co-text and co-discourse', to intertextual and interdiscur-

---

[5] 习近平新时代中国特色社会主义思想, the official formulation that encapsulates the political and ideological contribution of Xi Jinping; see Peters (2017) and Garrick and Bennett (2018). A related and relevant topic, which cannot be addressed here, is the role and use of ideology and propaganda in Xi's China; see Brown and Bērziņa-Čerenkova (2018) and Lams (2018).

sive relationships, the institutional context and, finally, the socio-political, historical context 'which discursive practices are embedded in and related to' (Reisigl and Wodak 2009: 93). The third element is the significance attributed to intertextuality: in other words, to how the texts are linked to other texts' (Reisigl and Wodak 2009: 90). As suggested by Devitt (1991: 337), the concept of intertextuality may be used 'to encapsulate the interaction of texts within a single discourse community'. In terms of field of action, the sources analysed in this chapter can be assigned to the field of the 'formation of public attitudes, opinion and will' (Reisigl and Wodak 2009: 91), as these include both the institutional discourse circulated through the state media and institutional websites as well as official textbooks meant to be integrated into the schooling practices. The extralinguistic context, and, particularly, both the institutional and broader socio-political and historical context of the study are represented by the PRC political domain, in the period 2012–22, corresponding to Xi Jinping's first two terms as Secretary General of the CPC.[6] In the case in point, intertextuality is addressed by looking at the repetition of the same sets of keywords (or even chunks of texts) throughout different texts and genres which, nonetheless, are produced within the same 'discourse community' (Devitt 1991;[7] Flowerdew 2013: 144–6), represented by the Party-State (Mottura 2021). In this respect, both the corpus of texts belonging to the field of institutional discourse and the textbook presented in the chapter can be regarded as belonging to different genres which, nevertheless, constitute integral parts of the same multifaceted landscape of the genres of contemporary political Chinese discourse. This is based on the assumption that political discourse in China may indeed be understood as a complex set of texts, issued by organs of the CPC and the state (Mottura 2021). In this sense, a wide range of texts belonging to different genres is thus produced by a variety of authors which, however, 'represent one single ideal institutional author, namely the Party-state in its broadest sense' (Mottura 2021: 209). From this perspective, the different genres of official political discourse synergically interact to build, disseminate and consolidate consistent discourses and narratives on specific macro-topics. In this particular case, the macro-topic under scrutiny is education and, notably, the principles and tasks assigned to it fall within the socio-political context of contemporary China.

Another useful concept for this study is frame (Goffman 1974; Entman 1993). Frames have been defined as 'schemata of interpretation' (Goffman 1974), and as 'organizing principles that are socially shared and persistent

---

[6] Since 2012–13, Xi has served as General Secretary of CPC, as President of the PRC, and Chairman of the Central Military Commission. During the Party 20th Congress, held in Beijing in October 2022, Xi Jinping was confirmed for a third term (five years) as General Secretary.
[7] In her analysis of texts produced in the setting of tax accounting, Devitt (1991) identifies three types of intertextuality: referential, functional and generic.

overtime, that work symbolically to meaningfully structure the social world' (Reese 2001: 11). Given that many of the signifying elements, or the 'structurally located lexical choices of codes constructed by following certain shared rules and conventions' (Pan and Kosicki 1993: 59), may function as rhetorical framing devices, particular attention should be given to the lexical choices in texts when analysing frames. In this respect, a widely studied feature of the discourse of Chinese politics is its frequent usage of recurring fixed formulations, standardised wordings typically created to condense the ideology and vision of the Party-State and the result of a process of crystallisation of the 'correct' meanings and linguistic forms in official discourse (Schoenhals 1992; Ji 2004). Therefore, it seems useful to look at lexical choices in the political discourse on education from the perspective of how both fixed formulations and recurrent sentences may function as framing devices. These may help us to make sense of the way education and its role in contemporary Chinese society is conceived by the political elite and comes to be represented in discourse.

The analysis of the selected sources blends elements of Corpus Linguistics with CDA (Baker et al. 2008), such as keyword extraction, analysis of concordances and collocations, and lexical bundles[8] are supported by discourse analysis carried out in a qualitative vein.

3.1 Data and method

The analysis presented in section 4 is based on a corpus of texts containing Xi Jinping's thoughts and observations on education, produced between 2012 and 2022 (hereinafter 'Xi Jinping Corpus') and, specifically, during his first two terms.[9] In most of the cases, the texts included in the corpus are excerpts from longer documents, and are regularly collected and organised chronologically as part of a special column published on the MOE official website, entitled 'Deepening the study and implementation of General Secretary Xi Jinping's important expositions on education'[10] (MOE n.d.) (see section 1, this chapter). The original sources of the documents (from which the excerpts were collected to form the special column) are official Party and state media. Prominent among these sources is Xinhua, followed by the Renmin Ribao (People's Daily), which are the official news agency of the Chinese government and the official newspaper of the Central Committee of the CPC respectively. The documents include letters and messages sent by Xi Jinping to different groups, institutions and representatives (including

---

[8] Lexical bundles are named 'N-grams' in the Sketch Engine tool, referring to the display of sequences of tokens.
[9] The first excerpt available is dated 7 December 2012, while the last excerpt considered for this study is dated 8 September 2022 (the last to be collected before the 20th Party Congress).
[10] 深入学习贯彻习近平总书记关于教育的重要论述.

students, teachers, for example), reports of visits he conducted in different contexts, and speeches delivered during important events. The words pronounced by Xi Jinping are either quoted verbatim (such as when the full text of a letter or a speech is included) or as reported speech. These constitute a typical example of how China's political discourse is circulated through official media online, republished on different media and systematised, as is the case here, on an institutional (governmental) website such as that of the Ministry of Education of the PRC. In this sense, the selection, by relevant institutions, of sources and excepts, their organisation and insertion in a specific frame (as is the special column on the website of the Ministry) to encapsulate Xi Jinping's vision on education acquires a particular significance. As such, it is believed that these excerpts deserve to be investigated. The collection of the excerpts for the present study has thus led to the compilation of a relatively small, yet specialised corpus for the analysis (Table 1.1)[11] which can provide a significant insight into what the political leadership of the PRC wants to highlight, circulate and submit to a process of canonisation within the vast discursive production of the past ten years on this topic by Chinese politics.

In this chapter, the Xi Jinping Corpus is analysed through the keywords extracted using Sketch Engine.[12] These keywords prove to be particularly significant in relation to the research questions set out in section 1, in that their meanings and usage in context relate to the relations between education, politics and the official ideology, as well as the cultivation of the youth through education as a political endeavour. The analysis is chiefly focused on collocations and concordances of the selected keywords, aiming to show their usage in contexts, also as part of recurrent lexical bundles or linguistic clusters. Due to space constraints, the analysis centres on the group of the first ten keywords included in the list extracted from Sketch Engine. For the same reason, only a limited number of examples for each keyword will be included, as prominence is given to concordance lines and collocations which most effectively reflect the issues under scrutiny.

With regard to the teaching material discussed in section 5, a chapter of one of the four textbooks issued in 2021 to teach Xi Jinping Thought is considered, specifically the volume addressed to younger students attending the first level of primary school in China (MOE 2021b). Compiled by a group within the MOE, these materials were published in the summer of 2021 by the People's Education Press – the publishing house under direct control of the Ministry – and entitled *Xi Jinping Thought on Socialism with Chinese Characteristics for a New Era. A Reader*.[13] In addition to providing

---

[11] The corpus size is of over 36,000 Chinese characters, or, based on the word segmentation and tokenisation by Sketch Engine, 18,418 words and 21,796 tokens.
[12] Sketch Engine: http://www.sketchengine.eu [accessed 28 February 2022]. See Kilgarriff et al. (2014).
[13] 习近平新时代中国特色社会主义思想学生读本.

Table 1.1 *Xi Jinping Corpus details*

Year	Number of excerpts per year
2012	2
2013	25
2014	14
2015	12
2016	11
2017	9
2018	11
2019	16
2020	20
2021	18
2022	9
	Total 147

some examples of how 'ideological-political education'[14] (Vickers 2009a; Chen 2021) is carried out in the textbook chapter analysed, the purpose of section 5 is to highlight the discursive continuity and elements of intertextuality between the more general discourse on education, as also exemplified by the keywords analysed in section 4, and the contents of this teaching material.

Examples from the Chinese sources analysed below are given in their translation (by the author of this chapter), but all original Chinese text is provided in the footnotes.

4 Keywords of Xi Jinping's discourse on education

Keywords from the Xi Jinping Corpus have been extracted through the software Sketch Engine, using *Chinese Web 2017* as a reference corpus. The first ten keywords include words and expressions whose meaning and usage in institutional discourse appear to be particularly relevant to the relationship between education, politics and ideology, as well as the task and objectives involved in cultivating people through education in China. Specifically, the keywords analysed below are: (1) 'builder'; (2) 'successor' (3) 'morality, intellect, physical fitness, aesthetics, love for labour' (or 'well-rounded development', see below); (4) 'fostering virtue through education'; (5) 'Marxism'; (6) 'patriotism'.[15] (The English

---

[14] 思想政治教育.
[15] (1) 建设者; (2) 接班人; (3) 德智体美劳; (4) 立德树人; (5) 马克思主义; (6) 爱国主义. Due to common imperfections in Chinese word segmentation by corpus analysis tools, 德智体 and 美劳 feature as separate words in the list, but they both appear among the first ten and are used as a single linguistic unit in concordance lines and therefore considered as a single keyword, as occurred with 立德 and 树人.

Education and political socialisation in China 33

translation is provided in this list; see the footnotes for the original keywords in Chinese.)

In Xi's discourse, the task of nurturing (young) people through education is presented as being aimed at the cultivation of a specific kind of individual who should be prepared to inherit and carry on China's socialist cause. In the corpus, the use of two keywords which translate as 'builder' and 'successors' constitute a clear example of this. As shown in examples (1) to (3), the most frequent lexical bundle containing both these keywords is 'socialist builders and successors',[16] typically featuring as the object of the verb 'to cultivate, to nurture':[17]

(1) Colleges and universities shoulder the great tasks of studying and disseminating Marxism, and cultivating socialist builders and successors with Chinese characteristics. (Xinhua 2014)

(2) The whole Party and society should continue to pay attention to and support Project Hope, so that young people can fully feel the care of the Party and the warmth of the big socialist family and strive to grow into socialist builders and successors. (Xinhua 2019a)

(3) ... strive to cultivate new people for this era who will take on the great task of national rejuvenation, and cultivate socialist builders and successors who are morally, intellectually, physically and aesthetically developed with a love for labour. (Xinhua 2019b)[18]

As is displayed in example (3), the 'socialist builder and successor' to be cultivated should have an all-round development in terms of morality, intellect, physical fitness, aesthetics and love for labour (keyword number 3). The original Chinese fixed formulation which constitutes keyword number 3 refers to the five dimensions on which, according to contemporary political and academic discourse on the topic, education should focus simultaneously as part of a 'proper' cultivation of the people[19] (Fan and Zou 2020; Qiushi 2021). This is shown by the fact that most of the occurrences of 'socialist builders and successors' (keywords 1 and 2) in the corpus appear (as in example 3) in the co-text with the five dimensions of education, which can be literally translated as 'cultivate socialist builders and successors who are

---

[16] 社会主义建设者和接班人.
[17] 培养.
[18] Original Chinese texts, examples (1) '高校肩负着学习研究宣传马克思主义、培养中国特色社会主义事业建设者和接班人的重大任务。' (2) '全党全社会要继续关注和支持希望工程，让广大青少年都能充分感受到党的关怀和社会主义大家庭的温暖，努力成长为社会主义建设者和接班人。' (3) '... 努力培养担当民族复兴大任的时代新人，培养德智体美劳全面发展的社会主义建设者和接班人。'.
[19] In contemporary Chinese discourse this is often connected to the idea of 'Educating the five domains simultaneously' 五育并举.

morally, intellectually, physically and aesthetically developed with a love for labour'.[20] Official sources (cf. Compilation and Translation Team 2022: 55) also translate this sentence as 'nurturing new generations of socialist builders with well-rounded development'.

The concept of the five domains of education places particular emphasis on moral integrity, which needs to be interpreted within the framework of the moralising function that, historically and today, has been assigned to education in China. Vickers (2009b: 67) also draws on Bakken's research (2000) to make the following observation: while the idea that education should pay attention to cultivating people characterised by moral integrity has its roots in ancient China (particularly in the Confucian tradition), throughout the decades the CPC has adopted and redefined such conceptualisation of education for political needs, including the need for social control.[21] In this context, both what 'moral' means, and which moral values and virtues which should characterise a 'good citizen', have been subject to redefinitions over several decades, reflecting ideological shifts (Vickers 2009b: 67).[22]

Keyword 4 extracted from the Xi Jinping Corpus is indicative of the relevance that 'virtue' and 'morality',[23] however defined, continue to bear in contemporary discourse addressing education (Feng and Shi 2019; Xue and Li 2021). A literal translation of this keyword may be 'establishing virtue and cultivating people', and has been translated into English in official sources as 'fostering virtue through education' (Xi 2022a, 2022b). This formulation was employed by former CPC General Secretary Hu Jintao in his Report to the 18th National Congress in 2012 (Hu 2012; Xue and Li 2021), and repeatedly used by Xi Jinping over the last ten years (cf. Xi 2017, 2022a). As seen in examples (4) and (5), 'fostering virtue through education' is repeatedly presented in the corpus as the 'fundamental task':

(4) Facing the future, Tsinghua University should adhere the fundamental task of fostering virtue through education ... (Xinhua 2021)

---

[20] Translation by the author of the chapter, based on official translations. For example: Compilation and Translation Team (2022: 56).
[21] This is achieved, for instance, by targeting 'unfettered individualism and lack of restraint' as being 'dangerous for social stability and therefore irrational' (Vickers 2009b: 67).
[22] Moreover, courses intended to cultivate the moral integrity, virtue of people and the adherence to a set of specific values deemed as 'correct' by the CPC have been an integral part of school curricula in the history of the PRC, as they are today. These have identified by different terms. On this subject, see Bakken (2000), Lee and Ho (2005), Vickers (2009a, 2009b) and Xu (2021).
[23] This translates as 德.

Education and political socialisation in China 35

(5) We should fully implement the Party's educational policy, fulfil the fundamental task of fostering virtue through education, develop quality-oriented education ... (Weiyan jiaoyu 2017)[24]

Finally, the keywords under scrutiny also include 'Marxism' and 'patriotism'. In the corpus, Marxism is presented as exerting a guiding role which should be supported, and as a thought which should be studied and disseminated in education. Collocations of this word occurring in the corpus thus include: 'to support the guiding role of Marxism'; 'to study Marxist theory'; 'to study, research, disseminate Marxism'.[25] As for patriotism, the words 'patriotism' and 'patriotic spirit'[26] are introduced in the corpus as elements and concepts which should be promoted and reinforced through education, especially when addressed to young generations, as shown by the occurrence of these words in collocation with verbs such as 'to strengthen', 'to enhance', 'to take root'.[27]

These examples show that these keywords commonly occur within a discursive frame which unequivocally reiterates the relationship which ties the task of educating the youth to the socialist cause, and, ultimately, to the political objectives of the leadership, as well as its guiding role in the field.

5 Xi Jinping Thought for textbooks

This section is concerned with the textbooks compiled by China's MOE to integrate the teaching of Xi Jinping Thought into school curricula and, namely, with the volume addressed at younger primary school students (MOE 2021b). The book is organised into six lessons (chapters), whose titles can respectively be translated as: 'I love China', 'Wholeheartedly follow the CPC', 'Entering the New Era', 'My Chinese Dream', 'We are the successors of Communism', and 'Being a good youth in the New Era'. This section focuses on the fifth lesson presented in the volume, 'We are the successors of Communism',[28] which is divided into two parts: 'Glorious Young Pioneers' and 'Grandpa Xi Jinping's expectations for us'.[29]

The lesson is constructed as a multimodal product, in which written and visual texts interact to create meaning and are designed to work synergically in engaging the reader with the represented knowledge (Weninger 2020). The written text is employed to introduce the discussion topics, in

---

24 Examples (4) '面向未来, 清华大学要坚持把立德树人作为根本任务 ...'; (5) '要全面贯彻党的教育方针, 落实立德树人根本任务, 发展素质教育, ...'.
25 坚持马克思主义指导地位; 学习马克思主义理论; 学习研究宣传马克思主义.
26 爱国主义 and 爱国主义精神.
27 加强, 弘扬, 扎根.
28 我们是共产主义接班人.
29 光荣的少先队 and 习近平爷爷对我们的期望.

captions to images, and as the written component of cartoons, framed within small balloons (words pronounced by students, portrayed in drawings). Images included in the lesson also feature pictures of a smiling Xi Jinping portrayed in different educational contexts and surrounded by young students. Although the multimodal dimension of the textbook cannot be explored in detail here, it should at least be noted that the linguistic representation of China's leader is ostensibly supported by the visual component, specifically by the interaction between the written texts and images in the creation of meaning.

The first part of the lesson focuses on Young Pioneers, the famous youth organisation in China, the members of which are described, in the text, as 'successors in building socialism and communism'[30] (MOE 2021b: 42). The second part addresses a related topic, but places particular emphasis on the person of Xi Jinping and his expectations of the youth. In terms of representational strategies, in the written text Xi Jinping is repeatedly referred to through nomination (van Leeuwen 1995: 52–4), from the students' perspective, as 'Grandpa Xi Jinping'. Moreover, in the short texts provided in the lesson, the first-person plural pronoun is employed, as if the students were speaking, describing Xi and his actions. For example, the first sentence of the text introducing this second part can be translated as 'We are the hope and future of the motherland'. The representation of Xi produced through the written text is aimed at portraying him as a caring and loving leader, holding hopes and expectations for the new generations 'to become qualified socialist builders and successors' (MOE 2021b: 44).[31] Linguistically, this is realised, for instance, through verbs which can be translated as 'to care', 'to earnestly hope', 'to give guidance',[32] of which 'Grandpa Xi Jinping' features as the grammatical subject and 'us'[33] as object.

Young students (and, specifically, children) are again presented as the 'builders' and 'successors' of the socialist cause, using the same formulations also found in the Xi Jinping Corpus discussed above. This constitutes a clear example of consistency and continuity across genres within Chinese (and, especially, Xi's) political discourse on education, also realised by means of intertextuality. In the textbook, instances of intertextuality may be found at different levels and in different forms, including in explicit references (in text and pictures) to specific events, such as the leader's visits to schools and the words he pronounced during these specific occasions. An instance of intertextuality as explicit reference to other texts is represented by the inclusion of the full text of a letter sent by Xi in October 2019 to congratulate Young Pioneers of China on the 70th anniversary of the organisation.

---

[30] 少先队员们是建设社会主义和共产主义的接班人.
[31] 成为合格的社会主义建设者和接班人.
[32] 关怀 and 关心, 期望, 教导.
[33] 我们.

This is the same letter which was circulated with its full text throughout state media at the time (see, for example, Xinhua 2019c).

6 Concluding remarks

This chapter has presented and discussed the results of the first phase of a research project which is concerned with the linguistic and discursive elements characterising the broad and multifaceted official discourse on education in the context of contemporary China. It has focused on the discourse by China's current political leader Xi Jinping and an instance of educational material designed to spread his canonised thought and theoretical contributions to the CPC ideology in the twenty-first century. Specifically, the chapter has looked at how the relationship between education, politics and the Party-State ideology is framed in the official discourse of the Xi Jinping Era, placing a particular emphasis on the role played by keywords and fixed formulations and on how these recur throughout different texts and genres, thereby reinforcing a specific interpretation and vision of education. Moreover, the analysis has shown that two dominant features characterise this discourse in contemporary China: the persistent emphasis on education as a means to contribute to the official political objectives (such as the 'socialist cause') and the moralising function assigned to education as the cultivation of people. Consequently, these may be regarded as discursive frames, of which recurring framing devices found at the textual level are (although not exclusively) keywords and fixed formulations as analysed in sections 4 and 5.

This contribution has focused on the first two terms of Xi Jinping, which formally began in 2012. However, the considerable number of policies, documents, teaching materials and speeches recently and currently produced by political and official media institutions to address principles, tasks and objectives of education in its wider sense unequivocally suggest that functions of education as a domain of political socialisation will continue to be assigned a prominent role in the years to come. In this respect, the words pronounced by Xi as part of his Report to the 20th National Congress of the CPC on 16 October 2022 acquire particular significance, as the report once more explicitly references the 'fundamental task' of 'fostering virtue through education', and the need to 'cultivate socialist builders and successors who are morally, intellectually, physically and aesthetically developed with a love for labour' (Xi 2022a, 2022b). This constitutes yet another example of how specific formulations are repeatedly employed in the texts and genres which form part of the multifaceted domain of contemporary political discourse. It also suggests that the framing of education both as a political tool and as carrying a strong moralising function will continue to remain significant during Xi Jinping's third term and that, as such, it deserves to be investigated further.

References

Baker, P., Gabrielatos, C., Khosravinik, M., Krzyżanowski, M., McEnery, T. and Wodak, R. (2008). A useful methodological synergy? Combining critical discourse analysis and corpus linguistics to examine discourses of refugees and asylum seekers in the UK press. *Discourse & Society*, 19 (3), pp. 273–306. doi: 10.1177/0957926508088962.

Bakken, B. (2000). *The Exemplary Society: Human Improvement, Social Control and the Dangers of Modernity in China*. Oxford: Oxford University Press.

Brown, K. and Bērziņa-Čerenkova, U. A. (2018). Ideology in the era of Xi Jinping. *Journal of Chinese Political Science*, 23 (3), pp. 323–39. doi: 10.1007/s11366-018-9541-z.

Cao, D. (2018). Xi calls on building China into education powerhouse. *China Daily*, 11 September. Available from: https://www.chinadaily.com.cn/a/201809/11/WS5b96c0eda31033b4f4655422.html [accessed 14 June 2023].

Cao, Q. (2014). Introduction: Legitimisation, resistance and discursive struggles in contemporary China. In: Qing, C. Tian, H. and Chilton, P., eds, *Discourse, Politics and Media in Contemporary China*. Amsterdam: John Benjamins, pp. 1–21.

Compilation and Translation Team (2022). *Understanding Xi Jinping's Educational Philosophy*. Beijing: Foreign Language Teaching and Research Press and Higher Education Press.

Chen, S. (2021). Ideological and political education. *China Media Project*, 17 December. Available from: https://chinamediaproject.org/the_CPC_dictionary/ideological-and-political-education/ [accessed 14 June 2023].

CPCCC & SC [CPC Central Committee & State Council] (2019). 中共中央、国务院印发《中国教育现代化 2035, 23 February [accessed 30 October 2022].

Devitt, A. (1991). Intertextuality in tax accounting: Generic, referential, and functional. In: Bazerman, C. and Paradis, J., eds, *Textual Dynamics of the Professions: Historical and Contemporary Studies of Writing in Professional Communities*. Madison: University of Wisconsin Press, pp. 336–57.

Doughty, J. J. (1978). The politics of education in the People's Republic of China. *Theory into Practice*, 17 (5), pp. 375–82.

Entman, R. M. (1993). Framing: Toward clarification of a fractured paradigm. *Journal of Communication*, 43 (4), pp. 51–8.

Fairclough, N. (1989). *Language and Power*. London: Longman.

Fairclough, N. (1995). *Critical Discourse Analysis. The Critical Study of Language*. London: Longman.

Fan, G. and Zou, J. (2020). Refreshing China's labor education in the new era: Policy review on education through physical labor. *ECNU Review on Education*, 3 (1), pp. 169–78. doi: 10.1177/2096531120903878.

Feng, G. and Shi, H. (2019). 新时代立德树人的理论内涵及其价值意蕴. 社会主义核心价值观研究, 5 (5), pp. 41–9.

Flowerdew, J. (2013). *Discourse in English Language Education*. London: Routledge.

Garrick, J. and Bennett, Y. C. (2018). 'Xi Jinping Thought': Realisation of the Chinese dream of national rejuvenation?' *China Perspectives*, 1–2. Available from: http://journals.openedition.org/chinaperspectives/7872 [accessed 14 June 2023].

Goffman, E. (1974). *Frame Analysis: An Essay on The Organization of Experience*. Cambridge, MA: Harvard University Press.

Hu, J. (2012). 胡锦涛在中国共产党第十八次全国代表大会上的报告. 8 November. Available from: http://cpc.people.com.cn/n/2012/1118/c64094-19612151-7.html [accessed 3 April 2023].

Ji, F. (2004). *Linguistic Engineering: Language and Politics in Mao's China*. Honolulu: University of Hawai'i Press.

Kilgarriff, A., Baisa, V., Bušta, J., Jakubíček, M., Kovář, V., Michelfeit, J., Rychlý, P. and Suchomel, V. (2014). The Sketch Engine: Ten years on. *Lexicography*, 1, pp. 7–36. doi: 10.1007/s40607-014-0009-9.

Lall, M. (2009). Introduction. In: Lall, M. and Vickers, E., eds, *Education as a Political Tool in Asia*. London and New York: Routledge, pp. 1–9.

Lall, M. and Vickers, E., eds. (2009). *Education as a Political Tool in Asia*. London and New York: Routledge.

Lams, L. (2018). Examining strategic narratives in Chinese official discourse under Xi Jinping. *Journal of Chinese Political Science*, 23 (3), pp. 387–411. doi: 10.1007/s11366-018-9529-8.

Law, W. W. (2013). Globalization, national identity, and citizenship education: China's search for modernization and a modern Chinese citizenry. *Frontiers of Education in China*, 8 (4), pp. 596–627. doi: 10.1007/BF03396993.

Lee, W. O. and Ho, C. H. (2005). Ideopolitical shifts and changes in moral education policy in China. *Journal of Moral Education*, 34 (4), pp. 413–31.

MOE [Ministry of Education] (n.d). 深入学习贯彻习近平总书记关于教育的重要论述. Available from: http://www.moe.gov.cn/jyb_xwfb/xw_zt/moe_357/s7865/s8417/ [accessed 30 October 2020].

MOE [Ministry of Education] (2020). 中共教育部党组关于印发《习近平总书记教育重要论述讲义》的通知. 16 July. Available from: https://www.hep.com.cn/news/show/zhonggong-jiao-yu-bu-dang-zu-guan-yu-yin-fa-xi-jin-ping-zong-shu-ji-jiao-yu-chong-yao-lun-shu-jiang-yi-de-tong-zhi-dadf2884-1736-1000-9d7d-c699b52f38d0 [accessed 30 October 2022].

MOE [Ministry of Education] (2021a). 开创用习近平新时代中国特色社会主义思想铸魂育人的新局面. 9 July. Available from: http://www.moe.gov.cn/jyb_xwfb/gzdt_gzdt/moe_1485/202107/t20210709_543465.html [accessed 30 October 2022].

MOE [Ministry of Education] (2021b). 习近平新时代中国特色社会主义思想学生读本, 小学低年级, 北京，人民教育出版社.

Mottura, B. (2021). The discursive creation of ideology in the contemporary Chinese political context. *Lingue e Linguaggi*, 42, pp. 195–212. doi: 10.1285/i22390359v42p195.

Pan, Z. and Kosicki, G. M. (1993). 'Framing analysis: An approach to news discourse.' *Political Communication*, 10 (1), pp. 55–75.

Pepper, S. (1996). *Radicalism and Education Reform in 20th-century China: The Search for an Ideal Development Model*. Cambridge: Cambridge University Press.

Peters, M. (2017). The Chinese Dream: Xi Jinping thought on Socialism with Chinese characteristics for a new era. *Educational Philosophy and Theory*, 49, pp. 1299–304. doi: 10.1080/00131857.2017.1407578.

Qiushi 求实 (2021). 德智体美劳全面发展，总书记这样说', 求实网. 19 September. Available from: http://www.qstheory.cn/zhuanqu/2021-09/19/c_1127880030.htm [accessed 30 October 2022].

Reese, S. (2001). Framing public life: A bridging model for media research. In: Reese, S., Gandy, O. and Grant, A., eds, *Framing Public Life*. Mahwah, NJ: Lawrence Erlbaum, pp. 7–31.

Reisigl, M. and Wodak, R. (2009). The discourse-historical approach. In: Wodak, R. and Meyer, M., eds, *Methods of Critical Discourse Analysis*. London: Sage, pp. 87–121.

Schoenhals, M. (1992). *Doing Things with Words in Chinese Politics: Five Studies*. Berkeley, CA: Institute of East Asian Studies, University of California.

Sketch Engine (2022). http://www.sketchengine.eu [accessed 28 February 2022].

van Leeuwen, T. (1995). The representation of social actors. In: Caldas-Coulthard, C. R. and Coulthard, M., eds, *Texts and Practices: Reading in Critical Discourse Analysis*. London: Routledge, pp. 32–70.

Vickers, E. (2009a). Selling socialism with Chinese characteristics. 'Thought and Politics' and the legitimization of China's developmental strategy. *International Journal of Educational Development*, 29, pp. 523–31. doi: 10.1016/j.ijedudev.2009.04.012.

Vickers, E. (2009b). The opportunity of China. In: Lall, M. and Vickers, E., eds, *Education as a Political Tool in Asia*. London and New York: Routledge, pp. 53–82.

Vickers, E. and Zeng, X. (2017). *Education and Society in Post-Mao China*. London: Routledge.

Weninger, C. (2020). Multimodality in critical language textbook analysis. *Language, Culture and Curriculum*, 34 (2), pp. 133–46. doi: 10.1080/07908318.2020.1797083.

Wodak, R. (2001). The discourse-historical approach. In: Wodak, R. and Meyer, M., eds, *Methods of Critical Discourse Analysis*. London: Sage, pp. 63–94.

Xi, J. 习近平 (2017). 在中国共产党第十九次全国代表大会上的报告. 18 October. Available from: http://www.gov.cn/zhuanti/2017-10/27/content_5234876.htm [accessed 30 October 2022].

Xi, J. (2022a). 在中国共产党第二十次全国代表大会上的报告. 16 October. Available from: http://www.gov.cn/xinwen/2022-10/25/content_5721685.htm [accessed 30 October 2022].

Xi, J. (2022b). Report to the 20th National Congress of the Communist Party of China. 16 October. Available from: https://www.fmprc.gov.cn/eng/zxxx_662805/202210/t20221025_10791908.html [accessed 30 October 2022].

Xinhua 新华网 (2019c). 习近平致中国少年先锋队建队70周年的贺信. 13 October. Available from: http://www.xinhuanet.com/politics/leaders/2019-10/13/c_1125098687.htm [accessed 18 January 2023].

Xinhua (2022). English version of 'Understanding Xi Jinping's Educational Philosophy' published. *Xinhuanet*, 9 October. Available from: https://english.news.cn/20221009/1b5723486e69453a8a40d82cdf91a88d/c.html [accessed 14 June 2023].

Xu, S. (2021). Citizenship education in China: Conceptions, curriculum, practices, and effects. In: Guo, Z., ed., *The Routledge Handbook of Chinese Citizenship*. London: Routledge, pp. 376–87.

Xue, E. and Li, J. (2021). What is the ultimate education task in China? Exploring 'strengthen moral education for cultivating people' ('Li De Shu Ren'). *Educational Philosophy and Theory*, 53 (2), pp. 128–39.

References for examples (1) to (5):[34]

Weiyan jiaoyu 微言教育 (2017). 习近平总书记：优先发展教育事业. 18 October. Available from: http://www.moe.gov.cn/jyb_xwfb/moe_176/201710/t20171018_316735.html [accessed 18 January 2023].

Xinhua 新华网 (2014). 习近平就高校党建工作作出重要指示强调 坚持立德树人思想引领 加强改进高校党建工作. 29 December. Available from: http://www.moe.gov.cn/jyb_xwfb/s6052/moe_838/201412/t20141229_182511.html [accessed 18 January 2023].

Xinhua 新华网 (2019a). 习近平寄语希望工程强调 把希望工程这项事业办得更好 让广大青少年充分感受到党的关怀和社会主义大家庭的温暖. 21 November. Available from: http://www.moe.gov.cn/jyb_xwfb/s6052/moe_838/201911/t20191121_409118.html [accessed 18 January 2023].

Xinhua (2019b). 习近平主持召开学校思想政治理论课教师座谈会强调用新时代中国特色社会主义思想铸魂育人 贯彻党的教育方针落实立德树人根本任务. 18 March. Available from: http://www.moe.gov.cn/jyb_xwfb/s6052/moe_838/201903/t20190318_373973.html [accessed 18 January 2023].

Xinhua (2021). 习近平在清华大学考察时强调 坚持中国特色世界一流大学建设目标方向 为服务国家富强民族复兴人民幸福贡献力量. 19 April. Available from: http://www.moe.gov.cn/jyb_xwfb/s6052/moe_838/202104/t20210419_527148.html [accessed 18 January 2023].

---

[34] The examples were all taken from the excerpts collected on the MOE website and can be consulted at https://www.moe.gov.cn/jyb_xwfb/xw_zt/moe_357/s7865/s8417/. This list provides the references to the documents to which the excerpts belong, in the version published in the 'news' section of the Ministry website.

CHAPTER 2

Smoothing processes in United Nations discourse on violence against women: A diachronic perspective

Célia Atzeni

1 Introduction

International organisations are institutions whose role is to discuss political issues in order to maintain international peace, security and peaceful relations among nations. When an international organisation happens to discuss controversial topics such as gender issues in order to fulfil their mission, they need to adapt their discourse in order to avoid offending their addressees. Discourse analysts have identified this tendency to adapt one's discourse to one's audience or readership as 'discursive smoothing' (Oger and Ollivier-Yaniv 2006: 64; Cussó and Gobin 2008: 8; Raus 2017: 95). Discursive smoothing is defined as the process of removing traces of heterogeneity, debate, difficulty, conflict or extreme positions from one's discourse, either by mitigating or by omitting elements which could generate opposition, thereby producing a consensual type of discourse. Discursive smoothing can take different forms. In this paper, a textometric approach is adopted which makes it possible to identify certain linguistic phenomena which point to discursive smoothing.

This study is conducted on the United Nations' (henceforth UN) discourse on the issue of violence against women. More specifically, it aims to identify the smoothing processes used by this international organisation in its discourse on such a political, controversial topic. The UN produces a large variety of documents which contribute to its discourse in many ways. Apart from the documents which serve internal, administrative purposes, UN discourse is composed of two kinds of documents: reference texts, which are official documents addressed to experts and political decision-makers, and mainstream texts, which are unofficial documents addressed to the media and the public. The present study relies on two discursive genres from each of these two kinds of documents: reports for reference texts, and press releases for mainstream texts. More precisely, we have built a corpus of UN reports and press releases on the topic of violence against women published between 1996 and 2019. The corpus is organised in such a way that our textometric tools are not only able to analyse the corpus as a whole, but also to compare data between the two genres and within the twenty-three years covered by the corpus. As a result, this has enabled us to conduct a diachronic study of UN discourse on violence against women in order to find linguistic evidence of smoothing processes which have occurred over time.

This chapter presents linguistic evidence which illustrates a process of discursive smoothing in UN discourse on violence against women through the replacement of the modal auxiliaries 'should' and 'must' with 'will' in the context of a diplomatic crisis. In section 2, the theoretical framework of the study will be presented. The corpus designed for the study and the methods used to analyse it will then be described in section 3. Section 4 will be devoted to the presentation of the results obtained from the corpus, and will be followed by a discussion of these results.

2 Theoretical framework

An essential aspect of this study is its reliance upon a corpus to analyse UN discourse. The school of Corpus-Assisted Discourse Studies was founded at the University of Bologna, and many discourse analysts have made use of corpora to achieve an enhanced understanding of discourse, especially those who are interested in political discourse, because of the importance of language in politics (Partington et al. 2013: 1–2). Nowadays, a great deal of research in discourse studies relies on corpora, and the present study is no exception. The use of a computerised corpus makes it possible to analyse a large amount of linguistic data, and offers analysts a high degree of objectivity (Stubbs 1994: 202–18; Hardt-Mautner 1995: 3; Baker et al. 2008: 277) as well as the opportunity to reveal phenomena which would otherwise remain undetectable (Sinclair 1991: 100; Partington et al. 2013: 11).

This paper aims to detect specific linguistic phenomena which can be observed in UN discourse. In order to better understand these phenomena and the reasons why they may occur in UN discourse, a few elements on the notion of discourse should be presented. First and foremost, from a socio-historical perspective, discourse can be defined as follows:

> 'discourse' refers to: . . . a cluster of context-dependent practices that are: situated within specific fields of social action; socially constituted and socially constitutive; related to a macro-topic; linked to the argumentation about validity claims such as truth and normative validity, involving several social actors who have different points of view.
> (Reisigl and Wodak 2009: 89, in Angermuller et al. 2009: 2–4)

As a result, a cluster of texts which belong to different genres can be considered as one type of discourse. In the present study, the corpus is made up of texts which belong to two different genres, deal with the same topic and were published by an institution which holds a certain point of view on this topic and claims that its discourse is valid and true. Therefore, this corpus constitutes a sample of UN discourse on violence against women. Analysing UN discourse also helps us understand how the organisation interacts with the other social actors involved in social issues, such as decision-makers, governments and their representatives. These interactions require UN discourse to be adapted in order to maintain peaceful relationships with all nations and their representatives. Our hypothesis is that they adapt their discourse by resorting to smoothing processes. In this respect, the theoretical frameworks of politeness and face theory, developed by Goffman (1967), Kerbrat-Orecchioni (1995) and Brown and Levinson (1999), are particularly enlightening and will be used to discuss the results obtained in this study. Face theory relies on the assumption that in verbal interaction a speaker's positive and negative faces are always under threat and that speakers do their best to protect their faces and those of their addressees:

> 'Face' [is] the public self-image that [every adult member of society] wants to claim for himself [*sic*] consisting in two related aspects:
> (a) negative face: the basic claim to territories ... to freedom of action and freedom from imposition.
> (b) positive face: the positive consistent self-image or 'personality' (crucially including the desire that this self-image be appreciated and approved of) claimed by interactants.
> (Brown and Levinson 1999: 311)

Negative faces of speakers are threatened by different types of acts such as orders, requests, suggestions, advice, reminders, threats or warnings, namely acts which put pressure on an addressee to do something, and therefore constitute an attempt to limit their freedom of action (Brown and Levinson 1999: 313). It is fairly common for speakers to try to protect their addressee's negative face – which is called tact, diplomacy, politeness or social skill – as well as their own positive face in order to keep the interaction going smoothly (Goffman 1967: 12; Kerbrat-Orecchioni 1995: 74).

This means that smoothing processes can be viewed as tools used by the UN to adapt its discourse so as to maintain its addressees' negative face and their own positive face. Maintaining these faces is crucial for the legitimacy of the UN on the international stage, especially in times of diplomatic tensions and crises, and when controversial topics like violence against women are discussed. This perspective on the evolution of UN discourse will be investigated in the Discussion section below.

3 Corpus and methods

A 3,487,687-word corpus was built to conduct the present study. It is made up of 253 press releases and 224 reports dealing with the theme of violence against women. They were published between 1996 and 2019. Details on the contents of the corpus are given in Table 2.1.

The press releases were collected from the United Nations' and UN Women's official websites using the advanced research option of these websites and a script written specifically to extract them from these websites. The reports were collected from the UN's digital library. Text selection was realised in two steps. First, the texts were selected whenever their titles contained both the words 'violence' and 'women'. This was followed by a second step to make sure that texts dealing with violence against women which did not contain both the words 'violence' and 'women' in their titles were not left out. In order to collect such texts, a term tree of violence against women was built using United Nations terminological resources. This term tree and the sources used to build it are presented in Atzeni (2022: 30, 42–3). All the terms which appear on this term tree were used as keywords to look for additional texts which should be added to the corpus. The latter was then organised in such a way that the texts can be separated according to their year of publication.

The corpus was analysed using Textometry (TXM), an open-source textual corpus analysis package (Heiden et al. 2010). TXM has different functions: a concordancer, several tools for performing statistical analyses, and a tool for multidimensional analysis called Correspondence Analysis (CA). This is a method which enables one to produce a graphical representation of a dataset in order to highlight the oppositions and correlations in the data. In our case, the dataset is made up of all the words in our corpus and their distribution across the different parts of our corpus. The apparent imbalance between the different areas of the corpus, due to the United Nations and UN Women not publishing the same number of texts every year, is corrected by the TXM's statistical computations in such a way that they do not have an adverse impact on the obtained results.

Our analysis of the corpus is mainly driven by the principles of the Discourse-Historical Approach (DHA) set out by Wodak (2001). This approach relies on the investigation of the historical context in which the texts under study were produced and intertextuality. In practice, the various tools provided by TXM are used to explore our two-year-based corpora and enable

Table 2.1 *Summary of the contents of the corpus*

	Reports	Press releases
Number of texts	224	253
Total word count	2,875,969	611,718
Average word count per text	12,839	2,418

us to identify linguistic traces of change of UN discourse on violence against women between 1996 and 2019. Furthermore, the historical context of production of the texts under study has been investigated in order to determine whether the observed change could be explained by the occurrence of certain historical events or the making of certain political decisions.

4 Results

The correspondence analysis carried out using TXM enables us to observe the distribution of the lexicon in the corpus. Firstly, we are able to observe the similarities and differences in terms of lexicon within the sub-corpora corresponding to the twenty-four years spanned by the corpus. A graphical representation of these similarities and dissimilarities is presented in Figure 2.1. Two clusters of sub-corpora can be identified. They indicate that there is a clear-cut separation of the corpus in terms of its lexicon between the texts published between 1996 and 2009 on the one hand, and those published between 2010 and 2019 on the other hand. In other words, the texts published between 1996 and 2009 are made up of the same words in the same frequencies, and the texts published between 2010 and 2019 are also very similar from a lexical point of view. Yet if one takes one text from the first period and one text from the second period, they will be very dissimilar in terms of their lexicon.

Secondly, we are able to identify words which best illustrate the dissimilarities between the two aforementioned periods using TXM's tool to compute specificity scores. Amongst these words, our attention is particularly drawn to the modal auxiliaries which are over-represented and under-represented in each of the two periods, namely 'should', 'must' and 'will'.[1] The exact behaviour of these words with regard to specificity actually depends on the textual genre under consideration, but highlights in both cases the separation between the two periods. In press releases, while 'should' and 'must' are over-represented in the 1996–2009 period, they are under-represented in the 2010–19 period. Moreover, 'will' is under-represented in the 1996–2009 period and it is over-represented in the 2010–19 period. The situation is, however, quite different in the reports: while 'must' is over-represented in the 1996–2009 period and under-represented in the 2010–19 period in press releases, 'should' displays both properties in the first period, as it is over-represented between 1996 and 2002 then under-represented between 2003 and 2009. As for the time frame from 2010 to 2019, 'should' fell in line with average usage and was neither over-represented nor under-represented.

---

[1] Over-represented words have positive specificity scores, whereas under-represented words have negative specificity scores. The specificity score of a word is computed by TXM using the frequency of this word, comparing it with its expected frequency, which is its frequency if it had been used uniformly in the corpus.

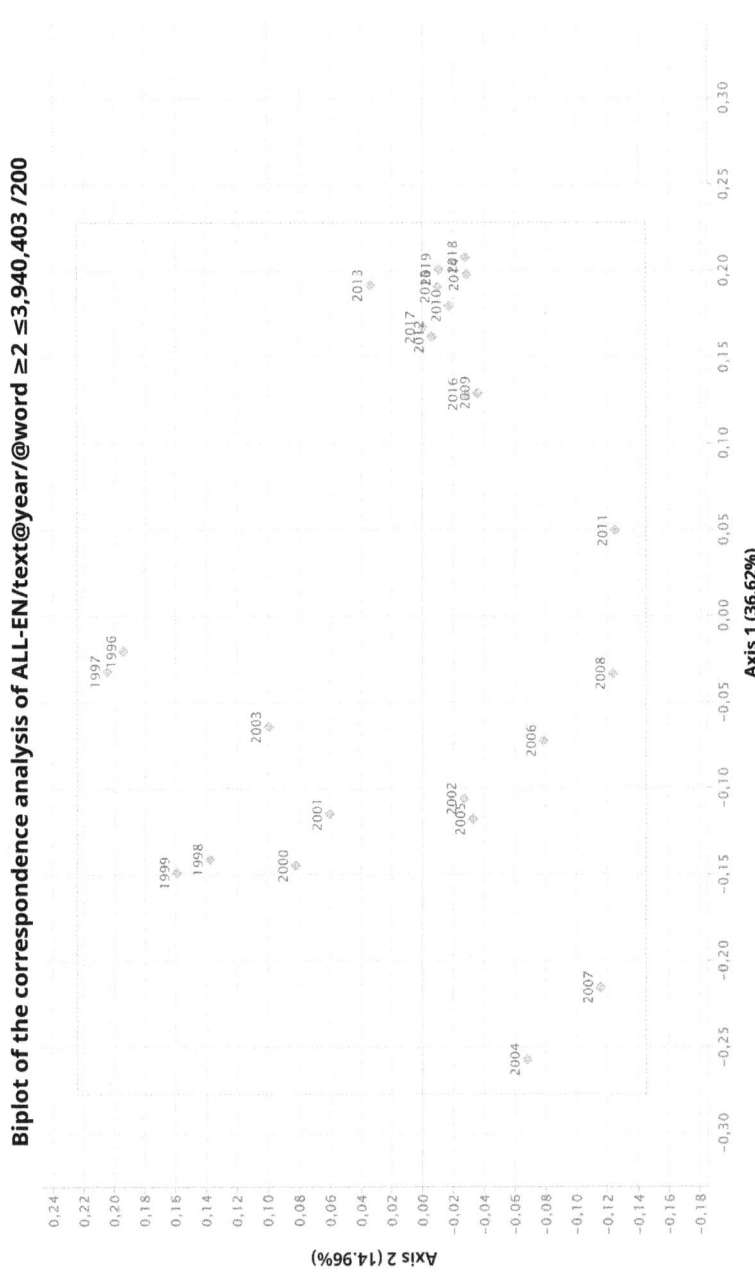

Figure 2.1 *Correspondence analysis of the corpus*

Finally, 'will' also has this banal behaviour in both periods. The specificity scores thus described correlate with the progression of these words, which is illustrated in Figure 2.2.

This figure shows the progression charts for the words 'will', 'should' and 'must' respectively in the two genre sub-corpora.[2] The correlation between specificity scores and progressions may be retrieved as follows: high positive scores, corresponding to over-representations, indicate a significant use of the words in a short period of time, which is illustrated by steeper gradients on the curve; conversely, high negative scores showing under-representations correspond to gentler slopes on the curve. Despite the apparent imbalance between the two textual genres in the corpus, the observations above support the hypothesis of a change in the use of modalities which occurred around 2010: in press releases, this change can be identified in the clear opposition between the representations of 'must' and 'should' and the representation of 'will'. In reports, however, such a change can only be observed in the evolution in the use of 'must' and, to a lesser extent, in the use of 'should', which is significantly over-represented, before stabilising to an average use in the time frame from 2010 to 2019. Modality expresses the speakers' attitudes towards their own discourse and towards their addressees. This is why we chose it as a starting point to investigate the UN's discursive strategy. Moreover, the opposition between 'should' and 'must' on the one hand, and 'will' on the other, has led us to formulate the hypothesis that a change in discursive strategy characterised by a change in the way the UN addresses its audience may have occurred.

In order to confirm or reject this hypothesis, it is necessary to take a closer look at the modalities expressed by these auxiliaries. As illustrated by examples (1), (2) and (3) extracted from the corpus, the auxiliaries 'should' and 'must' take on a deontic value in the UN's discourse on violence against women between 1996 and 2009. More specifically, they are used in contexts in which the UN says what it thinks states and governments should do to oppose violence against women between 1996 and 2009. As for 'will', it is used in contexts in which the UN affirms its commitment to addressing the issue of violence against women and eliminating it, as demonstrated by examples (4), (5) and (6):

(1) Moroccans **should** take a sincere, fair approach to this referendum as it was taking place under the auspices of the United Nations. (UN 1998)

(2) The [Chilean] Government **must** protect women. (UN 1999)

---

[2] The purpose of a progression chart is to display the evolution of the number of occurrences of a word or sequence of words by browsing the corpus texts in chronological order.

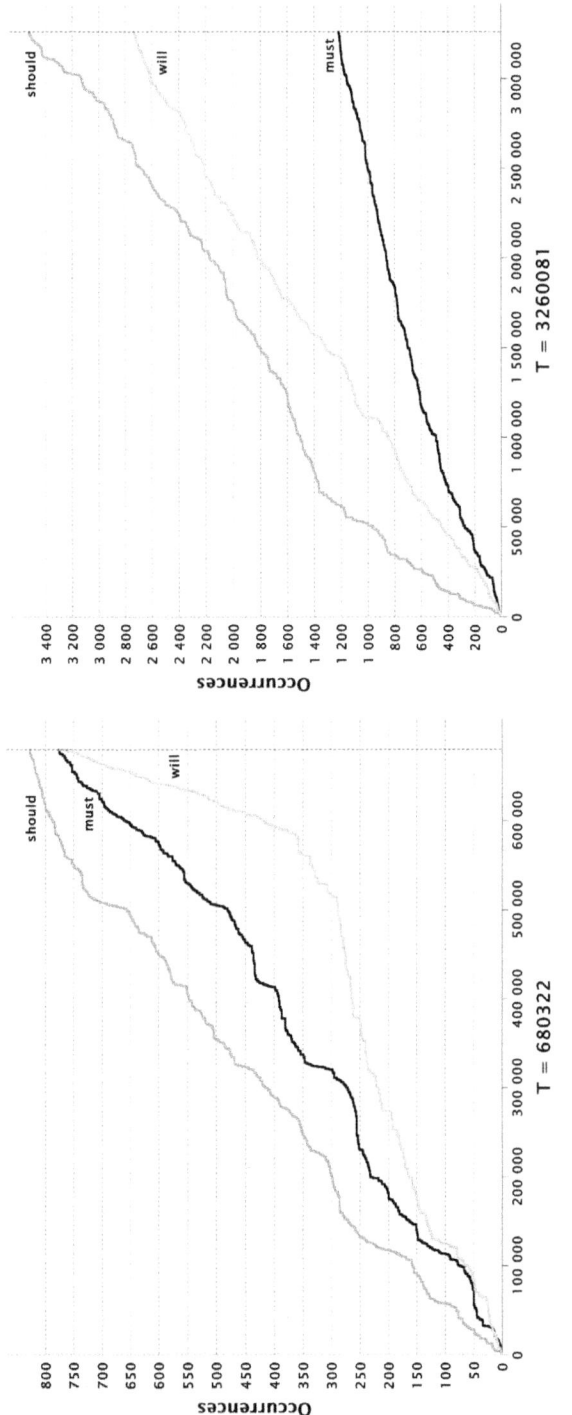

Figure 2.2 *Progression charts of 'will', 'must' and 'should' in press releases (left) and reports (right)*

(3) States **must** ensure that the perpetrators of such crimes were punished. (UN 2007)

(4) We declare that we **will** prosecute crimes against women. (UN 2013)

(5) ... funds **will** be used to address violence. (UN Women 2013)

(6) We **will** not relent until we stop all attacks against women and girls. (UN 2015)

It is worth noting that the verbs used with these modal auxiliaries are very similar semantically, and both denote general and vague actions. The ten most frequent verbs used with each of the modal auxiliaries, ordered by decreasing frequency, are presented in Table 2.2. The similarity between the lists is striking, and suggests that the UN has a unique way of denoting the actions which need to be taken to fight violence against women, independently of whether they occur in the context of a prescriptive statement with 'must' and 'should', or when expressing the commitment of the organisation itself with 'will'; and these actions are rarely described explicitly. The verbs which require nominal arguments mainly occur with unspecified suggestions such as 'measures', 'action', 'strategies' in the case of 'take', or with general concepts such as 'protection', 'information', 'services', 'assistance' in the case of 'ensure' (which is the eleventh most frequent verb used with 'will'), 'support', 'focus' and 'provide'. The verb 'include' occurs with both kinds, and the verb 'address' is generally followed by generic nouns such as 'issue', 'problem' or more often 'violence against women'. As for verbs with verbal arguments such as 'continue', they usually occur between the auxiliaries and the verbs listed in Table 2.2, as well as less frequent co-occurring verbs, such as 'implement' or 'strengthen'. The verbs which denote more precise actions, and take on a performative value as in example (4) above, remain exceptional in the corpus.

Two elements show through in the analysis of the verbs used with the modal auxiliaries conducted above. The first one is that the UN does not seem to enter into the details of the actions to be taken in the fight against violence against women. The description of these measures remains vague, which makes their statements consensual. This could be interpreted as part of a discursive strategy when used with the auxiliaries 'must' and 'should',

Table 2.2 *Lists of the ten most frequent verbs used with 'must', 'should' and 'will' ordered by frequency*

Auxiliary	Most frequently occurring lexical verbs
must	ensure, address, take, include, continue, account, work, provide, make, focus
should	ensure, include, take, provide, continue, support, work, consider, adopt, address
will	continue, provide, support, take, work, meet, include, require, focus, address

Smoothing processes in UN discourse 51

which carry a deontic value in the UN's discourse. Yet the second element which can be deduced from the previous observations is the fact that increase in the use of the modal auxiliary 'will' in the corpus is not accompanied by a change in the verbs used with this auxiliary: the UN's commitment relies on the same vague actions described in the prescriptive statements of the organisation, and only the agents of these actions and the modal auxiliaries undergo the observed change.

These remarks suggest that if our hypothesis is correct, then the observed change of strategy in UN discourse is characterised by a transition from a prescriptive position of the organisation towards member states and governments to a more self-centred position, where the organisation insists on its own plans of action and commitments. As a consequence, any other observation which supports the idea of such a transition supports our hypothesis as well. In this respect, evidence of the aforementioned transition may be found in the evolution in the use of other words in the corpus. The first example of such a word is the noun 'government', which, just like 'should' and 'must', is over-represented in the 1996–2009 period, and under-represented in the 2010–19 period. This evolution indicates that the UN's discourse is less and less focused on the actions of national governments over time, which suggests that the focus is directed to something else – the UN's own actions, for instance.

The latter idea is itself supported by another observation, namely the evolution in the use of the personal pronoun 'we' in the corpus: while under-represented in the first time period, this personal pronoun becomes significantly over-represented in the second period which we identified. In our corpus, it is used in three different ways:

(7) According to a 30-year-old Bangladeshi woman who was trafficked to Pakistan at the age of 27, '... **we** were taken to a secluded place in the jungle before crossing the border to Pakistan under police custody. The border officials kept the girls who were pretty and sexually abused them ...' (UN 1997)

(8) Testimony given to the Special Rapporteur by A: 12 'A group of armed men broke down the door of our home while **we** were sleeping; they knocked over the furniture and broke everything. They tied my father to a chair. They opened my legs and tied one leg to the wardrobe and the other to the bed ...' (UN 2002)

(9) Khunying Supatra Masdit, Minister, Office of the Prime Minister of Thailand: Thailand has made substantial progress in the implementation of the Beijing commitments since 1995. **We** have been giving mindful attention to all areas of concern as addressed in the Platform for Action, prioritizing the urgency of the problems and the people ... (UN 2000)

(10) Following is the text of Secretary-General Kofi Annan ... Gender-based violence is perhaps the most shameful human rights violation. As long as it continues, **we** cannot claim to be making real progress towards equality, development and peace. (UN 2003)

(11) Full Statement of UN Women Executive Director Phumzile Mlambo-Ngcuka ... This is the terror that contributes to the high levels of displacement **we** are discussing today. (UN Women 2014)

(12) Following are UN Secretary-General Ban Ki-moon's remarks ... United, **we** can end violence against women! (UN 2010)

Between 1996 and 2002, 'we' is frequently used in contexts of reported speech in which it refers to people who were the victims of acts of violence or witnessed such acts, as illustrated in examples (7) and (8). 'We' is also used by representatives of certain states during meetings and assemblies at the UN, to refer to themselves and their country, as shown in example (9). This use of the pronoun 'we' is the least frequently observed in the corpus, especially from 2010 onwards. On the contrary, the use of 'we' by UN personnel and representatives to refer to the organisation and its different organs, which can be seen in examples (10) and (11), is the most frequent use of this pronoun observed in our corpus, so much so that it becomes the only use of the pronoun after 2010. A number of occurrences also extend the reference of 'we' to humanity as a whole, under the aegis of the UN, in examples such as (12).

These results suggest that from 2010 onwards, the UN has a stronger tendency to represent itself and the actions it will take as an organisation to fight violence against women, than to state what should be done by states or governments. Thus, the concurrent decrease in the use of 'government' and increase in the use of 'we' to refer to the UN can be analysed as evidence that the UN has adopted a new communication strategy in which the organisation itself plays a leading role, supporting the idea of a transition from a prescriptive position to a self-centred position, as described above. This is aligned with the hypothesis of a change in discursive strategy based on an evolution in the use of modal auxiliaries and the pronoun 'we' in the corpus.

5 Discussion

The hypothesis defended in this chapter is that a change occurred in the UN's discursive strategy in the time frame from 1996 to 2019. More precisely, between 1996 and 2009, the organisation's discourse was noticeably prescriptive. In contrast, its discourse became less prescriptive and more focused on the organisation's commitment and actions from 2010 onwards. This hypothesis relies on the linguistic evidence presented in the previous section: a decrease in the use of the modal auxiliaries 'should' and 'must', which are mostly used in contexts where they have a deontic value, as well as a simultaneous increase in the use of the modal auxiliary 'will' used with verbs similar to those used with 'should' and 'must', and a concomitant increase in the use of the pronoun 'we'. In this section, the historical context of production of the texts under study as well as the relationships between the different social actors interacting with the UN will be investigated and analysed as evidence to support this hypothesis. Our aim is to answer the following two questions: why does this discursive change occur in UN discourse, and why is it specifically noticeable from 2010 onwards?

The decline in the use of prescriptive statements in UN discourse is likely to occur for diplomatic reasons, especially since it can be observed from 2010 onwards. Indeed, the second half of the 2000s paved the way for a decade of international diplomatic crises and conflicts on human rights issues which endangered the UN's legitimacy. An early example of such a crisis is the case of the UN's Human Rights Commission. Over the years, this UN body was criticised due to the membership of many countries which were accused of violating human rights, and this criticism culminated in the election of Libya as chair of the Commission in 2003. At that point, the Commission's legitimacy had been definitively lost, which resulted in its dissolution in 2006. The second half of the 2000s was also marked by several armed conflicts which took place around the world. In this context, the UN deployed several peacekeeping operations. Some of these operations have had a very negative impact on the UN's public image. For example, during the UN peacekeeping mission conducted in 2006 in the Republic of the Congo, the UN's peacekeeping personnel sexually exploited and abused women and girls in the countries they were supposed to protect. When these crimes were exposed, the UN's public image and legitimacy was, unsurprisingly, severely damaged (Notar 2006; UN 2006; Ndulo 2009; Moncrief 2017).

In addition to the UN's image and legitimacy being damaged in this period, the organisation found itself having to face a decade of exits from international treaties on the protection of human rights and women's rights and from organs meant to protect and defend these rights from 2010 onwards (Bugorgue-Larsen 2021). In 2012, Israel refused to be reviewed by the Human Rights Council, a body which had been created to replace the Human Rights Commission and to pursue its mission to protect and defend human rights. It was the first time that a state had ever refused to appear to be reviewed, which created a dangerous precedent for the Council and elicited strong criticism from the other member states (Elizalde 2019: 83–106). In 2018, the USA decided to leave the Human Rights Council in reaction to the Council's denunciation of their immigration policy at the Mexico border.[3] This withdrawal was unprecedented in the Council's history.

---

[3] The American ambassador Nikki Haley called the Council 'a protector of human rights abusers and a cesspool of political bias' and a 'so-called Human Rights Council',

In 2021, Turkey decided to exit from the Convention on preventing and combating violence against women and domestic violence, better known as the Istanbul Convention.[4] All these exits contributed to setting up a climate of distrust which threatened the international consensus to an extent that it can now hardly be called a consensus. Some international figures have expressed their concerns with regard to this situation, including the ex-Chancellor of Germany, Angela Merkel, who stated in 2018:

> The world witnessed Germany unleash World War II and commit the Shoah, whereby it betrayed all civilised values and shook faith in humanity. Afterwards, nothing was the same. Granted, nothing could be. The answer was to create the United Nations. The international community established a legal order and a framework for international cooperation. The foundation for this was laid with the Universal Declaration of Human Rights that the UN General Assembly adopted 70 years ago. I often wonder if, today, we were again called on as an international community to adopt such a declaration of human rights – would we be up to the task? I fear not.
>
> (Merkel 2018)

The UN, as the symbol of international cooperation and consensus, has become endangered by such a climate of diplomatic crises on human rights issues. As an international organisation, the only way for it to maintain its legitimacy and authority with regard to its member states is to rely on its rhetoric: indeed, the power of the organisation is mainly applied through its resolutions and recommendations, and any state which ceases to respect them or ignores them undermines the organisation's power and legitimacy. As a result, the UN faces the difficult task of promoting human rights and pointing out the failures of member states to defend them while trying not to offend them. This is where processes of discursive smoothing prove particularly useful: since the efficiency of UN discourse depends on its ability to lead to a consensus (Maingueneau 2002: 129), the strategy of remaining vague about the responsibilities of states or avoiding mentioning them makes this consensus easier to reach.

Face theory and politeness, which were introduced in the theoretical framework, explain how the diplomatic situation of the UN could have led to

---

accusing it of being biased against the State of Israel and overlooking the abuses condoned by certain states in terms of human rights. See the articles from the *New York Times* (Cumming-Bruce 2018) and CNN (Koran 2018).

[4] Although the Istanbul Convention is a European initiative, it has been promoted by the UN since the beginning of its elaboration. According to Purna Sen, executive coordinator and spokesperson on addressing sexual harassment and other forms discrimination at UN Women, this treaty implements the international standards defended by the UN in terms of women's rights at a regional level (Lilleslåtten 2021).

the results obtained in section 4. Let us remind ourselves here that the negative face of speakers designates their claim for freedom of actions, while their positive face designates the self-image which a speaker needs to maintain in order to be approved by their addressees. From this perspective, when the UN affirms what certain states or governments should or must do to protect women from violence, they threaten the negative faces of these states and governments. These pieces of advice and orders may be interpreted as attempts at limiting their freedom of action. Moreover, as illustrated by the aforementioned criticism the UN faced in the 2000s and 2010s, targeting certain states or governments on certain issues which they may have regarding human rights can lead to reactions of opposition and reproaches about the alleged bias the organisation has against them. As a consequence, it is in the organisation's interest to limit its use of linguistic structures involving the modal auxiliaries 'should' and 'must' in combination with the names of states or nouns such as 'state' or 'government', in the plural or in the singular. This is because these structures directly express this prescriptive stance which threatens the negative face of the targeted states and governments.

Besides protecting the negative faces of the addressees of its discourse, the UN has to protect its own positive face. The strategy which consists in reducing the possible breaches of the negative face of the other states also serves this purpose: indeed, any case of a state exiting an international body or a treaty on human rights supported by the UN is a threat to the UN's public image and its very legitimacy. Thus, limiting the opportunities for such an event to occur by making these changes in the organisation's discourse contributes to preserving its positive face. However, this strategy alone cannot be sufficient when considering the many events which have already damaged the UN's image since the second half of the 2000s. In order to retrieve a more satisfying image, the UN must actively work to rebuild its positive face in its discourse. This second strategy is linguistically realised through the increasing use of the modal auxiliary 'will' in conjunction with the pronoun 'we', which enables the organisation to depict itself as an active force on the diplomatic stage in the same way as its member states, and to reaffirm its commitment to addressing the issue of violence against women. This contributes to maintaining the positive face of the organisation. As such, this discursive strategy can be interpreted as an attempt by the UN to regain its authority and legitimacy on the international stage.

In our theoretical framework, we defined discursive smoothing in the light of the framework of face theory and politeness as discursive strategies for the UN to maintain the negative faces of its addressees as well as its own positive face. As discussed above, we can reasonably consider the observed changes in UN discourse as a case of discursive smoothing, which was used by the organisation to maintain its legitimacy on the international stage. Moreover, the historical context helps us understand why this discursive change occurred from 2010 onwards: in this period, the organisation needed to preserve its public image after several events which threatened its legitimacy, and then had to keep using this strategy as more and more diplomatic crises occurred.

6 Conclusion

In this chapter, we have studied the UN's discourse on the controversial topic of violence against women and presented linguistic evidence which suggests that the UN resorted to discursive smoothing processes in the 1996 to 2019 period, and more precisely in the time frame since 2010. Our textometric results have shown a decrease in the use of the modal auxiliaries 'should' and 'must', which carry a deontic value as they are mainly used by the UN to formulate prescriptions and recommendations to other states, and a simultaneous increase in the use of 'will' which is mainly used by the organisation to reaffirm its commitment to fighting violence against women. The difference in the modalities expressed by the two sets of auxiliaries has led us to the hypothesis that there was a change in the UN's discursive strategy: the organisation tends to reduce its advice to other states and to put itself and its commitments more in the spotlight.

We have found some possible explanations for such a change in the historical, social and political contexts of the period under study. The organisation's legitimacy was indeed threatened by a succession of diplomatic crises which aroused criticism against the UN and withdrawals of member states from treaties and initiatives on human rights and violence against women conducted or supported by the UN. In order to preserve its authority, the UN may have resorted to discursive smoothing processes to avoid opposition and criticism by states and their representatives. Reducing recommendations and orders would thus be a way of giving fewer opportunities to states and governments to feel attacked and react with diplomatic breaks. Furthermore, by putting itself in the spotlight, the UN represents itself as an active force in the fight for human rights and women's rights, a force which has the potential to lead its member states towards the achievement of this task. Consequently, the UN maintains a positive self-image which is less likely to be challenged.

We may therefore conclude that the UN resorts to smoothing processes to reinforce its legitimacy on the international political stage. However, the use of such processes in discourses on controversial topics like human rights and violence against women may have the side effect of reducing the visibility of such topics. As a consequence, the UN's attempt at preserving its legitimacy may be done at the expense of the fight against violence used against women itself. In this respect, discursive smoothing leads the UN to adopt a paradoxical position in which discursive smoothing processes are used to maintain its authority and legitimacy in the eyes of member states and governments, while weakening the scope of the organisation's discourse on violence against women and thus its potential impact on these states and governments.

References

Angermuller, J., Maingueneau, D. and Wodak, R., eds. (2009). *The Discourse Studies Reader: Main Current in Theory and Analysis*. Amsterdam: John Benjamins.

Atzeni, C. (2022). From 'violence against women' to 'violence against women and girls'. The reconceptualisation of violence against women in United Nations discourse. *The ESSE Messenger*, 30, pp. 28–43.

Baker, P., Gabrielatos, C., KhosraviNik, M., Krzyżanowski, M., McEnery, T. and Wodak, R. (2008). A useful methodological synergy? Combining critical discourse analysis and corpus linguistics to examine discourses of refugees and asylum seekers in the UK press. *Discourse & Society*, 19 (3), pp. 273–306. doi: 10.1177/0957926508088962.

Brown, P. and Levinson, S. C. (1999). Politeness: Some universals in language usage. In: Jaworski, A. and Coupland, N., eds, *The Discourse Reader*. London: Routledge, pp. 311–23.

Burgorgue-Larsen, L. (2021). Le basculement de l'Histoire ? Les attaques contre l'universalisme des droits de l'homme. *Revue des Droits et Libertés Fondamentaux*, 6. Available from: http://www.revuedlf.com/droit-international/le-basculement-de-lhistoire-les-attaques-contre-luniversalisme-des-droits-de-lhomme/ [accessed 14 June 2023].

Cumming-Bruce, N. (2018). U.N. rights chief tells U.S. to stop taking migrant children from parents. *New York Times*, 18 June. Available from: https://www.nytimes.com/2018/06/18/world/europe/trump-migrant-children-un.html [accessed 14 June 2023].

Cussó, R. and Gobin, C. (2008) Du discours politique au discours expert: le changement politique mis hors débat ? *Mots. Les Langages du Politique*, 88, pp. 5–11. doi: 10.4000/mots.14203.

Elizalde, P. (2019). A horizontal pathway to impact? An assessment of the Universal Periodic Review at 10. In: Brysk, A. and Stohl, M., eds, *Contesting Human Rights: Norms, Institutions and Practice*. Cheltenham: Edward Elgar, pp. 83–106.

Goffman, E. (1967). On face-work. In: Goffman, E., ed., *Interaction Ritual: Essays on Face-to-Face Behavior*. Garden City, NY: Doubleday.

Hardt-Mautner, G. (1995). Only connect. Critical Discourse Analysis and Corpus. *UCREL Technical Papers*, 6.

Heiden, S., Magué, J.-P. and Pincemin, B. (2010). TXM: Une plateforme logicielle open-source pour la textométrie – conception et développement. In: Bolasco, S., Chiari, I. and Giuliano, L., eds, *Proceedings of the 10th International Conference on the Statistical Analysis of Textual Data – JADT 2010*. Milan: Edizioni Universitarie di Lettere Economia Diritto, pp. 1021–32. Available from: https://halshs.archives-ouvertes.fr/halshs-00549779 [accessed 14 June 2023].

Kerbrat-Orecchioni, C. (1995). La construction de la relation interpersonnelle: quelques remarques sur cette dimension du dialogue. *Cahiers de linguistique française*, 16, pp. 69–88.

Koran, L. (2018). US leaving UN Human Rights Council – 'a cesspool of political bias'. *CNN Politics*, CNN, 20 June. Available from: https://www.cnn.com/2018/06/19/politics/haley-pompeo-human-rights-bias/index.html [accessed 14 June 2023].

Lilleslåtten, M. (2021). Fighting gender inequality and violence with the Istanbul Convention. *Synergy*, 22 May 2019 [updated 29 September 2021]. Available from:

https://www.eeagender.org/the-synergy-network/news/fighting-gender-inequality-and-violence-with-the-istanbul-convention/ [accessed 14 June 2023].

Maingueneau, D. (2002). Les rapports des organisations internationales: un discours constituant ? In: Rist, G., ed., *Les Mots du Pouvoir: Sens et Non-Sens de la Rhétorique Internationale*. Geneva: Cahiers de l'IUED, 13, pp. 119–32.

Merkel, A. (2018). Speech by Federal Chancellor Angela Merkel at the opening of the Paris Peace Forum on 11 November 2018. Presse- und Informationsamt der Bundesregierung, 11 November 2018. Available from: https://www.bundesregierung.de/breg-en/news/speech-by-federal-chancellor-angela-merkel-at-the-opening-of-the-paris-peace-forum-on-11-november-2018-1549780 [accessed 14 June 2023].

Moncrief, S. (2017). Military socialization, disciplinary culture, and sexual violence in UN peacekeeping operations. *Journal of Peace Research*, 54 (5), pp. 715–30. doi: 10.1177/0022343317716784.

Ndulo, M. (2009). The United Nations responses to the sexual abuse and exploitation of women and girls by peacekeepers during peacekeeping missions. *Berkeley Journal of International Law*, 27 (1), pp. 127–61.

Notar, S. A. (2006). Peacekeepers as perpetrators: Sexual exploitation and abuse of women and children in the Democratic Republic of the Congo. *Journal of Gender, Social Policy & Law*, 14 (2), pp. 413–29.

Oger, C. and Ollivier-Yaniv, C. (2006). Conjurer le désordre discursif. Les procédés de « lissage » dans la fabrication du discours institutionnel. *Mots. Les Langages du Politique*, 81 (2), pp. 63–77. doi: 10.4000/mots.675.

Partington, A., Duguid, A. and Taylor, C. (2013). *Patterns and Meanings in Discourse. Theory and Practice in Corpus-Assisted Discourse Studies (CADS)*. Amsterdam: John Benjamins.

Raus, R. (2017). 'Les rapports d'initiative au Parlement européen ou comment la traduction influe sur les aspects performatifs d'un genre discursif.' *Mots. Les Langages du Politique*, 114, pp. 95–115. doi: 10.4000/mots.22810.

Reisigl, M. and Wodak, R. (2009). 'The Discourse-Historical Approach (DHA).' In Wodak, R. and Meyer, M., eds, *Methods of Critical Discourse Analysis*. 2nd edn. London: Sage, pp. 87–121.

Sinclair, J. (1991). *Corpus, Concordance, Collocation*. Oxford: Oxford University Press.

Stubbs, M. (1994). Grammar, text, and ideology: Computer-assisted methods in the linguistics of representation. *Grammar, Text, and Ideology: Computer-Assisted Methods in the Linguistics of Representation*, 15 (2), pp. 201–23.

United Nations (UN) (2006). Problem of sexual abuse by peacekeepers now openly recognized, Broad strategy in place to address it, Security Council told. UN Press Release SC/8649, 23 February 2006.

Wodak, R. (2001). The discourse-historical approach. In: Wodak, R. and Meyer, M., eds, *Methods of Critical Discourse Analysis*. London: Sage, pp. 63–94.

Sources from the corpus

UN (1997). *Further Promotion and Encouragement of Human Rights and Fundamental Freedoms, Including the Question of the Programme and Methods of Work of the Commission.* Report of the Special Rapporteur on violence against women, its causes and consequences E/CN.4/1997/47, Commission on Human Rights, 12 February 1997.

UN (1998). High commissioner for Human Rights calls for greater efforts at crisis prevention, more action to prevent violence against women. UN Press Release HR/CN/822, 23 March 1998.

UN (1999). Chile ending 'gender order' based on exclusion, violence against women, Women's Anti-Discrimination Committee told. UN Press Release WOM/1144, 22 June 1999.

UN (2000). Persistence of violence against women should be matter both of shame and concern, 'Beijing+5' Special Assembly Session told. UN Press Release GA/9716, 5 June 2000.

UN (2002). *Integration of the Human Rights of Women and the Gender Perspective. Addendum: Mission to Colombia (1–7 November 2001).* Report of the Special Rapporteur on violence against women, its causes and consequences E/CN.4/2002/83/Add.3, Commission on Human Rights, 11 March 2002.

UN (2003). Secretary-General calls for transformation in men's attitudes to end all forms of violence against women. UN Press Release SG/SM/9030-OBV/396-WOM/1418, 24 November 2003.

UN (2007). Security Council deeply concerned about 'pervasive' gender-based violence as it holds day-long debate on women, peace, security. UN Press Release SC/9151, 23 October 2007.

UN (2010). Secretary-General, at International Day Commemoration, Invites Proposals for 'Innovative' Projects in Campaign to Combat Violence against Women. UN Press Release SG/SM/13270-OBV/939-WOM/1835, 23 November 2010.

UN (2013). Give response to sexual violence priority in peace activities, Secretary-General instructs senior advisers in message for International Women's Day. UN Press Release SG/SM/14843-OBV/1185-WOM/1939, 4 March 2013.

UN (2015). Being serious about ending violence against women means greater efforts to protect their rights, Secretary-General says at commemoration of International Day. UN Press Release SG/SM/17361-OBV/1557-WOM/2054, 25 November 2015.

UN Women (2013). UN trust fund to end violence against women announces over USD 8 million in grants in 18 countries and territories. UN Women Press Release, 22 November 2013.

UN Women (2014). As nature of conflicts change, UN Women urges swifter action to protect targets of violence. UN Women Press Release, 28 October 2014.

CHAPTER 3

Who calls whom a populist? A pragmatic analysis of the uses of *populism(s)* and *populist(s)* in French and Spanish parliamentary debates

Nadezda Shchinova

1 Introduction: A linguist's eye view on populism

Populism is a highly contested term in academic and public debate. For the past few decades, it has been frequently discussed within various fields as a vague term, which refers to a multiplicity of phenomena in different socio-political and geographical contexts (Canovan 1999). Previous research has addressed populism as an ideology (Mudde 2004) and as a communication phenomenon (de Vreese et al. 2018). In addition, discourse analysts have examined populist discourses and the language of populist politicians in a variety of countries (Hidalgo-Tenorio et al. 2019; Zienkowski and Breeze 2019).

Several definitions of the term are found in academic literature, although there seems to be a consensus among scholars on the two main features of populism: the representation of the people and the criticism of the elites (Mudde 2004). However, recent research on populism points out that the concept is still contested and that the conceptualisations of populism largely depend on 'geographical foci, methods, and host ideologies' (Hunger and Paxton 2021: 617).

While academic conceptualisations of the term have been extensively examined, the actual use of the term in public debate has attracted much less attention. Recent scholarship points to the 'need to engage with the rhetoric *about* populism' (De Cleen et al. 2018: 649, original emphasis) and draws the attention to the investigation of the 'non-scholarly use of the term' (Demata et al. 2020: 9). Several studies in line with Discourse Theory, which have analysed discourses about populism, view the term as 'empty' or as a 'floating signifier' (Laclau 2005), or a word without a clear referent and one meaning. However, in his cognitive linguistic analysis of the occurrences of the word *people* in populist discourse, Chilton (2017) points out that this view on the meanings of 'vague' words is tantamount to 'ignoring a century of linguistic research' (Chilton 2017: 583).

Previous research on populism has suggested that the term is used to establish the divides between in-groups and out-groups (Eklundh 2020). A detailed linguistic analysis will help us to understand the strategies of legitimisation of the in-group and de-legitimisation of the out-group, and to enhance our understanding of the pragmatic functions or the communicative goals behind the use of 'the main political buzzword of the 21st century' (Mudde and Kaltwasser 2017: 1).

Kranert (2020) has compared the uses of the terms *populism* and *populist* in the German and British press in the period between 2012 and 2017. Kranert's corpus-based study focuses on the discursive functions of the uses of the terms by journalists and politicians, as well as on the semantic prosody of the terms, in other words, 'the part of the lexical meaning produced through consistent collocation patterns with evaluative expressions' (Kranert 2020: 36). Kranert argues that the meanings attributed to such loaded terms in political and media discourses are not stable and follow from a 'semantic struggle that strategically chooses programme terms to signify the group's own position or stigma terms to describe and devalue the position of the political opponent' (Kranert 2020: 34).

Furthermore, studies adopting the linguistics perspective on the analysis of the uses of *populism* in discourse (Kranert 2020; Thornborrow et al. 2021) show that the term is far from being empty or vague, as its 'sematic scope ... appears to be very firmly anchored in common negative frames of reference' across different contexts (Thornborrow et al. 2021: 9). However, these studies are rare, therefore making it necessary to further investigate the uses of the term by focusing on who calls whom a populist in discourse. Examining the uses of the term in political discourse from a linguistic and discursive perspective can develop our understanding of why the term is extensively used by politicians, why it appears in a multitude of contexts, and what forms the purpose of the use of the term in political discourse.

Through a linguistic perspective, this chapter adds to our understanding of the uses and meanings of widely used political terms by adopting the discursive pragmatics perspective. It presents some of the results from the ongoing research on the uses of the terms *populism(s)* and *populist(s)* in French and Spanish in political and media discourses. Specifically, it compares the occurrences of the terms *populism(s)* and *populist(s)* – henceforth *populis** – in French and Spanish parliamentary debates during 2019.

The terms *populism(s)* and *populist(s)* are approached as 'discourse keywords' (Schröter et al. 2019), which make them 'one of the most interesting concepts for its ability to really bring corpus and discourse work together' in the study of political discourse (Taylor 2022: 609). Discourse keywords are often polysemic, versatile and controversial. These words play a crucial role in political discourse because they participate in the processes of classification or categorisation related to political leanings and ideologies (Heller and McElhinny 2017: 4–9). Establishing the discursive divides between who or what fits into the category of *populism* or *populist* is a way to categorise, and therefore to justify and legitimise, or devalue and de-legitimise. Analysing the way discourse keywords are employed in specific lexical and pragmatic contexts in political discourse is the window to understanding why people use them the way they do in contemporary socio-political debates.

This chapter begins by presenting the context of the present study and by describing the data and the method. Then analysis of the occurrences of *populis** in French and Spanish is provided by focusing on the comparison between the uses of the singular and plural nouns *populism(s)* and the singular and plural adjectives *populist(s)* in each dataset.

2 Context: Populism in France and Spain

This chapter focuses on how populism is shaped by political discourses in two European democracies in 2019, a year characterised by several politically and socially significant events, and a year of political crises and protests. In France, the European elections took place in May 2019. In Spain, there were national, regional and local elections. In both countries, the far right made electoral gains in 2019. Moreover, several social protests took place, such as the 'Yellow Vests' in France and protests following the trial of Catalonia independence leaders in Spain.

In political science, populism in France and Spain is associated with both left- and right-wing political parties (Rooduijn et al. 2019). In the context of France, two political parties are primarily referred to as populist in academic literature: the far-right party Le Rassemblement national (RN) and the far-left party La France insoumise (LFI).[1] Examining academic literature on populism in France, Hubé and Truan (2016: 181) emphasise the 'relatively infrequent use of the word, its quasi-systematic association with right-wing parties, and the critical tone adopted by French authors when referring to populism as a concept'. Hubé and Truan (2016) point out that the far-right Front national (since 2018 Le Rassemblement national) is mainly associated with populism. However, in French academic literature this political party is not analysed as predominantly populist. As for the far-left LFI, which has been classified as a populist party by some scholars (Rooduijn et al. 2019), Hubé and Truan state that its leader, Jean-Luc Mélenchon, 'has not been examined through this lens in any academic paper, even if he is constantly presented as a populist in the media' (Hubé and Truan 2016: 182). Moreover,

---

[1] We employ the terms 'far left' and 'far right' in this analysis following the classification in Rooduijn et al. (2019).

the uses of the term in French are characterised by the association with other words and concepts, such as 'boulangism, cesarism, poujadism, bonapartism' and every combination of these words (Hubé and Truan 2016: 190).

In the context of Spain, since the emergence of the far-left Podemos in the Spanish political landscape in 2014, the term *populism* has been largely used to refer to this party and its former leader Pablo Iglesias. In addition to Podemos, the party on the opposite side of the political spectrum, the far-right Vox, is also classified as a populist party (Rooduijn et al. 2019). A diachronic study of the uses of the terms *populismo* and *populista* in the Spanish press (de Santiago Guervós 2015) shows how the infrequent uses of the terms in Spanish political language before the 1990s have gradually increased. These uses were mainly related to political movements classified as populist in Latin America, and the emergence of the left-wing political party Podemos in Spain. The analysis of the uses of the terms in the Spanish press shows that the meanings of the terms have changed over time and that the process of relexicalisation has resulted in the predominance of the pejorative uses of the terms which are extensively employed to attack political opponents (de Santiago Guervós 2015: 481).

3 Data and method

This comparative study analyses parliamentary discourse containing the token *populis** in the French National Assembly (l'Assemblée nationale) and the Spanish Congress of Deputies (Congreso de los Diputados) during 2019. The token *populis** is a search word which allows for a comparative analysis of the following terms: *populisme(s)* and *populiste(s)* in French and *populismo(s)* and *populista(s)* in Spanish. This study is guided by the main research question: How are the terms *populism(s)* and *populist(s)* employed in parliamentary debates in France and Spain in 2019? More specifically, this study aims to compare the uses of the singular and plural forms of the nouns *populism(s)* and the singular and plural forms of adjectives *populist(s)* in each dataset by examining (1) which form of *populis** was used, by whom, and how frequently; (2) what are the collocations and the semantic prosody of *populis**; (3) for what purpose politicians use *populis** in this parliamentary context.

This comparative analysis is part of a larger research project entitled TrUMPo: **Tr**acking the **U**ses of Populism in **M**edia and **Po**litical Discourse (UCLouvain, Belgium). The data was extracted from the webpages of the French National Assembly and the Spanish Congress of Deputies using Python script, and includes all plenary debates held in 2019 with at least one token of *populis**. The data is publicly available and can be accessed online.[2] The French corpus contains 47 plenary debates with *populis**;

---

[2] Publicly available data can be found at: https://www.assemblee-nationale.fr/dyn/15/comptes-rendus/seance and https://www.congreso.es/es/busqueda-de-publicaciones [accessed 10 November 2022].

the Spanish corpus contains 19 plenary debates with *populis**. All parliamentary debates with the search word were stored in a shared database of the TrUMPo project. We then manually compiled two datasets containing only the selected parts of the parliamentary interventions, consisting mainly of the sentence with the token *populis** and five sentences which precede and follow the one with *populis**. The dataset with the occurrences of *populis** in French contains 14,481 words and the dataset in Spanish contains 14,134 words. These datasets were used to analyse the collocations and the semantic prosody of the terms with the help of the Word sketch function of the Sketch Engine software. In addition, each occurrence of *populis** was stored in an Excel database, which was used to manually annotate the data. Analytical categories were established inductively, taking into account previous research on the uses of the term in discourse (de Santiago Guervós 2015; Hubé and Truan 2016; Kranert 2020), and on (de)legitimisation strategies (van Leeuwen 2007; Reyes 2011).

Specifically, we have employed the following analytical categories: (1) topic of the message containing *populis**, (2) grammatical category, (3) lexical items which co-occur with *populis**, (4) speaker ID (identification) (namely the person who used the term), (5) object ID (meaning to what object *populis** is attributed), (6) the target of the use of *populis**, (7) the connotation of *populis** (positive, negative or neutral), (8) the pragmatic function of *populis** (namely the disqualification of others, or self-legitimisation). The analysis of the uses of *populis** by French and Spanish politicians follows a qualitative method focusing mainly on the results of the collocation analysis and the annotated database.

4 Analysis

First, we provide a comparison of the two datasets focusing on who used *populis** and which term was used. The description of the frequencies and the distribution of the terms in each dataset contains absolute numbers. In order to draw conclusions on the frequency of occurrence of *populis** by each political party, a proportion of the allocated time for each party is required. The amount of speaking time in the parliaments under analysis is not in direct proportion to the number of members of parliament. As the main aim of this chapter is to focus on the implied meanings and the pragmatic functions of *populis** by French and Spanish politicians, the analysis mainly provides the results of the collocation analysis and the annotated database. However, the description of who uses *populis**, how frequently, and which term is used all helps to further understand the similarities and differences in the uses of each term under study within the specific political landscape.

The French dataset contains 91 occurrences of *populis** (Figure 3.1). The Spanish dataset contains 72 occurrences of *populis** (Figure 3.2). In both

Uses of populism(s) *and* populist(s) *in parliamentary debates* 65

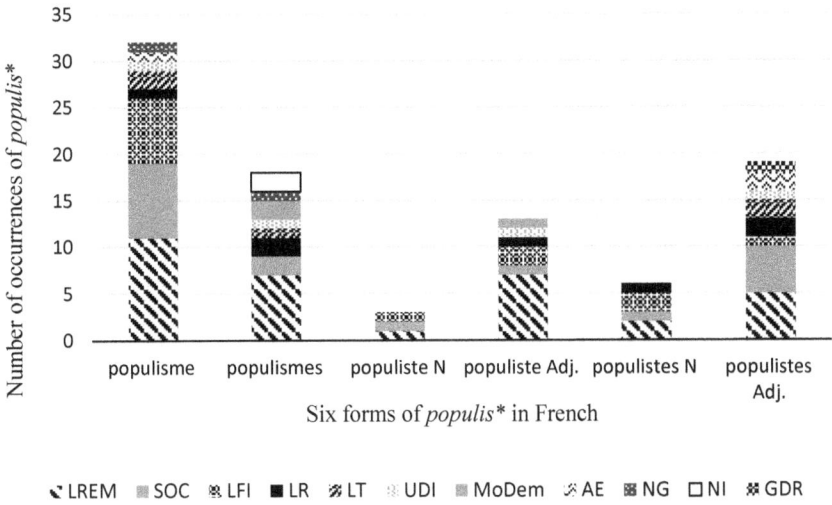

Figure 3.1 *The distribution of* populis* *in the French dataset*

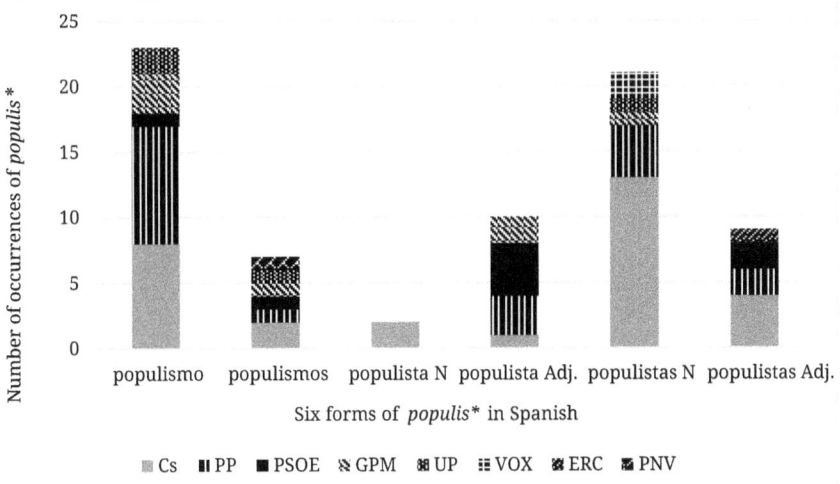

Figure 3.2 *The distribution of* populis* *in the Spanish dataset*

datasets, all four terms are used by politicians from across the whole political spectrum. However, the trends in the use of a concrete term and the extent to which it is employed by each political party are different. In the French dataset, most of the uses of *populis** (n = 33) were produced by the politicians from the majority La République en marche (LREM), often classified as a catch-all party and self-positioned as a centrist and pro-European party. In the Spanish dataset, most of the uses of *populis** (n = 32) were by the politicians from the opposition, the centre-right party Ciudadanos (Cs). This party, founded in Catalonia in 2006, positions itself as the alternative for the traditional two-party system of the PSOE (Spanish Socialist Workers' Party) and PP (People's Party) and promotes discourses of opposition to the Catalan independence movement.

Additionally, in the French dataset, there are more uses of *populis** by the parties to the left of the ruling LREM, mainly SOC, a parliamentary group including representatives of the Socialist Party (n = 18) and LFI, France Unbowed (n = 13). Furthermore, there are six occurrences of *populis** by the centre-right LR (The Republicans).[3] The uses of *populis** by other parliamentary groups are rare (less than five occurrences). In the Spanish dataset, there are more uses of *populis** by the parties to the right of the ruling PSOE: Cs (n = 33) and PP (n = 18).[4] Cs and PP are two political parties competing to become the leader of the centre-of-the-right, as well as being competitors in the 2019 legislative elections. Other parliamentary groups (UP, Vox, GPM, ERC, PNV) used *populis** to a lesser extent.

The distribution of the four terms presents several similarities and differences. For the most part, the singular noun *populism* is the most used form in both datasets, while the singular noun *populist* is the least employed term by French and Spanish politicians. Moreover, the plural noun *populisms* was employed more frequently in the French dataset than in the Spanish dataset. The occurrences of the singular adjective *populist* present similar frequencies in both datasets. A significant difference can be observed in the use of the terms *populistes* and *populistas*. In the French dataset, the occurrences of the plural adjective (n = 19) are higher than the occurrences of the plural noun (n = 6). On the contrary, in the Spanish dataset, the occurrences of the plural noun (21) are higher than the occurrences of the plural adjective (n = 9).

4.1 The uses of the terms *populism(s)*

The singular and plural nouns *populism(s)* co-occur with other concepts: (1) words which denote ideologies and political leanings; (2) negatively charged nouns; (3) metaphors. In the French dataset, negatively charged words such as 'nationalism' (*le nationalisme*), 'Euroscepticism' (*l'euroscepticisme*), 'anti-parliamentarism' (*l'antiparlamentarisme*), all occur with *populism(s)*. In addition to negatively charged words, there are

---

[3] Other parliamentary groups in the French dataset are: LT (Liberties and Territories), UDI (Union of Democrats and Independents), MoDem (Democratic Movement), AE (Act Together), NG (New Left), NI (Non-attached members), GDR (Democratic and Republican Left).
[4] Other parliamentary groups in the Spanish dataset are: UP (United We Can), Vox (Voice), GPM (Multiple Parliamentary Group), ERC (The Republican Left of Catalonia), PNV (The Basque Nationalist Party).

occurrences of 'democracy' (*la démocratie*), 'the people' (*le peuple*). The occurrences of 'nationalism' or 'democracy' are not surprising. Several studies have already pointed out that populism is represented as 'a threat to democracy' (Pappas 2016; Goyvaerts and De Cleen 2020). Moreover, the three concepts – populism, nationalism and democracy – revolve around the idea of the representation of 'the people', which is another recurrent political keyword and a 'basic component of political discourse' (Truan 2019: 205). As De Cleen and Stavrakakis argue, there is 'an ultimately confusing overlap between the concepts of populism and nationalism' due to the emergence of several cases of populist politics with traits of nationalism, 'including – mainly European – populist radical right and most Latin American populisms' (De Cleen and Stavrakakis 2017: 301).

The association of 'populism' and 'nationalism' in the French context might be linked to the far-right Le Rassemblement national, the party which surged in the European elections in May 2019. The collocation 'Euroscepticism' also relates to the contexts of the European Union and the rise of the far right. In the Spanish dataset, such political leanings as 'nationalism' (*el nacionalismo*), 'socialism' (*el socialismo*), 'communism' (*el comunismo*) occur alongside with *populism(s)*, thereby suggesting the association with the concepts referring to the left-wing ideologies, and the Latin American populisms often linked to Podemos. Moreover, in both datasets, the term 'national populism' was used: the hyphenated form 'national populism' (*le national-populisme*) in French, alluding to the historical context of Germany, and the same term (*el nacionalpopulismo*) in Spanish, referring in some instances to the left-wing leaning in Spain, and in others to national populism in Germany.

As for the second category, namely the collocates of *populism(s)* with negatively charged nouns, the nouns employed in the French dataset include 'xenophobia' (*la xénophobie*), 'exasperation' (*l'exaspération*), 'domination' (*la domination*), 'national egoisms' (*les égoïsmes nationaux*), 'doubt' (*le doute*), 'religious hatred' (*la haine religieuse*), 'chaos' (*le chaos*) and 'danger' (*le danger*). Let us consider the following excerpt:

(1) ... in a context of **rising xenophobia and populisms that threaten common European values**, the Union must fully contribute to deconstructing fears and alleviating them.[5] (Stella Dupont, LREM, majority, 7 October 2019; author's translation)

While talking about the migration politics and policies in France and in Europe, the member of parliament uses 'the rising' as the head of the noun

---

[5] Original quotation: '... dans un contexte de **montée de la xénophobie et des populismes qui menacent les valeurs européennes communes,** l'Union doit pleinement contribuer à déconstruire les peurs et à apaiser' (Stella Dupont, LREM, majority, 7 October 2019).

phrase (NP) in a coordination construction of two nouns: 'xenophobia' and 'populisms'. The use of the plural noun *populisms* implies that there is more than one populism but leaves it unclear whether this refers to the political leanings, the left- and the right-wing populisms, or about some political parties, and whether those populisms belong to the context of France, Europe or both. This negative representation is recurrent in discourses containing *populism* by the ruling LREM, whose discourses do not target a specific political actor, but rather send a message of warning.

This appeal to negative emotions is often constructed using metaphors, such as 'the rising' (*la montée*), 'the surge' (*la poussée*), 'the drift' (*la dérive*), and 'the wave' (*la vague*), which discursively represent populism as the force of nature or an illness. Excerpt (2) illustrates how *populism* is portrayed as a major threat to European democracies, as indicated by two linguistic cues, namely the use of *populism* as the subject of the utterance and the use of *populis** in metaphorical descriptions. Here, populism 'takes root' and 'infects, turns gangrenous' in the current political situation:

(2) In a troubled political context, **where populism is trying to take root and infect modern democracies**, our country is trying to move forward on a narrow path. One of the challenges of the stability program is precisely to trace it. (Philippe Chassaing, LREM, majority, 30 April 2019; author's translation)[6]

The use of the singular and plural nouns *populism(s)* suggests that *populis** is used as an abstract phenomenon which is negatively connoted. Populism is presented as an already existing threat which needs to be taken seriously and urgently addressed. Such uses of *populis** exemplify an indirect self-legitimisation strategy, which is present in discourses characterised by an abstract use of *populis**, as well as in discourses which target a concrete object associated with populism – for example, a citizens' initiative referendum.

Another context-bound characteristic of discourses containing the singular noun 'populism' (*le populisme*) and the plural noun 'populisms' (*les populismes*) is linked to debates concerning different conceptions of democracy. These discourses include references to concrete political measures, such as 'shared initiative referendum' (*référendum d'initiative partagée*) and 'citizens' initiative referendum' (*référendum d'initiative citoyenne*). The latter is a proposal for a constitutional amendment in France to allow citizens to be consulted by referendum concerning the proposition or abrogation of laws. For example, a plenary debate concerning the privatisation

---

[6] Original quotation: 'Dans un contexte politique troublé, **où le populisme cherche à s'enraciner et à gangrener les démocraties modernes**, notre pays s'efforce d'avancer sur une voie étroite. L'un des enjeux du programme de stabilité est précisément de la tracer' (Philippe Chassaing, LREM, majority, 30 April 2019).

of the Airports of Paris and the proposition of the Business Growth and Transformation Action Plan (*Loi PACTE*) contained thirteen occurrences of *populis**. Specifically, the singular and plural nouns were employed in utterances such as 'indulging in populism(s)' (*faire le jeu du/des populisme(s)*), used by the Minister of the Economy and Finance, Bruno Le Maire.

Excerpt (3), from the plenary debate about the proposition of the *Loi PACTE* illustrates how a direct democratic process is referred to as populist, again showing its threat to democracy and using the phrase *faire le jeu de*, meaning 'to play into someone's hands; to do exactly what an opponent or enemy wants one to do'. Again, political opponents are not mentioned explicitly. However, considering the socio-political context, it becomes clear that it is the left wing, and specifically LFI, which is targeted by the use of 'populism' (*le populisme*). However, this does not mean that all the left-wing parties are targeted as being populist. In this excerpt, Bruno Le Maire employs the first-person plural pronoun 'we' (*nous*), which may be interpreted as reference to LREM, and evokes the fear caused by this referendum. However, as illustrated in excerpt (4), he specifies that the fear comes from populism and not from 'the French people' (*le peuple français*). The uses of *populism* in this excerpt shows how a measure of direct democracy is referred to as populist measure and is contrasted with 'democracy in Europe in France':

(3) **We live in dangerous times for democracies**. In France, as in Europe, representative democracy has never been so **threatened**. I find any initiative that would **play into the hands of populism** and fuel the contestation of parliamentary democracy unfortunate. (Bruno Le Maire, Minister of the Economy and Finance, LREM, majority, 11 April 2019; author's translation.)[7]

(4) ... it is **not the French people** that we are afraid of, but **populism**. (Bruno Le Maire, Minister of the Economy and Finance, LREM, majority, 11 April 2019; author's translation.)[8]

The debate concerning the privatisation of the Airports of Paris activated different uses of *populis** related to the role and the place of the people in contemporary European democracies who are currently witnessing

---

[7] Original quotation: '**Nous vivons une période dangereuse pour les démocraties**. En France comme en Europe, jamais la démocratie représentative n'a été aussi **menacée**. Je trouve malencontreuse toute initiative qui viendrait **faire le jeu des populismes** et alimenter la contestation de la démocratie parlementaire' (Bruno Le Maire, Minister of the Economy and Finance, LREM, majority, 11 April 2019).
[8] Original quotation: 'ce n'est pas **du peuple français** dont nous avons peur, **mais du populisme**' (Bruno Le Maire, Minister of the Economy and Finance, LREM, majority, 11 April 2019).

political polarisation and the rise of the extremes on both sides of the political spectrum. Conflicting opinions about what is democratic and what is populist are expressed by different uses of *populis** during this debate. Excerpt (5) shows how the member of LFI contests Bruno Le Maire's use of *populism*. Alexis Corbière counter-attacks Le Maire by retaking his use of *populis** and attributing the label 'Macronist' to him (referring to the politics of the President, Emmanuel Macron) with an implied negative meaning. In this example, *populis** is used to directly discredit the addressee and the government of Macron and to provide a counter-argument in a debate:

(5) A minister dared to say that **using the law was a populist drift**. Mr. Mayor, you are amazing! We should put you under glass! You are the reference macronist [*sic*], the one who sees in a call for the law so that the sovereign **people** speak out a **populist drift!** (Alexis Corbière, LFI, opposition, 11 April 2019; author's translation.)[9]

In the Spanish dataset, the singular and plural nouns *populism(s)* collocate with negatively charged nouns which include 'repression' (*la represión*), 'regression' (*el retroceso*), 'demagogy' (*la demagogia*), 'threat' (*la amenaza*). Metaphorical descriptions are also used to represent populism, such as 'the breeding ground' (*el caldo de cultivo*), 'the wave' (*la oleada*), 'the toll towards national populism' (*el peaje al nacionalpopulismo*). In addition, the noun *populism* is modified by negatively charged adjectives, such as 'cheap' (*barato*), 'musty' (*rancio*), 'the worst' (*el peor*), as well as by qualifying adjectives as *económico* ('economic'), *institucional* ('institutional'). In the French dataset, the uses of the singular and plural *populism(s)* appeared in discourses which represented populism as a negative but obscure political phenomenon without explicitly targeting political actors. In the Spanish dataset, however, the recurrent context of the appearance of the noun *populismo* is in reference to Catalonia. Alternatively, it is associated with the left-wing ideologies, such as socialism and communism, much more than with right-wing politics.

Most of the discourses containing the terms *populismo(s)* belong to two right-wing parties, Cs and PP, who strongly oppose the politics of the ruling PSOE and specifically the idea of a coalition government between PSOE and the left wing. As 2019 was the year of numerous elections in Spain, it seems natural to find occurrences of *populism* in discourses related to the elections to self-promote and self-legitimise, as well as to discredit political opponents. Both Cs and PP follow two strategies: (1) using the NP 'populism

---

[9] Original quotation: 'Un ministre a osé dire qu'utiliser **la loi était une dérive populiste.** Monsieur Le Maire, vous êtes incroyable ! On devrait vous mettre sous verre ! Vous êtes le macroniste de référence, celui qui voit dans un appel à la loi pour que **le peuple** souverain se prononce **une dérive populiste!**' (Alexis Corbière, LFI, opposition, 11 April 2019).

Uses of populism(s) *and* populist(s) *in parliamentary debates*

of Podemos' (*populismo de Podemos*), explicitly attributing populist politics to the left-wing party; (2) using the noun 'populism' (*populismo*) together with other concepts which can be interpreted in the Spanish contexts as implicitly attributing populist politics to specific Spanish actors. In concrete terms, they associate *populism*, on the one hand, with concepts related to left-wing politics, mainly in Venezuela and Bolivia, which evoke the politics of Podemos and its links with the Latin American socialist politics and, on the other hand, with such terms as 'independence movement' (*independentismo*) and 'separatism' (*separatismo*), referring to the Catalan context.

Excerpt (6) illustrates the use of the singular noun in the discourse of the member of the right-wing PP:

(6) Ladies and gentlemen, in Spain, **Catalan nationalism practices the most stale and anti-democratic populism in Europe** . . . (Dolors Montserrat, PP, opposition, 19 February 2019; author's translation).[10]

The subject of the utterance is the noun 'nationalism' (*el nacionalismo*) modified by the adjective 'Catalan', and 'populism' (*el populismo*) is the object of the utterance. *El populismo* is characterised as being 'musty' and 'anti-democratic'.

4.2 The uses of the terms *populist(s)*

In both Spanish and French, the terms *populiste(s)* and *populista(s)* can be employed as nouns and as adjectives. The analysis has determined the tendency to use *populiste(s)* as a qualifying adjective in the French dataset. *Populiste(s)* appeared as a qualifying adjective of nouns such as 'discourses' (*les discours*), 'parties' (*les partis*), 'formations' (*les formations*), 'movements' (*les mouvements*), 'currents' (*les courants*), 'measures' (*les mesures*) and 'strategies' (*les stratégies*). These uses appear in similar contexts to the occurrences of the nouns *populisme(s)*, namely in discourses concerning the negative portrayal of populism as a major threat to European politics, as well as in instances of the debates regarding the representation of 'the people' in European democracies. For example, the citizens' initiative referendum (RIC) was qualified by a member of LREM as 'a simplistic and populist tool, a tool not of citizen democratic participation but of popular democratic consumption'.[11] Labelling this measure as *populist*, the politician de-legitimises it, by using it together with the negatively charged adjective 'simplistic'.

---

[10] Original quotation: 'Señorías, en España **el nacionalismo catalán practica el populismo más rancio y antidemocrático de Europa** . . .' (Dolors Montserrat, PP, opposition, 19 February 2019).

[11] Original quotation: 'un outil simpliste et populiste, un outil non de participation démocratique citoyenne mais de consommation démocratique populaire' (Guillaume Gouffier-Cha, LREM , majority, 21 February 2019).

However, in the Spanish dataset the use of the nouns *populista(s)* prevails over the adjective. The only use of the singular noun 'populist' targeting a concrete person occurs exclusively in the Spanish dataset and is used by the leader of Cs for the most part of 2019, Albert Rivera (excerpt 7):

(7) Mr. Sánchez, it is that this economic policy has also been marked by **Mr. Iglesias**. If we have seen him signing; we have seen **a populist** signing an agreement in Moncloa. You are the first president to sign a government agreement with a populist in Moncloa. (Albert Rivera, Cs, opposition, 12/02/2022; author's translation).[12]

The leader of Cs directly addresses the leader of PSOE and explicitly criticises the government and the decision to form a coalition with Podemos, attracting attention to the apparently scandalous fact that a populist politician should allegedly share the official residence of the Prime Minister of Spain. Several linguistic strategies are used, such as the use of the first-person plural 'we' in 'we have seen' (*hemos visto*), the nomination strategy (van Leeuwen 1995) by explicitly naming the leader of Podemos, and highlighting the fact that Pedro Sánchez is the only Prime Minister to make such a decision. This example illustrates the use of *populis** as a stigma term attributed to a political actor classified as populist. However, the de-legitimisation is addressed to another politician, the leader of the government which had allowed a populist to enter Moncloa, the official residence of the Prime Minister of Spain.

As in excerpt (7), the uses of 'populist' and 'populists' demonise Podemos and its leader and construct a negative image primarily of Pedro Sánchez by de-legitimising him because of negotiation with 'the evil'. The label is applied to Podemos either explicitly by naming the political party (*populistas de Podemos*), or implicitly. However, it is clear from the context that the label *populists* is applied to Podemos. The plural noun 'populists' (*populistas*) collocates with other terms, such as 'independentists' (*independentistas*), 'nationalists' (*nacionalistas*), 'separatists' (*separatistas*), 'putschists' (*golpistas*), and the pro-ETA Basque nationalist terrorist group, referred to in the corpus as '*filoetarras*', thus associating populism with the regionalist discourses, and the Catalan and Basque autonomist movements.

The following excerpt illustrates a combination of recurrent strategies employed in the discourses containing the term *populistas* in the Spanish dataset:

---

[12] Original quote: 'Señor Sánchez, es que además esa política económica se la ha marcado **el señor Iglesias**. Si es que le hemos visto firmando; hemos visto **a un populista firmando** en la Moncloa un acuerdo. Es usted el primer presidente que firma con **un populista** un acuerdo de Gobierno en la Moncloa' (Albert Rivera, Cs, opposition, 12 February 2022).

Uses of populism(s) *and* populist(s) *in parliamentary debates* 73

(8) We Spaniards will decide – yes, in two shifts – whether in the summer we put the Socialist Party of **the triple alliance of nationalists, populists and socialists**, the alliance of the worst ideas of the 19th century, the worst sentiments of the 20th century and the fake news of the 21st, or if, on the contrary, we put the PP, which creates jobs, increases well-being and brings progress, to govern, to the ideas of humanity, humanism, freedom and democracy. In other words, we will decide whether we are governed by the bloc of the supremacist Quim Torra, the terrorist Arnaldo Otegi, the dictator Nicolás Maduro or the ultra-radical Sánchez Pérez-Castejón, or a PP government, in favor of the European Union, of peace and Spain. (Jordi Roca, PP, opposition, 21 February 2019; author's translation).[13]

Excerpt (8) shows the discursive representation of the dichotomy 'us' (PP) versus 'them' (PSOE) or the dichotomy 'good' and 'evil' in the context of the upcoming elections. The member of PP emphasises the collective nature of the group using the reference to the nationality 'Spaniards' (*los españoles*) and the omitted first-person plural pronoun 'we' (*nosotros*), which is the strategy of backgrounding an individual and assimilating them to a collective identity, in this case, specific nationality (van Leeuwen 1995). The negative image of PSOE is discursively achieved by targeting the coalition, referring to it with a military term, 'the alliance' (*alianza*), of the plural nouns which denote groups of individuals categorised as 'populists', 'nationalists' or 'socialists'. The coalition is furthermore de-legitimised by attributing to it such characteristics as 'the worst ideas', 'the worst sentiments', repeating the evaluative adjective and employing the pejorative label 'fake news'. The de-legitimisation of PSOE and an even more negative portrayal of the coalition is achieved through the nomination strategy, giving the names of the politicians along with attributing to them such categories as 'supremacist', 'terrorist' or 'dictator', while the target and the head of the coalition, Pedro Sánchez, is classified as 'ultraradical'. Nonetheless, this excerpt also illustrates the self-legitimisation strategy, as PP is discursively associated with positive actions such as 'creating jobs' and 'increasing well-being', and positively charged nouns as 'progress', 'humanism', 'freedom', 'democracy' and 'peace'.

---

[13] Original quotation: 'Los españoles decidiremos – eso sí, en dos turnos – si en verano ponemos a gobernar toda España y sus ciudades **al Partido Socialista de la triple alianza de nacionalistas, populistas y socialistas**, la alianza de las peores ideas del siglo XIX, los peores sentimientos del siglo XX y las fake news del XXI, o si por el contrario ponemos a gobernar al PP, que crea empleo, aumenta el bienestar y trae progreso, al de las ideas de humanidad, humanismo, libertad y democracia. En otras palabras, decidiremos sobre si nos gobierna el bloque del supremacista Quim Torra, el terrorista Arnaldo Otegi, el dictador Nicolás Maduro o el ultrarradical Sánchez Pérez-Castejón, o un Gobierno del PP, a favor de la Unión Europea, de la paz y la España' (Jordi Roca, PP, opposition, 21 February 2019).

The examples presented in this section have shown some of the recurrent linguistic and discursive strategies employed in discourses containing the terms *populism(s)* and *populist(s)*. However, the present analysis is not exhaustive and provides only some of the results concerning the strategies of (de)legitimisation employed in political discourse containing the terms under study.

5 Conclusion

This chapter has aimed to analyse the uses of the terms *populism(s)* and *populist(s)* in parliamentary discourse by French and Spanish politicians during 2019. The examination of the collocations of *populis** in each dataset points to the negative semantic prosody of the terms in both Spanish and French parliamentary discourse during the studied period. In both datasets, the terms were used with negative implied meaning, as suggested by the collocation analysis. *Populis** occurs in conjunction (1) with words which denote ideologies and political leanings; (2) with negatively charged nouns; (3) in metaphorical descriptions. In this study, there are no occurrences of *populis** associated with positive connotations either in the French or in the Spanish corpus.

The analysis reveals the specific contexts of the uses of the terms *populism(s)* and *populist(s)*, as well as the set of concrete associations with populism. In the French dataset, the singular and plural nouns 'populism' (*populisme*) and 'populisms' (*populismes*) are mostly used to refer to a kind of abstract phenomenon, but which can then be associated with specific proposals from particular political parties. The abstract use of *populis** in the French dataset is characterised as presenting populism as a threat to democracy and as a dangerous phenomenon which needs to be stopped urgently. This abstract use of the term and the negative representation of populism as a political phenomenon is linked to other concepts which are often related to political agendas perceived as extremist, such as 'nationalism', 'Euroscepticism' and 'xenophobia'. The study shows that even though the abstract use of *populis** implies a pejorative meaning, it does not plainly target political actors often regarded as populist or explicitly question their legitimacy. On the contrary, discourses containing the labels *populism* and, in some cases, the adjective *populist*, function as a means of self-legitimisation and self-positioning as antagonistic and anti-populist forces.

The occurrences of the adjectives 'populist' (*populiste*) and 'populists' (*populistes*) in the French dataset also show the tendency towards the abstract use which does not have the de-legitimising function, but instead is used to qualify and to categorise objects, entities and ideas, such as 'populist drift' or 'populist measure'. However, this abstract use of the term can also be indirectly aimed at concrete political actors and may occur in de-legitimising discourses. An example of such use is the attribution of the label *populist* to a direct democratic process proposed by the left wing (namely the citizens' initiative referendum), by appealing to fear and qualifying it as dangerous, simplistic and contrary to European democracies.

In the Spanish dataset, *populis** is mainly characterised as the association with concrete political actors and specific features attached to the meaning of populism. The association with populism, as well as the target of the use of the negative label, differ according to the political leaning of the speaker. The labels *populismo(s)* and *populista(s)* are attached mainly to the left-wing Podemos and are associated with a range of concepts, such as socialism, communism, independentism and terrorism. The contexts of the occurrences of the terms are linked to regional nationalisms (primarily, in Catalonia and the Basque country) and the 2019 elections. The plural noun *populistas* was the most used term in the Spanish dataset. It implies a group of individuals and labels, either explicitly by using the strategy of nomination, or implicitly, suggesting a specific political party, namely Podemos. The main target of the discourses of de-legitimisation is the leader of the ruling political party and the coalition between PSOE and the left wing. In addition to de-legitimising discourses, the uses of *populis** in the Spanish dataset are also common in self-legitimising discourses. In such cases, the opponents of the ruling party employ *populis** to discredit the coalition and to praise and position themselves as the only alternative to the populist government.

This chapter shows how such contested terms such as *populism* and *populist* are used by politicians in parliamentary discourse and reveal that the implied meaning depends on the context and the communicative goal of the speaker. *Populis** can be used as a tool for explicit or implicit disqualification, as well to self-praise, self-position and self-legitimise. The analysis demonstrates that in the specific context of this study, *populis** can indeed be used as a stigma term to discredit populist political opponents, as shown in previous research (Kranert 2020). However, this study reveals that *populis** is mainly used in self-legitimising discourses with the purpose of self-promotion as the only legitimate political actor in the existing political landscape. Ultimately, the findings point to the need for further investigation into discourses containing *populis** and into the pragmatic function of the terms in political discourse from a linguistic perspective. In addition, a detailed comparative analysis of the occurrences of *populis** in metaphorical descriptions can help us to understand whether there are similar or different conceptual patterns in the use of the terms with concrete implied meanings.

References

Canovan, M. (1999). Trust the people! Populism and the two faces of democracy. *Political Studies*, 47 (1), pp. 2–16. doi: 10.1111/1467-9248.00184.

Chilton, P. (2017). 'The people' in populist discourse: Using neuro-cognitive linguistics to understand political meanings. *Journal of Language and Politics*, 16 (4), pp. 582–94. doi: 10.1075/jlp.17031.chi.

De Cleen, B., Glynos, J. and Mondon, A. (2018). Critical research on populism: Nine rules of engagement. *Organization*, 25 (5), pp. 649–61. doi: 10.1177/1350508418768053.

De Cleen, B. and Stavrakakis, Y. (2017). Distinctions and articulations: A discourse theoretical framework for the study of populism and nationalism. *Javnost – The Public*, 24 (4), pp. 301–19. doi: 10.1080/13183222.2017.1330083.

Demata M., Conoscenti M. and Stavrakakis Y. (2020). Riding the populist wave: Metaphors of populism and anti-populism in the *Daily Mail* and *The Guardian*. *Iperstoria*, 15, pp. 8–35. doi: 10.13136/2281-4582/2020.i15.686.

de Santiago Guervós, J. (2015). La relexicalización en el discurso político actual: El ejemplo de populismo a través de la prensa española. *Boletín de la Real Academia Española*, 95, pp. 471–500. Available at: http://revistas.rae.es/brae/article/view/118/227 [accessed 15 June 2023].

de Vreese C. H., Esser F., Aalberg T., Reinemann, C. and Stanyer, J. (2018). Populism as an expression of political communication content and style: A new perspective. *The International Journal of Press/Politics* 23 (4), pp. 423–38. doi: 10.1177/1940161218790035227.

Eklundh, E. (2020). Excluding emotions: The performative function of populism. *Partecipazione e Conflitto*, 13 (1), 107–31. doi: 10.1285/i20356609v13i1p107.

Goyvaerts, J. and De Cleen, B. (2020). Media, anti-populist discourse and the dynamics of the populism debate. In: Krämer, B. and Holtz-Bacha, C., eds, *Perspectives on Populism and the Media: Avenues for Research*. Baden-Baden: Nomos Verlagsgesellschaft, pp. 83–108.

Heller, M. and McElhinny, B. S. (2017). *Language, Capitalism, Colonialism: Toward a Critical History*. Toronto: University of Toronto Press.

Hidalgo-Tenorio E., Benítez-Castro, M.-Á. and De Cesare F., eds. (2019). *Populist Discourse: Critical Approaches to Contemporary Politics*. London: Routledge.

Hubé, N. and Truan, N. (2016). France: The reluctance to use the word populism as a concept. In: Aalberg, T., Esser, F., Reinemann, C., Stromback, J. and de Vreese, C., eds, *Populist Political Communication in Europe: A Cross-National Analysis of European Countries*. London: Routledge, pp. 181–95.

Hunger, S. and Paxton, F. (2021). What's in a buzzword? A systematic review of the state of populism research in political science. *Political Science Research and Methods*, 10 (3), pp. 617–33. doi: 10.1017/psrm.2021.44.

Kranert, M. (2020). When populists call populists populists: 'Populism' and 'populist' as political keywords in German and British political discourse. In: Kranert, M., ed., *Discursive Approaches to Populism Across Disciplines: The Return of Populists and the People*. Cham: Springer, pp. 31–60.

Laclau, E. (2005). Populism: What's in a name? In: Panizza, F., ed., *Populism and the Mirror of Democracy*. London: Verso, pp. 32–49.

Mudde, C. (2004). The populist zeitgeist. *Government and Opposition*, 39 (4), pp. 541–63. doi: 10.1111/j.1477-7053.2004.00135.x.

Mudde, C. and Kaltwasser, C. R. (2017). *Populism: A Very Short Introduction*. Oxford: Oxford University Press.

Pappas, T. (2016). The specter haunting Europe: Distinguishing liberal democracy's challengers. *Journal of Democracy*, 27 (4), pp. 22–36. doi: 10.1353/jod.2016.0059.

Reyes, A. (2011) Strategies of legitimization in political discourse: From words to actions. *Discourse & Society*, 22 (6), pp. 781–807. doi: 10.1177/0957926511419927.

Rooduijn, M., van Kessel, S., Froio, C., Pirro, A., De Lange, S., Halikiopoulou, D., Lewis, P., Mudde, C. and Taggart, P. (2019). The PopuList: An overview of populist, far right, far left and Eurosceptic parties in Europe. Available from: https://populist.org [accessed 15 June 2023].

Schröter, M., Veniard, M., Taylor, C. and Blätte, A. (2019). A comparative analysis of the keyword multicultural(ism) in French, British, German and Italian migration discourse. In: Viola, L. and Musolff, A., eds, *Migration and Media: Discourses about Identities in Crisis*. Amsterdam: John Benjamins, pp. 13–44.

Taylor, C. (2022). Corpus linguistics in the study of political discourse: recent directions. In: O'Keeffe, A. and McCarthy, M. J., eds, *The Routledge Handbook of Corpus Linguistics*. 2nd edn. London: Routledge.

Thornborrow, J., Ekström, M. and Patrona, M. (2021). Discursive constructions of populism in opinion-based journalism: A comparative European study. *Discourse, Context & Media*, 44 (100542). doi: 10.1016/j.dcm.2021.100542.

Truan, N. (2019). The discursive construction of the people in European political discourse: Semantics and pragmatics of a contested concept in German, French, and British parliamentary debates. In: Zienkowski, J. and Breeze, R., eds, *Discourse Approaches to Politics, Society and Culture*. Amsterdam: John Benjamins, pp. 201–28.

van Leeuwen, T. (1995). The representation of social actors. In: Caldas-Coulthard, C. R. and Coulthard M., eds, *Texts and Practices: Readings in Critical Discourse Analysis*. London: Routledge, pp. 32–70.

van Leeuwen, T. (2007). Legitimation in discourse and communication. *Discourse & Communication*, 1 (1), pp. 91–112. doi: 10.1177/1750481307071986.

Zienkowski, J. and Breeze, R., eds. (2019) *Imagining the Peoples of Europe: Populist Discourses across the Political Spectrum*. Amsterdam: John Benjamins.

Corpus

Assemblée nationale (2019). *Comptes rendus des débats en séance*. Available at: https://www.assemblee-nationale.fr/dyn/15/comptes-rendus/seance [accessed 15 June 2023].

Congreso de los Diputados (2019). *Diario de sesiones del Congreso de los Diputados. Pleno y diputación permanente*. Available at: https://www.congreso.es/es/busqueda-de-publicaciones [accessed 15 June 2023].

CHAPTER 4

The Brexit saga: Stancetaking, control and identity in political discourse

Juana I. Marín-Arrese

1 Introduction

Stance resources indicate the epistemic, evaluative or attitudinal positionings of speakers or writers, and may also be said to index the interactional construction of identities in the discourse (Biber and Finegan 1989; Bucholtz and Hall 2005; Du Bois 2007; Englebretson 2007; Johnstone 2007, inter alia). This chapter focuses on the speaker's or conceptualiser's positioning in striving for epistemic control in the discourse, through the expression of justificatory support for their claims, 'epistemic support' and 'epistemic justification' (Boye 2012). The paper also examines subject positioning in striving for effective control in the discourse, as persuasive and coercive intent regarding action plans and the realisation of events, thereby expanding the notion of stance (see Marín-Arrese 2011, 2021). It will be argued that the joint deployment of epistemic and effective resources in the discourse results in those complementary legitimisation strategies whereby the politician presents some situation as true or likely and urges for some justifiable action.

The framework for the analysis of stance posits two macro-categories, epistemic and effective stance (Marín-Arrese 2011, 2021), which reflect the systematic opposition in discourse between striving for control of conceptions of reality and striving for control of relations at the level of reality (Langacker 2009, 2013). These two categories draw on Langacker's (2008, 2009) distinction between the epistemic and the effective level in grammar, exemplified among other linguistic elements in the contrast between root and epistemic modals, which 'are distinguished by whether the modal force pertains to occurrences or knowledge of occurrences' (Langacker 2008: 485). As Langacker (2009: 291) notes, 'Epistemic relations are those which hold at the level of knowledge, and thus involve conceptions of reality. By contrast, effective relations hold at the level of reality per se.'

The chapter explores the joint deployment of epistemic and effective stance expressions in the discourse of two key actors in the Brexit process:

Theresa May and Boris Johnson. Their specific and recurrent stancetaking patterns are assessed in comparison with the discourse stance of a group of key members in the Conservative Party during the Brexit process in the United Kingdom (UK). The ad hoc corpora for this study comprise texts from political speeches, during the period 2016–20. The paper presents a quantitative study of the following discourse features: (1) variation in the use of epistemic and effective stance resources in the discourse of key actors in the Brexit process (May vs Johnson); (2) variation in stance resources in relation to the indexing of identity construction (May/Johnson vs Conservative Party members).

From a critical discourse perspective, it will be argued that the deployment of these resources serves the strategic functions of legitimisation and coercion, that is, support for the validity of the communicated information and persuasive intent regarding preferred actions and action goals (van Dijk 2003; Chilton 2004, 2017; Marín-Arrese 2011, 2015, 2021; Bennett 2019).

This chapter is organised as follows. Section 2 discusses stance and identity, and the main features and functions of the categories of epistemic and effective stance strategies. Section 3 gives a brief account of the Brexit process. Section 4 provides a description of methodological decisions and research procedures. In section 5, the results and discussion of the study are presented. The conclusions are found in section 6.

2 Epistemic and effective stance in the discourse of Brexit

2.1 Stance, identity and (inter)subjectivity

The multifaceted nature of stance, the expression of beliefs, evaluations or value judgements, attitudes or emotions, or the way we align or disalign with particular positions or information advanced by others in social interaction, has been addressed from diverse and often overlapping perspectives and frameworks, such as the work on stance (Biber and Finegan 1989; Biber 2015), affect and emotion (Ochs and Schieffelin 1989; Kärkkäinen and Du Bois 2012), evaluation (Thompson and Hunston 2000; Thompson and Alba-Juez 2014), attitude and engagement (Martin and White 2005), stancetaking and dialogicality (Du Bois 2007; Englebretson 2007), and the sociolinguistics of stance (Jaffe 2009).

Du Bois (2007: 163) describes stance in the following terms: 'Stance is a public act by a social actor, achieved dialogically through overt communicative means, of simultaneously evaluating objects, positioning subjects (self and others), and aligning with other subjects, with respect to any salient dimension of the sociocultural field.' According to Englebretson (2007: 17), stance can be subdivided into the following categories: evaluation (value judgements, assessments and attitudes), affect (personal feelings) and epistemicity (commitment). In this chapter, our framework focuses on epistemic stance and on the category of effective stance (Marín-Arrese 2011, 2021).

Variation in the choice of stance resources and preferred types of stance may be linked to identity construction and style in interaction. Identity has been defined as 'the social positioning of self and other', as 'a discursive construct that emerges in interaction' and contributes to persona construction within the discourse (Bucholtz and Hall 2005: 586–7). Du Bois (2002) has posited the concept of 'stance accretion', that is, the process whereby more stable structures of identity are configured through the repetition of stances; that is, interactional stances may create consistent personas, and this process is ultimately linked with styles (cited in Bohmann and Ahlers 2022: 67). According to Bucholtz and Hall (2005: 597), micro-level linguistic structures like stance markers and style features may index identity categories. Similarly, Johnstone (2007: 52) has observed that 'identities can be associated with individually-embodied speakers', and argues that 'a repeated stancetaking move or pattern of moves may emerge as an identity'. In this chapter we will show that certain politicians display preferences for specific stances and recurrent choices of epistemic and effective stance resources, and we will argue that these patterns of preferred stance choices for epistemic persuasion and coercive intent may point to varying forms of interactional identity construction thus indexed in the discourse.

In addition to their contentful meaning,[1] epistemic and effective stance expressions are also indexical of the speaker's or writer's subjectivity and intersubjectivity. These stance expressions are indexical of the extent to which the communicated proposition is implicitly grounded in the perspective of the speaker as subject of conception, in contrast to objectivity, whereby the subject of conception or some other facet of the ground is explicit and salient (Langacker 1991, 2009). Langacker (1991: 93) identifies a continuum in terms of degrees of salience that the ground elements, the speech-act participants, have in a particular predication, and the extent to which speakers or writers are explicitly or implicitly present in the discourse. Consequently, in the case of pronouns like *I* or *you*, as in expressions like *I think*, which profile the speech-act participants, the role of the speaker or hearer as conceptualiser is 'rendered maximally salient and minimally subjective', while the object of conception, the propositional content, is explicitly subjective. With epistemic modals, the roles of speaker or hearer remain implicit, and therefore non-salient and maximally subjective, while the object of conception, the communicated proposition, is implicitly subjective.

---

[1] For the notion of and the continuum from contentful to procedural meaning, see Traugott (2017).

The expression of stance also relates to issues of speaker or writer[2] commitment to and responsibility for the communicated proposition or proposal. Nuyts (2001) conceives the dimension of subjectivity vs intersubjectivity as the degree to which the speaker assumes personal responsibility for the evaluation of the evidence (subjectivity) or whether the assessment is 'potentially' shared by others (intersubjectivity). As a result, these stance expressions index the ways speakers or writers take overt or covert responsibility for the expression of knowledge or for the expression of social force (Nuyts 2001, 2012; Langacker 2009; Marín-Arrese 2011, 2015).

2.2 Epistemic and effective control in discourse

Epistemic stance pertains to control of 'conceptions of reality' (see Langacker 2008, 2009, 2013). Speakers will strive for epistemic control in the discourse, by providing 'justificatory support' ('epistemic support' and 'epistemic justification'; Boye 2012: 2–3) for their assertions or claims, in order to legitimise the truth or validity of the communicated information and overcome hearers' cognitive mechanisms for epistemic vigilance (Sperber at al. 2010; Hart 2011; Marín-Arrese 2011). The speaker's striving for control of conceptions of reality involves their estimation of the veracity of the event designated and the likelihood of its realisation, and/or their specification of the sources whereby they feel entitled to make an assertion (Marín-Arrese 2011, 2015, 2021).

Effective stance pertains to control of 'relations at the level of reality' (see Langacker 2008, 2009, 2013). Speakers will strive for effective control by positioning themselves with respect to the realisation of events and action plans. Effective stance strategies aim to exert direct control over the course of reality itself, by exerting social force on hearers or readers and persuading them of the necessity, advisability or requirement, social desirability or righteousness of the proposed plans of action, or alternatively by expressing intention or determination to carry out those action plans, or more indirectly by indicating their feasibility or enabling circumstances (Marín-Arrese 2011, 2021).

In discussing the notion of control, Langacker (2008: 473) notes a number of features which distinguish the 'statement scenario' from the 'order scenario' (cf. Langacker 2008: 474). In a usage event in which the speaker produces a statement, he or she assumes the role of the conceptualiser (C) and subscribes to the proposition by adopting 'an epistemic stance (e) toward the profiled occurrence (primarily by the presence or absence of a modal)'. The speaker's intended outcome is that 'the hearer will momentarily join the speaker in attending to the proposition', and the 'potential result of the usage event is that the hearer also identifies with C and subscribes

---

[2] Henceforth, 'speaker' will refer to both speakers and writers, and 'hearer' to hearers and readers.

to the proposition' (Langacker 2008: 473). By extension, epistemic stance resources, such as those studied in this chapter, thus serve their purpose as legitimising strategies, in persuading the hearer to acknowledge the truth or validity of the communicated information.

In the prototypical 'order scenario', as Langacker (2008: 474) observes, 'the content expressed (for example: *Leave!*) is not a proposition but simply a process'. The prototypical clause in the order scenario, the imperative, 'does not contain a separate grounding element: its verb cannot be inflected for tense (**Left!*) or take a modal (**Will leave!*)'. As with root modals, the element which counts as grounding is the act of ordering, since 'it relates the profiled process to the interlocutors' (Langacker 2008: 474). In the order scenario, effective stance involves the speaker's intention of bringing about the occurrence of the profiled process. The speaker realises this intent by subjecting 'the hearer to social and psychological force', with the projected outcome 'that the hearer will share this intent and act accordingly' (Langacker 2008: 474). Similarly, other effective stance resources studied in this chapter serve to exert social force on hearers and persuade them of the adequacy of the proposed plans of action.

We may sum up the main features of epistemic and effective stance in the following terms:

1. *Epistemic stance*
    - Communicated content: proposition.
    - Source of epistemic stance: The speaker as conceptualiser (C) subscribes to the proposition by assessing the epistemic status (location vis-à-vis reality) of the profiled occurrence.
    - Target: The hearer, who identifies with C and subscribes to the proposition.
    - Potential result: The hearer 'identifies with C and subscribes to the proposition' (Langacker 2008: 473). Hence the speaker's control of conceptions of reality (Langacker 2009), that is, the legitimisation of the beliefs, knowledge or evidence that support or justify their claims.

2. *Effective stance*
    - Communicated content: process (or proposition).
    - Source of effective stance: The speaker as conceptualiser (C), or by proxy some 'deontic controller' (Chilton 2020), exerts social or psychological force on the hearer with regard to the realisation of some action or event.
    - Target: The hearer, who shares intent with the speaker and acts accordingly.
    - Potential result: The 'hearer will share this intent and act accordingly' (Langacker 2008: 474). Hence the speaker's control of relations at the level of reality (Langacker 2009), and the legitimisation of the realisation of some event or action plan.

2.3 Epistemic stance (EP)

Epistemic stance resources comprise a variety of lexico-grammatical elements or 'devices' which 'overtly express an evaluative frame for some other proposition' (Biber at al. 1999: 967). The conceptual domain of epistemicity, as Boye (2012: 2–3) consistently argues, comprises the 'subcategories evidentiality and epistemic modality'. Epistemic modality has been defined in the literature in terms of speaker's degree of certainty or degree of commitment concerning the proposition, or as Boye (2012: 21) argues, the degree of 'epistemic support' for a proposition. Evidentiality pertains to speaker's reference to the modes of knowing, or access to evidence or information (Aikhenvald 2004), on the basis of which they feel entitled to make a statement or claim (Anderson 1986), or in the words of Boye (2012: 2–3) as 'epistemic justification' for the proposition (see Marín-Arrese et al. 2022 for a detailed study on evidentiality in English). Within epistemic stance resources our framework also includes verbs of mental state or cognitive attitude (Capelli 2007), and cognitive factive predicates, which are generally defined as presupposing the truth of the proposition designated by their complement clause (Kiparsky and Kiparsky 1970), or impersonal factives.

For epistemic stance, we have identified the following sub-categories:

1. *Personal cognitive factives (PFV)*: Expression of knowledge about events, and assignment of factual status to the complement proposition (strong 'epistemic support'; Boye 2012). Expressions used are factive mental predicates, which presuppose the truth of the proposition designated by their complement clause (cf. Kiparsky and Kiparsky 1970).

   Linguistic resources include personal cognitive factives such as: *I or we know, I realise, I remember, I acknowledge; We have learned; I am aware* ...

   (1) When I speak of Global Britain – and the need <EF, DM> for us to commit ourselves to the peace and prosperity of the world. **I know** <EP, PFV> that there will <EP, EM> be some who are wary that this sounds pretentious, in a nation that comprises less than one per cent of the world's population. **I know** <EP, PFV> there will <EP, EM> be cynics who say we can't afford it. I say we can't <EF, POT> afford not to. (Boris Johnson, Foreign Secretary: 'Beyond Brexit: a Global Britain', speech, 2 December 2016)

2. *Impersonal factives (IFV)*: Expression of factivity involving the presupposition of the truth of the proposition designated by their complement clause (cf. Kiparsky and Kiparsky 1970). Linguistic resources include impersonal factive expressions, such as: *The truth is, the fact is, the reality is; It is true, it is a fact; in truth, in fact, in reality* ...

(2) Free trade has been blamed for all sorts, but we must <EF, DM> not unfairly scapegoat it and lurch towards protectionism. **The fact is** <EP, IFV> that the UK's industrial heartlands have not been failed by bad trade, but rather by bad policy. (Liz Truss, International Trade Secretary: Chatham House speech, 29 October 2020)

3. *Cognitive attitude (CGA)*: Expression of subjective beliefs and epistemic evaluations regarding the reality of the event designated ('epistemic support'; Boye 2012). Expressions include non-factive mental predicates, which indicate speakers' reflective attitudes or beliefs regarding the described event (Capelli 2007). Linguistic resources include epistemic complement-taking predicates and adverbs of cognitive attitude such as: *I* or *we think, believe, suppose, suspect, assume, imagine, expect, guess, doubt; I am sure, I am certain, I have no doubt, I am confident; It seems to me; supposedly, presumably, no doubt, undoubtedly, doubtless* . . .

(3) **I'm sure** <EP, CGA> your assessment of the British government is quite different. But **I suspect** <EP, CGA> that a certain word beginning with 'B' has appeared in a thousand diptels over the past 3 years. Thanks to Brexit, British politics has certainly <EP, EM> not been dull. (Jeremy Hunt, Foreign Secretary: speech at Lord Mayor's Banquet, 14 May 2019)

4. *Epistemic modality (EM)*: Expression of speaker's degree of certainty concerning the reality of the event designated, its actual occurrence or the likelihood of its realisation (cf. 'epistemic support' for the proposition; Boye 2012). Linguistic resources include epistemic modals, adverbs and predicative adjectives such as: *must, should, will, could, may, might; perhaps, maybe, possibly, probably, certainly, surely; certain, possible, likely, bound to* . . .

(4) And on the great environmental issue of our time, **perhaps** <EP, EM> the greatest issue facing humanity, Britain was the first major economy in the world – let alone the EU – to place upon our own shoulders a legal obligation to be carbon neutral by 2050. That **will** <EP, EM> put huge strains on our system, it **will** <EP, EM> require full effort and change but we know <EP, PFV> we can <EF, POT> do it. (Boris Johnson, Prime Minister [PM]: speech in Greenwich, 3 February 2020)

5. *Indirect-inferential evidentiality (IIE)*: Within the domain of evidentiality, we focus here on indirect-inferential evidentiality, where we may distinguish perception-based, conception-based and communication-based inferences (cf. Marín-Arrese 2017). Inferences may be triggered through access to various types of information source: perceptual evidence,

conceptual knowledge (logical reasoning, assumption or general knowledge), or knowledge acquired through social communication sources (reports, documents, other speakers, and so on). Linguistic resources include evidential predicates, sentence adverbs and predicative adjectives such as: *It seems, appears, looks (like); It is clear, evident, obvious; apparently, seemingly, clearly, obviously, palpably* ...

(5) They want the continued ability to control our legislative freedom, our fisheries, in a way that is **obviously** <EP, IIE> unacceptable to an independent country. And since we have only ten weeks until the end of the transition period on January 1, I have to <EF, DM> make a judgment about the likely outcome and to get us all ready. And given that they have refused to negotiate seriously for much of the last few months, and given that this summit **appears** <EP, IIE> explicitly to rule out a Canada-style deal, I have **concluded** <EP, IIR> that we **should** <EF, DM> get ready for January 1 with arrangements that are more like Australia's based on simple principles of global free trade. (Boris Johnson, PM statement on negotiations with the EU, PM's Office, 10 Downing Street, 15 October 2020)

6. *Indirect interpretation/reformulation (IIR)*: Expressions indicating inferences or deductions based on some kind of 'proof' or interpretation of information previously available to the speaker. This category is akin to inferential evidentiality, since it involves inferential work which Bednarek (2006: 650) describes as some form of 'backings for the speaker's knowledge', and is typically derived from contextual knowledge. Linguistic resources include lexical verbs, typically with a deictic subject element such as: *That suggests, that means; it indicates, it tells, it shows* ...

(6) And unfortunately history **tells** <EP, IIR> us that centralised state control, socialist management, and the absence of effective price signals and functioning markets, and indeed <EP, IFV> the expropriation of private property and collectivisation have led, not just to economic misery but also to environmental degradation. The example of Mao's China, Soviet Russia and Maduro's Venezuela, **shows** <EP, IIR> that that path leads to poisoned soils and contaminated rivers, toxic air and wrecked habitats. (Michael Gove, Environment Secretary: 'Green Brexit: A New Era for Farming, Fishing and the Environment', speech, Prosperity UK, 15 March 2018)

2.4 Effective stance (EF)

Effective stance pertains to the positioning of the speaker with respect to the realisation of events, to the ways in which the speaker carries out a stance act aimed at determining or influencing the course of reality itself. Effective stance resources include a variety of lexico-grammatical elements: deontic modals, expressions of directivity, such as imperatives and hortatives and various forms of directive speech acts, personal and impersonal predicates expressing normativity, or expressions of intentionality, or inclination, as well as expressions of possibility or potentiality.

The sub-categories of effective stance identified in our framework are the following:

1. *Directivity (DIR)*: Expression of directive illocutionary force regarding the realisation of the event. Linguistic resources include the imperative mood with a conventional directive force or with a hortative value, and directive utterances involving direct force scenarios such as: *Look, Remember, Do not, Don't*; *Let us, Let's*; *I/we urge you to, I want you to, I ask you to* . . .

    (7) **Let's** <EF, DIR> get Brexit done on October 31. **Let's** <EF, DIR> get it done because of the opportunities that Brexit will <EP, EM> bring not just to take back control of our money and our borders and our laws. To regulate differently and better, and to take our place as a proud and independent global campaigner for free trade. **Let's** <EF, DIR> get it done because delay is so pointless and expensive. **Let's** <EF, DIR> get it done because we need <EF, DM> to build our positive new partnership with the EU, because it cannot <EF, DM> be stressed too much that this is not an anti-European party and it is not an anti-European country. (Boris Johnson, PM and Party Leader: Conservative Party conference speech, Manchester, 2 October 2019)

2. *Deonticity (DM)*: These are expressions of necessity, duty or obligation, such as deontic necessity regarding the realisation of the event, and 'advisability' (*should, ought to*), a weak form of deonticity (cf. Traugott and Dasher 2002). Deontic meanings are likewise expressed by so-called semi-modals or quasi-modals (*have to, need to*) (cf. Leech 2003). Linguistic resources include deontic modals and modals of possibility and necessity, and adverbs, predicative adjectives and nominals such as: *must, should, can, cannot, can't*; *have to, need to, ought to*; *It is necessary to*; *there is a need to, it is our duty to* . . .

    (8) The sovereignty of Parliament does not come to Parliament out of a void. It comes to Parliament from the people. Yet this Parliament is now holding the people in contempt. They are holding you in contempt. Hence we **must** <EF, DM> have a general election. It is time for a new Parliament. A new egg **must** <EF, DM> be laid that will <EP, EM> not be addled. We trust the people. Our opponents do not. (Jacob Rees-Mogg, Leader of the House of Commons: Conservative Party conference speech, 29 September 2019)

3. *Intentionality (INT)*: Expression of intention, commitment or determination with respect to the realisation of the event designated. The speaker participates as both source and target of the intent regarding the realisation of the event. Linguistic resources include personal complement-taking predicates expressing intention, or determination, modals and 'emerging' modals of intention (*I am/we are going to*) (Krug 2000), as well as modals of volition with a commissive illocutionary force such as: *I/We intend to, mean to, want to; I am/We are determined to, resolved to; I/we shall/will/'ll/won't; I am/we are going to . . .*

   (9) So, let us <EF, DIR> send a clear message from this hall today: **we will** <EF, INT> never accept either of those choices. **We will** <EF, INT> not betray the result of the referendum. And **we will** <EF, INT> never break up our country. I have treated the EU with nothing but respect. The UK expects the same. (Theresa May, PM and Conservative Leader: Conservative Party conference, 3 October 2018)

4. *Inclination (INC)*: Expression of speaker's inclination or volition for the realisation of an event. This category is related to intentionality (INT), the distinction being that the target of the intent is not the speaker, though they may be strategically included in the reference to the target. Linguistic resources include personal predicates expressing volition and inclination, and modals of volition such as: *I/We want, hope, wish, would like . . .*

   (10) My answer is clear. **I want** <EF, INC> the United Kingdom to emerge from this period of change stronger, fairer, more united and more outward-looking than ever before. **I want** <EF, INC> us to be a secure, prosperous, tolerant country – a magnet for international talent and a home to the pioneers and innovators who will shape the world ahead. **I want** <EF, INC> us to be a truly Global Britain – the best friend and neighbour to our European partners, but a country that reaches beyond the borders of Europe too. (Theresa May, PM: speech outlining Britain's 12-point plan for Brexit, Lancaster House, 17 January 2017)

5. *Normativity (NRM)*: Expression of judgements of social desirability, instrumentality, appropriateness or fit to social norms, as well as social consequentiality and righteousness regarding the event designated and its realisation. Linguistic resources include impersonal complement-taking predicates and adverbials such as: *It is important, essential, crucial, vital; It is time to; It is right, best; quite rightly; it will not do . . .*

   (11) **It is time** <EF, NRM> to stop treating the referendum result as though it were a plague of boils or a murrain on our cattle or an

inexplicable aberration by 17.4 m people. **It is time** <EF, NRM> to be bold, and to seize the opportunities, and there is no country better placed than Britain. (Boris Johnson, Foreign Secretary: 'Let that lion roar', Conservative Party conference speech, Manchester, 3 October 2017)

6. *Potentiality (POT)*: Expression of judgements of possibility or feasibility regarding the realisation of the event designated. Linguistic resources include modal auxiliaries and semi-modals of 'participant-external possibility', and 'non-prototypical generalised possibility' (van der Auwera and Plungian 1998; Traugott and Dasher 2002) such as: *I/We can, you can, cannot, could; able to; It is possible (to), impossible (to)* . . .

(12) And we have that same opportunity today. To show the world that **we can** <EF, POT> be the strongest global advocate for free markets and free trade, because we believe <EP, CGA> they are the best way to lift people out of poverty. But that **we can** <EF, POT> also do much more to ensure the prosperity they provide is shared by all. To demonstrate that **we can** <EF, POT> be the strongest global advocate for the role businesses play in creating jobs, generating wealth and supporting a strong economy and society . . . (Theresa May, PM: speech to the Lord Mayor's Banquet, 14 November 2016)

3 The context: The Brexit saga

In a referendum held on 23 June 2016, the UK voted to leave the European Union (EU)³ by a 52% to 48% majority. David Cameron, who led the campaign to remain in the EU, resigned as Prime Minister (PM) in July 2016, and Theresa May became Leader of the Conservative Party and Prime Minister.

May's new cabinet was formed by prominent pro-Brexit campaigners. On 29 March 2017, the PM May formally triggered Article 50, which set into motion the Brexit process and the two-year countdown for the UK to exit the EU ('Brexit'). After a period of deadlock in the Brexit talks, the UK and EU reached an agreement for the withdrawal in November 2018, which required the approval of the UK and EU parliaments in order to take effect. In January 2019, the PM tried to pass the Withdrawal Agreement through parliament, but lost that first vote as well as other subsequent

---

[3] Information from the following sources: Balkan (2020), Sandford (2020) and Walker (2021).

votes, which obliged her to ask the EU for a series of delays on Brexit. In June 2019, Theresa May finally announced her resignation as Conservative Party leader and PM.

In July 2019, Boris Johnson won the Conservative leadership contest, and was appointed new Prime Minister. In the 2019 Conservative Party conference, he set in motion the campaign 'Get Brexit done'. In October 2019, a new Brexit deal was agreed with the EU in Brussels, which was then turned down in the Commons. This led to a further Brexit extension to 31 January 2020, granted by the EU.

The House of Commons then approved a UK General Election to take place on 12 December 2019, where Boris Johnson won by an ample majority. By 23 January 2020, the European Union (Withdrawal Agreement) Act 2020 gained Royal Assent, and on 31 January 2020, the UK left the EU and entered a transition period. This transition period ended on 31 December 2020, when the United Kingdom ceased to be a member of the EU.

4 Methodology

4.1 Hypotheses

The chapter explores the following research issues mentioned above: (1) variation in the use of epistemic and effective stance resources in the discourse of key actors in the Brexit process (May vs Johnson); (2) variation in stance resources in relation to the indexing of identity construction (May/Johnson vs Conservative Party members).

Following the work on stance and identity construction (Du Bois 2002; Bucholtz and Hall 2005; Johnstone 2007), it is assumed that key actors in the political arena such as Theresa May and Boris Johnson may well have developed interactional identities which are linguistically indexed in the discourse through specific preferred stances and recurrent stancetaking moves or patterns. It is further hypothesised that these specific and recurrent stancetaking choices are more likely to emerge in a crucial political situation for the UK, such as the Brexit process, which requires them to put into action their best learned legitimisation and persuasive strategies. These specific features of stance are compared to those of a 'control' group consisting of key Conservative members in the May and Johnson cabinets.

The paper therefore posits the following hypotheses:

1. In relation to the degree to which there is variation in the deployment of epistemic and effective stance markers (dependent variable) in the discourse of two key actors in the Brexit process, May vs Johnson (independent variable), which might reflect features of speaker stance identity, the following null hypothesis is posited:

H_{01}: There will be no significant variation in the use of epistemic and effective stance expressions between the two key actors in the Brexit process: no significant difference in the sub-categories of stance and the frequency of stance tokens involving overuse in the May vs Johnson speeches.

The null hypothesis is expressed as H_{01}: $\pi 1 = \pi 2$

2. In relation to the degree to which there is variation in the use of epistemic or effective stance expressions (dependent variable), which might reflect features of speaker stance identity, in the discourse of each of the two key actors in the Brexit process, May or Johnson, in comparison to the group of Conservative Party members (independent variable), the following null hypothesis is posited:

H_{02}: There will be no significant variation in the use of epistemic and effective stance expressions between each of the two key actors in the Brexit process, May or Johnson, and the group of Conservative Party members: no significant difference in the sub-categories of stance and the frequency of stance tokens involving overuse in the speeches of May/Johnson vs Conservative Party members.

The null hypothesis is expressed as H_{02}: $\pi 1 = \pi 2$

4.2 Corpus

In order to test the above hypotheses, a corpus of speeches was collected from the following websites:

GOV.UK: News and communications: https://www.gov.uk/search/news-and-communications

BREXITCentral: https://brexitcentral.com

The corpus consists of political speeches involving the topic of Brexit during the period (2016–20):

Theresa May, PM: 50,114 words (12 texts)

Boris Johnson, Foreign Secretary and PM: 34,272 words (15 texts)

Key Conservative members in the May and Johnson cabinets: 33,713 words (14 texts):

- Secretary of State for Exiting the European Union: David Davis, Dominic Raab and Stephen Barclay
- Chancellor of the Exchequer: Philip Hammond
- Foreign Secretary: Jeremy Hunt
- Secretary of State for International Trade: Liam Fox and Liz Truss
- Environment Secretary: Michael Gove
- Business Secretary: Sajid Javid
- Leader of the House of Commons: Andrea Leadsom and Jacob Rees-Mogg

4.3 Research objectives and stance categories

The following research objectives were set in relation to the above hypotheses:

1. Identification of expressions of epistemic and effective stance in our corpora.
2. Classification according to the framework of epistemic and effective stance categories and for (inter)subjectivity described above, and annotation of tokens in the corpus.
3. Frequency comparison of use of stance expressions across political actors.

Epistemic and effective stance categories and resources in the texts were annotated and grouped into the categories shown in Table 4.1.

4.4 Procedure and statistical analysis

4.4.1 Analysis and annotation
The analysis and annotation procedure was carried out as follows:

1. An initial search, using Monoconc, was carried out for those expressions of epistemic and effective stance judged to be more prototypical (introspective, top-down process).

Table 4.1 *Epistemic and effective stance: Categories and expressions*

EPISTEMIC STANCE (EP)		EFFECTIVE STANCE (EF)	
Category	Expressions	Category	Expressions
Personal cognitive factives (PFV)	*I/we know, I realise, I remember,...*	Directivity (DIR)	*Remember! Do not, Don't!; Let us, Let's; I/we urge you to...*
Impersonal factive predicates (IFV)	*The truth/fact/reality is; It is true...*	Normativity or social desirability (NRM)	*It is important, crucial; It is time to; It is right, best...*
Cognitive attitude (CGA)	*I/we think, believe, suppose, suspect...*	Potentiality (POT)	*I/We/you can, cannot; able to; It is possible (to)...*
Epistemic modality (EM)	*must, should, will, could, may, might; perhaps, maybe, possibly, probably, certainly...*	Deonticity (DM)	*must, should, cannot, can't; have to, need to; It is necessary to...*
Indirect-inferential evidential expressions (IIE)	*It seems, appears; It is clear, obvious; apparently, clearly, obviously...*	Intentionality (INT)	*I/We intend to, want to; I am/We are determined to; I/we shall/will/'ll/won't...*
Interpretation or reformulation of information (IIR)	*That suggests, that means, it indicates, it tells, it shows...*	Inclination (INC)	*I/We want, hope, would like...*

2. The texts were then examined closely and the tokens of effective and epistemic expressions present were tagged manually (text-driven, bottom-up process).
3. Annotation procedure: The texts were independently annotated by two annotators, who swapped texts and carried out a first revision. The second revision of the annotation in all the texts was carried out by a third annotator.
4. Quantification of data, comparison and statistical analysis of the quantitative results across political actors (May vs Johnson vs Conservative Party members).

4.4.2 Statistical analysis

For the analysis of the significance of the quantitative results, a set of statistical tests was used:

1. Social Sciences Statistics: Chi Square Calculator – Up To 5x5, With Steps, http://www.socscistatistics.com
   The Chi-square test (Chi^2) test provides a method for testing the degree to which there is association between the variables in a contingency table, by measuring the divergence of the observed values from the expected values under the null hypothesis of no association. The test compares the observed frequencies to the frequencies one would expect if the two variables are unrelated. If the p-value is significant, it indicates that there is some association between the variables, so that the observed frequencies are not due to random variation. The test was applied to results in Table 4.2.
2. Statistical Inference: *A Gentle Introduction for Linguists* (SIGIL): Corpus Frequency Test Wizard, http://sigil.collocations.de/wizard.html
   This test was used to measure the relative frequencies of tokens for each category (per thousand words, and per ten thousand words). The test was applied to measure the chi-squared distribution, with one degree of freedom ($df = 1$), of each of the sub-categories in relation to two of the speaker types and the size of the sample or subcorpora. The test was applied to results in Tables 4.3 and 4.4.
3. University Centre for Computer Corpus Research (UCREL): Log likelihood wizard, http://ucrel.lancs.ac.uk/llwizard.html
   The log-likelihood (LL) test measures the relative overuse or underuse of the observed frequency for each sub-category in one of the corpora in comparison to the observed frequency for same category in another corpus (O1: observed frequency in corpus 1; O2: observed frequency in corpus 2). The test was applied to results in Tables 4.3 and 4.4.

5 Results and discussion

5.1 Results for epistemic and effective stance in political speeches: May vs Johnson

Table 4.2 shows the results for the two macro-categories of stance (epistemic vs effective) in the discourse of May, Johnson, and key Conservative members.

Table 4.2 *Epistemic and effective stance in speeches: May vs Johnson vs Conservatives (N and ratio per thousand words) (Chi^2 = 23.6065; p-value < 0.00001)*

Stance	T. May (50,114 words)		B. Johnson (34,272 words)		Conservatives (33,713 words)	
EP vs EF	N	R‰	N	R‰	N	R‰
Epistemic	481	9.598	418	12.196	302	8.958
Effective	1,060	21.152	621	18.120	509	15.098
TOTAL	1,541	30.750	1,039	30.316	811	24.056

The results for the Chi-square test (Chi^2) are significant at p < 0.05, which indicates that we are dealing with dependent variables, that is, the observed values are not due to random variation and there is association between the speaker involved and the differences in the frequencies of the stance resources in the two corpora.

Effective stance is the preferred mode of stance in all the speakers, but there is a clear cline in use, with May showing the highest figures (21.152 per 1,000 words [ptw]), and the group of Conservatives the lowest figures (15.098 ptw). With respect to epistemic stance, Johnson shows the highest ratio of use (12.197 ptw).

There is a clear difference in use in the discourse of both PMs and that of the other Conservative members, which might be attributed to their role as PMs, and their higher responsibility in achieving the goals of Brexit. Both speakers show a higher degree of striving for both epistemic and effective control in discourse, and a greater display of persuasive and coercive strategies.

5.2 Results for epistemic stance in political speeches: May vs Johnson vs Conservative Party members

The figures in Table 4.3 show the results for each of the sub-categories of epistemic stance in the discourse of May, Johnson, and the group of Conservative members. The Chi-square test,[4] sensitive to the size of

---

[4] The value of significance for the Chi-square test was established at p < 0.05. The following values were observed and coded by using asterisks: *** difference significant at p < .001; ** significant at p < .01; * significant at p < .05.

Table 4.3 Categories of epistemic stance in speeches: May vs Johnson vs Conservatives (N and ratio per ten thousand words)

Stance	T. May (50,114 words)		B. Johnson (34,272 words)		Conservatives (33,713 words)	
Epistemic	N	R‰	N	R‰	N	R‰
PFV	79	15.764	69	20.133	41	12.161
IFV	40	7.982	37	10.796	39	11.568
CGA	107	21.351	90	26.260	54	16.017
EM	230	45.895	195	56.898	144	42.714
IIE	14	2.794	19	5.544	5	1.483
IIR	11	2.195	8	2.334	19	5.636
TOTAL	481	95.981	418	121.965	302	89.580

the corpus, and the log-likelihood test,[5] were applied to the results. The latter test shows the relative frequencies of stance expressions, indicating either overuse or underuse of tokens for each sub-corpus in relation to another sub-corpus.

The comparison between the results for May and those of Johnson shows a significant difference and marked overuse of epistemic stance resources on the part of Johnson ($X^2 = 12.79267$***, LL = –12.74), and more specifically in the category of epistemic modals (EM: $X^2 = 4.69963$*, LL = –4.84). The relative distribution and cline of preference is equivalent for both politicians: EM (epistemic modality) > CGA (cognitive attitude) > PFV (personal cognitive factives) > IFV (impersonal factives) > IIE (inferential evidentiality) > IIR (indirect interpretation/reformulation).

The comparison of the discourse of Johnson with that of the control group of Conservative members shows that there is a significant overuse of epistemic expressions in his discourse ($X^2 = 16.70360$***, LL = +16.91), and more specifically in the three major sub-categories: personal cognitive factives (PFV: $X^2 = 6.20115$*, LL = +6.75), cognitive attitude predicates (CGA: $X^2 = 7.95851$**, LL = +8.51) and epistemic modals (EM: $X^2 = 6.60871$*, LL = +6.89). However, the comparison between the discourse of May with that of other Conservative members reveals only a significant underuse by May in a minor sub-category: indirect interpretation or reformulation of information (IIR: $X^2 = 5.74268$*, LL = –6.50). We may thus conclude that while May seems to conform to the standard use of epistemicity in the political discourse of Conservatives, Johnson's significant overuse of epistemicity may be a distinct feature of his interactional identity.

Both politicians opt for implicitness (EM) and obfuscation of responsibility for their 'epistemic support' with regard to the communicated proposition. However, they also favour, and especially Johnson, stance expressions (CGA, PFV) in which their role as speaker or conceptualiser is visible, thereby

---

[5] A plus sign (+) indicates overuse in O1 (results in column 1) relative to O2 (results in column 2); a minus sign (–) indicates underuse in O1 relative to O2.

taking personal responsibility and explicitly vouching for the content of the communicated proposition. The least preferred categories involve impersonal expressions and inferential markers of 'epistemic justification', that is, those which presumably require more complex cognitive processes on the part of the decoder.

5.3 Results for effective stance in political speeches: May vs Johnson vs Conservative Party members

The results in Table 4.3, together with those in Table 4.2, show that effective stance is markedly preferred in political discourse. The Chi-square test, sensitive to sample size, and the log-likelihood test were likewise applied to the results in Table 4.4, showing the relative frequencies of stance expressions, indicating either overuse or underuse of tokens for each category in relation to the discourse domain.

The comparison of the results for May and Johnson shows a significant overuse of effectivity stance resources in the case of May ($X^2 = 9.42907^{**}$; LL = +9.49). With respect to the sub-categories of effective stance, May makes a marked overuse of two categories: deontic modality (DM: $X^2 = 12.33260^{***}$, LL = +13.01) and potentiality (POT: $X^2 = 14.25812^{***}$, LL = +15.02). Johnson outranks May in the category of directivity (DIR: $X^2 = 8.53674^{**}$, LL = –8.88) and normativity (NRM: $X^2 = 2.93397$, LL = –3.21). However, the relative distribution and cline of preference is similar in both politicians:

- *May*: INT (intentionality) > POT (potentiality) > DM (deonticity) > INC (inclination) > NRM (normativity) > DIR (directivity)
- *Johnson*: INT (intentionality) > POT (potentiality) > DM (deonticity) > INC (inclination) > DIR (directivity) > NRM (normativity)

The comparison of the discourse of May with that of the control group of Conservative members shows a highly significant overuse in effectivity

Table 4.4 *Categories of effective stance in speeches: May vs Johnson vs Conservatives (N and ratio per ten thousand words)*

Stance	T. May (50,114 words)		B. Johnson (34,272 words)		Conservatives (33,713 words)	
Effective	N	R‰	N	R‰	N	R‰
DIR	54	10.775	64	18.674	25	7.415
DM	268	53.478	125	36.473	174	51.612
INT	297	59.265	179	52.229	124	36.781
INC	96	19.156	65	18.966	38	11.272
NRM	61	12.172	58	16.923	37	10.975
POT	284	56.671	130	37.932	111	32.925
TOTAL	1,060	211.517	621	181.197	509	150.980

expressions on the part of May (X^2 = 39.88597***, LL = +40.50). More specifically, May makes very significant overuse of expressions in the categories of intentionality (INT: X^2 = 19.94177***, LL = +21.09), and potentiality (POT: X^2 = 23.72806***, LL = +25.24), and to a lesser degree in the expression of inclination (INC: X^2 = 7.36460**, LL = +8.19).

The comparison of the results for Johnson and for the Conservative group yields similar results. Johnson makes a significant overuse of effective stance expressions in general (X^2 = 9.30993**, LL = +9.35), more specifically in the categories of directivity (DIR: X^2 = 15.62735 ***) and intentionality (X^2 = 8.79602**, LL = +9.16), and to a lesser degree of inclination (X^2 = 6.15224*, LL = +6.72) and normativity (X^2 = 3.89376*, LL = +4.34). The only sub-category where Conservatives show significantly higher results is in deontic modality (DM: X^2 = 8.55345**, LL = –8.89).

In terms of her interactional identity, May thus emerges as a particularly effective speaker in terms of 'getting things done', and also as quite inclined to exerting more direct forms of social control, as shown by the overuse of deontic modality (DM: 'must') in comparison to Johnson. Results also show that May favours overtly marking her personal or interpersonal responsibility in expressing commitments and promises (INT: 'I will', 'we are going to'), and inclination (INC: 'I want', 'we want') regarding the realisation of events. For potentiality (POT), we find both expressions of interpersonal responsibility ('we can'), and expressions of implicit responsibility in judgements of capability ('Britain can').

For his part, Johnson emerges as a speaker seeking to involve the audience in expressing directivity by intersubjectivity markers (DIR: 'Let's'), and also in the expression of commitments and promises (INT: 'We will'). He also makes explicit his personal responsibility in the expression of inclination (INC: 'I want').

The fact that both May and Johnson clearly favour intentionality (INT), and potentiality (POT) and deontic modality (DM), albeit these latter categories to a lesser degree in the case of Johnson, may point to their interactional roles as prime ministers. In comparison with the Conservative group, they have both the power and the responsibility to carry out commitments and promises, and the capacity or power and social control for setting in motion particular plans for action.

5.4 Discussion of results in political discourse

We may conclude that political discourse is characterised by a distinct preference for effective stance, in particular expressions of deontic modality (DM), intentionality (INT) and potentiality (POT). Politicians show a tendency to make their roles as speakers or conceptualisers explicit ('I will') and also to take shared responsibility for the expression of intentionality, commitments and promises ('we will'), as well as in the expression of potentiality ('we can'). However, when exerting social or psychological force on the target or hearer, they opt for implicit expressions of deontic modality ('must', 'should').

The presence of epistemic stance is comparatively low in the present corpus of political discourse, and mostly involves the categories of epistemic modality (EM), cognitive attitude predicates (CGA) and personal factive verbs (PFV). There is a preference either for epistemic modality markers ('may', 'perhaps') involving implicit personal responsibility in the expression of epistemic support for their claims, and for explicit personal responsibility in the expression of beliefs ('I think') or both personal and interpersonal responsibility in reference to knowledge ('I know', 'we know') regarding the propositional content.

6 Conclusions

This chapter has focused on two macro-categories of stance: epistemic and effective. Epistemic stance pertains to the positioning of the speaker with respect to knowledge regarding the veracity of the proposition, and their commitment to the communicated information, that is, to stance acts aimed at persuading hearers to subscribe to the beliefs, knowledge or evidence that support or justify their claims. Effective stance resources involve the positioning of the speaker with respect to the realisation of events, to stance acts aimed at persuading hearers to share their intent, thereby determining or influencing the course of reality itself. This chapter has presented a corpus-based study on the use of stance expressions in political discourse – specifically, in the genre of political speeches involving the Brexit process from 2016 to 2020.

Politicians have a vested interest in justifying their assertions or claims, since they may be held politically accountable for the communicated information. In addition, politicians may have specific political interests in carrying out certain actions or plans of action. Striving for epistemic control in the discourse is realised *indirectly* by vouching for claims based on knowledge and information crucially related to those actions and plans of actions involving specific political aims. Striving for effective control is realised more *directly* by claiming the necessity, desirability or righteousness of the proposed plans of action, or expressing their commitment to or the feasibility of the realisation of those actions or events. Thus, the joint deployment of epistemic and effective stance resources effects a combined strategy of striving for control in the discourse, both by the legitimisation of knowledge about events and by coercive persuasion concerning the realisation of events.

Acknowledgements

I am grateful to the anonymous reviewers and to the editor for their valuable comments on the chapter.

References

Aikhenvald, A. (2004). *Evidentiality*. Oxford: Oxford University Press.
Anderson, L. B. (1986). Evidentials, paths of change, and mental maps: Typologically regular asymmetries. In: Chafe, W. and Nichols, J., eds, *Evidentiality: The Linguistic Coding of Epistemology*. Norwood, NJ: Ablex, pp. 273–312.
Balkan, A. (2020). The Brexit timeline simplified – Why are we leaving? Get Britain Out campaign. http://getbritainout.org.
Bednarek, M. (2006). Epistemological positioning and evidentiality in English news discourse: A text-driven approach. *Text & Talk*, 26 (6), pp. 35–60.
Bennett, S. (2019). 'Crisis' as a discursive strategy in Brexit referendum campaigns. *Critical Discourse Studies*, 16 (4): pp. 449–64. doi: 10.1080/17405904.2019.1591290.
Biber, D. (2015). Stance and grammatical complexity: An unlikely partnership discovered through corpus analysis. *Corpus Linguistics Research*, 1, pp. 1–19.
Biber, D. and Finegan, E. (1989). Styles of stance in English: Lexical and grammatical marking of evidentiality and affect. In: Ochs, E., ed., *The Pragmatics of Affect*. Special issue. *Text*, 9 (1), pp. 93–124.
Biber, D., Johansson, S., Leech, G., Conrad, S. and Finegan, E. (1999). *Longman Grammar of Spoken and Written English*. London: Longman.
Bohmann, A. and Ahlers, W. (2022). Stance in narration: Finding structure in complex sociolinguistic variation. *Journal of Sociolinguistics*, 26, pp. 65–83. doi: 10.1111/josl.12533.
Boye, K. (2012). *Epistemic Meaning: A Crosslinguistic and Functional-Cognitive Study*. Berlin: Mouton de Gruyter.
Bucholtz, M. and Hall, K. (2005). Identity and interaction: A sociocultural linguistic approach. *Discourse Studies* 7 (4–5), pp. 585–614. doi: 10.1177/1461445605054407.
Capelli, G. (2007). *'I reckon I know how Leopoldo da Vinci must have felt...': Epistemicity, Evidentiality and English Verbs of Cognitive Attitude*. Pari: Pari Publishing.
Chilton, P. (2004). *Analysing Political Discourse*. London: Routledge.
Chilton, P. (2017). 'The People' in populist discourse: Using neuro-cognitive linguistics to understand political meanings. *Journal of Language and Politics*, 16 (4), pp. 582–94. doi: 10.1075/jlp.17031.chi.
Chilton, P. (2020). Stance, truth and lies in a post-truth discourse environment. Paper presented at the International Conference on Stance, (Inter)Subjectivity and Identity in Discourse (STANCEDISC'20), Universidad Complutense de Madrid, Madrid, 9–11 September.
Du Bois, J. W. (2002). Stance and consequence. Paper presented at the 101st Annual Meeting of the American Anthropological Association, New Orleans, 20–24 November.
Du Bois, J. W. (2007). The stance triangle. In: Englebretson, R., ed., *Stancetaking in Discourse*. Amsterdam: John Benjamins, pp. 139–82.
Englebretson, R. (2007). Introduction. In: Englebretson, R., ed., *Stancetaking in Discourse*. Amsterdam: John Benjamins, pp. 1–26.

Hart, C. (2011). Legitimising assertions and the logico-rhetorical module: Evidence and epistemic vigilance in media discourse on immigration. *Discourse Studies*, 13 (6), pp. 751–69.
Jaffe, A., ed. (2009). *Stance: Sociolinguistic Perspectives*. Oxford: Oxford University Press.
Johnstone, B. (2007). Linking identity and dialect through stancetaking. In: Englebretson, R., ed., *Stancetaking in Discourse*. Amsterdam: John Benjamins, pp. 49–68.
Kärkkäinen, E. and Du Bois, J. W., eds. (2012). *Stance, Affect, and Intersubjectivity in Interaction: Sequential and Dialogic Perspectives*. Special issue. *Text & Talk* 32 (4).
Kiparsky, P. and Kiparsky, C. (1970). Fact. In: Bierwisch, M. and Heidolph, K. E., eds, *Progress in Linguistics*. The Hague: Mouton de Gruyter, pp. 143–73.
Krug, M. G. (2000). *Emerging English Modals: A Corpus-based Study of Grammaticalization*. Berlin and New York: Mouton de Gruyter.
Langacker, R. W. (1991). *Foundations of Cognitive Grammar: Vol. 2: Descriptive Application*. Stanford, CA: Stanford University Press.
Langacker, R. W. (2008). *Cognitive Grammar. A Basic Introduction*. Oxford: Oxford University Press.
Langacker, R. W. (2009). *Investigations in Cognitive Grammar*. Berlin: Mouton de Gruyter.
Langacker, R. W. (2013). Modals: Striving for control. In: Marín-Arrese, J. I., Carretero, M., Arús, J. and van der Auwera, J., eds, *English Modality: Core, Periphery and Evidentiality*. Berlin: Mouton de Gruyter, pp. 3–55.
Leech, G. (2003). Modality on the move: The English modal auxiliaries 1961–1992. In: Facchinetti, R., Palmer, F. and Krug, M., eds, *Modality in Contemporary English*. Berlin: Mouton de Gruyter, pp. 225–40.
Marín-Arrese, J. I. (2011). Effective vs. epistemic stance and subjectivity in political discourse: Legitimising strategies and mystification of responsibility. In: Hart, C., ed., *Critical Discourse Studies in Context and Cognition*. Amsterdam: John Benjamins, pp. 193–224.
Marín-Arrese, J. I. (2015). Epistemic legitimisation and inter/subjectivity in the discourse of parliamentary and public inquiries: A contrastive case study. *Critical Discourse Studies*, 12 (3), pp. 261–78. doi: 10.1080/17405904.2015.1013484.
Marín-Arrese, J. I. (2017). Multifunctionality of evidential expressions in discourse domains and genres: Evidence from cross-linguistic case studies. In: Marín-Arrese, J. I., Hassler, G. and Carretero, M., eds, *Evidentiality Revisited: Cognitive Grammar, Functional and Discourse-Pragmatic Perspectives*. Amsterdam and Philadelphia: John Benjamins, pp. 195–223.
Marín-Arrese, J. I. (2021). Stance, emotion and persuasion: Terrorism and the press. *Journal of Pragmatics* 177, pp. 135–48. Available from: https://psycnet.apa.org/doi/10.1016/j.pragma.2021.01.022 [accessed 15 June 2023].
Marín-Arrese, J. I., Carretero, M. and Usoniene, A. (2022). Evidentiality in English. In: Wiemer, B. and Marín-Arrese, J. I., eds, *Evidential Marking in European Languages. Toward a Unitary Comparative Account*. Berlin: Mouton de Gruyter, pp. 57–94.
Martin, J. R. and White, P. R. R. (2005). *The Language of Evaluation. Appraisal in English*. Basingstoke and New York: Palgrave Macmillan.
Nuyts, J. (2001). *Epistemic Modality, Language, and Conceptualization: A Cognitive-Pragmatic Perspective*. Amsterdam: John Benjamins.

Nuyts, J. (2012). Notions of (inter)subjectivity. *English Text Construction* 5 (1), pp. 53–76. doi: 10.1075/etc.5.1.04nuy.

Ochs, E. and Schieffelin, B. (1989). Language has a heart. In: Ochs, E., ed., *The Pragmatics of Affect*. Special issue. *Text* 9, (1), pp. 7–25.

Sandford, A. (2020). Brexit Timeline 2016–2020: Key events in the UK's path from referendum to EU exit. *Euronews*. Available from: https://www.euronews.com/2020/01/30/brexit-timeline-2016-2020-key-events-in-the-uk-s-path-from-referendum-to-eu-exit [accessed 15 June 2023].

Sperber, D., Clement, F., Heintz, C., Mascaro, O., Mercier, H., Origgi, G. and D. Wilson (2010). Epistemic vigilance. *Mind and Language*, 25 (4), 359–93. Available from: https://psycnet.apa.org/doi/10.1111/j.1468-0017.2010.01394.x [accessed 15 June 2023].

Thompson, G. and Alba-Juez, L., eds. (2014). *Evaluation in Context*. Amsterdam: John Benjamins.

Thompson, G. and Hunston, S. (2000). Evaluation: An introduction. In: Hunston, S. and Thompson, G., eds, *Evaluation in Text: Authorial Stance and the Construction of Discourse*. Oxford: Oxford University Press, pp. 1–27.

Traugott, E. C. (2017). Semantic change. *Oxford Research Encyclopedias: Linguistics*. Oxford: Oxford University Press. doi: 10.1093/acrefore/9780199384655.013.323.

Traugott, E. C. and Dasher, R. (2002). *Regularity in Semantic Change*. Cambridge: Cambridge University Press.

van der Auwera, J. and Plungian, V. (1998). Modality's semantic map. *Linguistic Typology*, 2 (1), pp. 79–124.

van Dijk, T. A. (2003). Knowledge in parliamentary debates. *Journal of Language and Politics*, 2 (1), pp. 93–129. doi: 10.1075/jlp.2.1.06dij.

Walker, N. (2021). Brexit timeline: Events leading to the UK's exit from the European Union. *House of Commons Briefing Paper*, Number 7960, 6 January 2021. Available from: https://commonslibrary.parliament.uk/research-briefings/cbp-7960/ [Accessed 27 March 2023].

Part II

Legitimisation and new media

CHAPTER 5

Political discourse and the new media: New architectures of communication

Mariya Chankova

1 Introduction

The new media have opened up immense opportunities for communication and information exchange. The early days of the Participative Web 2.0 were inspired by visions of unlimited access to information and communication tools which could magnify the voices of ordinary citizens who can now claim their rightful place in political exchange and make their voices count. Political actors can engage directly with their electorate, unhindered by facilitators and traditional mediators, providing much-needed uptake on what the electorate has to say. More than a decade later, participative platform pioneers still paint the picture of a global virtual community, transcending offline existence, having conquered the problems of the real world, exemplified by Mark Zuckerberg's open letter published on Facebook in 2017 (Wagner and Swisher 2017). The reality of the new kind of online–offline nexus is hard to capture: the daily production of content is impossibly large, with video content accounting for 53.72% of all traffic according to Sandvine (2022); daily screen consumption is increasing, largely facilitated by hand-held smart devices, for an average of over seven hours per day predominantly for recreational purposes for young adults (Desmurget 2019); researchers note a declining demand for political news and, at the same time, a declining quality of political news, which constitutes a serious challenge for democracy (van Aelst et al. 2017). The echo chamber effects associated with social media act in a similar manner to coloured spectacles, creating an illusory parallel world for users, either consciously or accidentally (Nguyen 2020).

Understanding digital communication channels is central to understanding the time we live in, as, according to Debray's theory of the mediasphere (2007), any time period is defined by the dominant form of communication channels. Novelty is welcomed and reviled with equal passion. At the beginning of the twenty-first century, techno-optimists, to borrow Shullenberger's (2020) term, praised the liberating and democratising effects of social media, mostly for their perceived pivotal role in social uprisings,[1] arguing that 'reality has a well-known liberal bias' (Shullenberger 2020: 47) and emphasising the advent of citizen journalism which was there to bear witness, to relate a lived experience (Allan 2009) without gatekeepers and censors. At the same time, others told a cautionary tale, reminding optimists that the effects (real or perceived) were due not to alleged inherent democratising qualities of the tools, but due to the tools' users and the intentions they had in using them: Morozov (2011) shows that the same tools can be put to use by authoritarian dictators for manipulation and control. If digital tools are to be the epitome of freedom and democracy, they ought to be available for all users regardless of their ideological or political makeup. However, as Shullenberger (2020: 48) notes, 'Previously, much of the Western commentariat believed that democratized information would enable people to counter top-down misinformation. Now, it denounces the information free-for-all for unleashing a flood of "fake news" and conspiracy theories.' Accordingly, something has changed. The Internet platforms have provided grounds for a wide range of phenomena: alternative facts, misinformation, disinformation, conspiracy theories, censorship and self-censorship, echo chambers and epistemic bubbles, political advertising, trolling and social media mobs (the list is not exhaustive). All of these phenomena seem to have one thing in common: the information which gets to be propagated. Top-down information conduits, which used to be exemplified by mainstream media and political and social authorities, have been widely discredited; and bottom-up information spread does not appear to work as a reliable information spread alternative. The latter is not as devoid of constraints as one would believe, as digital platforms apply filters – 'terms of use' – which lay down rules on acceptable speech.[2] Some of these platforms were adopted for political discourse across the entire political spectrum for ease of access, providing a qualitatively different type of control over discourse: the speaker can act as news creator and commentator, filling in a self-created informational void. This aspect of the study has been reported elsewhere (Chankova, forthcoming). In an effort to capture the dynamics of alternative political communication online, this case study focuses on the use of digital platforms by politicians.

2 Aims and methodology

The general axes of interest which drive this study are the following: first, how the affordances of platforms influence the production of political discourse; second, how political discourse integrates the digital environment.

---

[1] See, for example, Chebib and Sohail (2011).
[2] The possibility of abusing or manipulating the moderation system has been demonstrated by the 2022 release of the so-called Twitter files by freelance journalist Matt Taibbi in December 2022 (Taibbi 2022).

In particular, this contribution presents a case study of political communication on digital platforms, exploring the Facebook posts of a political newcomer – Slavi Trifonov,[3] the founder of the political party Ima Takav Narod (ITN, meaning 'There is such a people') – in order to grasp the challenges and the new architectures of political communication across digital platforms. Facebook was selected for its popularity among the Bulgarian population: 4.4 million users in 2021 (Statista 2021). The data consist of the Facebook posts harvested between July and early November 2021, a period between two parliamentary elections in Bulgaria, from Trifonov's publicly accessible Facebook page,[4] amounting to a total of 3,446 words in Bulgarian. Additionally, Trifonov's electoral campaign was only deployed on the Internet, according to his own statement (see section 4 below), providing an almost unique opportunity to understand how politicians may construe the digital environment as a communicative and political arena. Our focus is on the construction of the social actor and the legitimisation strategies used in the online political discourse. The analytical approach is pragmatic: discourse analysis to identify the strategies of legitimisation; Goffman's (1974) frames to grasp the process of social actor construction. In what follows, the data analysis will be presented in a thematic manner, starting with a section on legitimisation techniques in the context of strategic interaction, along with a discussion of the features that validate this type of discourse as strategic. Then, in section 4, a discussion of frames and switching between frames will be connected to the construction of the social actor. The Conclusions section will put forward a proposition about the new architectures of digitally based political communication.

3 Strategic interaction and legitimisation

Based on game theory,[5] we define strategic interaction as any kind of interaction in which the participants have a particular strategic goal driving the contribution (Chankova 2019). Participants will typically attempt to anticipate and predict their interlocutors' contributions in order to shape their own, in reference to game theory models (Camerer 2003). Strategic interaction is usually opposed to cooperative interaction, in which the interests of the participants converge and they work towards a common goal – in game-theoretic terms, this is called a 'partnership game' (Jaeger 2008: 408). Habermas's understanding of strategic action also involves the idea of calculating success which motivates the action aimed at influencing

---

[3] Slavi Trifonov (Trifonov/Facebook) has been a public figure, showman and TV show host for over 30 years and is now the owner of the private television channel 7/8 (Wikipedia 2022).
[4] The official page name is facebook.com/STTrifonov.
[5] For an overview of game-theoretic studies in pragmatics, see Jaeger (2008).

other participants' decisions (Habermas 2000: 120). Political discourse is the epitome of strategic interaction: the speaker who engages in political discourse has strategic goals to attain, which is at least partly achieved by anticipating the interlocutors' (and the audience's) responses. In election campaigns, its ultimate goal would be to influence the decision-making process of the voters. Chilton (2004) notes that political discourse is Machiavellian in that the person who engages in political discourse seeks to maximise their own advantage. He identifies three main strategic functions of discourse (and political discourse in particular) – coercion, legitimisation and de-legitimisation, and representation and misrepresentation – which are interconnected in practice (Chilton 2004: 45–6). For Cap (2013: 8), one overarching strategic goal dominates political discourse production: legitimisation, which he describes as mixture of justification and support for the politician's actions, presented as being in the interest of the audience. Van Leeuwen (2007: 92) distinguishes four categories of legitimisation in discourse: authorisation, moral evaluation, rationalisation and mythopoesis.

Legitimisation techniques have been well-documented in the literature; for example, proximisation, which plays on the fear of an imminent catastrophe which only the speaker can avert, with its spatial, temporal and axiological dimensions (Chilton 2004; Cap 2013). Reyes (2011) explores strategies of legitimisation through emotions, rationality, voices of expertise and altruism. Another technique is suggested here, at the crossroads between moral evaluation and emotion: relying on the emotional response of the audience, the speaker produces content of the type that Nguyen and Williams (2020) call 'moral outrage porn'. They define it as 'representations of moral outrage engaged with primarily for the sake of the resulting gratification, freed from the usual costs and consequences of engaging with morally outrageous content' (Nguyen and Williams 2020: 148). The gratification consists in experiencing feelings of moral superiority and the sense of clarity that stems from it, along with 'the sheer pleasure of the feeling of outrage itself' (Nguyen and Williams 2020: 149). The speaker who elicits the feelings of moral outrage by evoking what she believes to be morally outrageous content has several gains in this enterprise: she projects the assumption of decency, clarity or righteousness (the list is not exhaustive) over her audience, excluding by definition the people targeted by the content itself, thus inviting the audience to share in the outrage, and establishing group identity. This technique can be observed in many of the posts from the dataset:

(1) (Oct. 15) Is it possible that the biggest and the most prestigious university in Bulgaria has been headed by a man without honour and dignity?[6]

---

[6] Възможно ли е години наред начело на най-големия и престижен университет в България да е бил човек без чест и достойнство? This and the subsequent examples are translated from Bulgarian by the author.

(2) (Oct. 5) ... what [Boyko Borisov] said horrified me ... Ok, people, tell me, what kind of a person you have to be to say something like that?! First, to even think it, then to actually say it.[7]

(3) (Nov. 5) Now what? What now, huh? What is going to happen? Will those who took the money be punished?[8]

The basis for the moral judgement is a popular understanding of common decency, with the speaker (Slavi Trifonov) positioning himself as one of the ordinary people. This trait has been emphasised as a populist characteristic by Pasquino (2008): the speaker expresses his outrage at the deeds and words of his political opponents. He underlines his non-belonging to the political elite, who are at the opposite moral pole to the people. As a strategic move, the moral outrage is the mirror image of what he anticipates the regular person's moral response would be. As a whole, this strategy bears the characteristics of populism in De Cleen's definition (2017): the populist conceptualises the people as the underdog who cannot be properly represented by an inept (corrupt, without honour and dignity) elite. The speaker seeks legitimisation and political legitimacy through the claim that he shares the common decency of the people and positions himself to be the common people's champion.

The populist overtones are to be found throughout the dataset: the electorate is referred to as 'sovereign', and the speaker vows to uphold the 'sovereign will of the people';[9] the motif of the underdog has its roots deep in Bulgarian culture and history, evoking the dire times of the Ottoman rule when Hajduks fought against all odds for the liberation of an enslaved population. In modern times, after the regime change in the late 1980s and early 1990s when Bulgarian society made the transition to democracy, this imagery was revived to describe in a symbolic way the change in Bulgarian society. The idea of the underdog was used to promote non-conformity and the struggle for individual freedoms. This heavy imagery is exploited even in the very political slogan of the ITN party today – 'Alone against every one. Together with you'[10] – as the party explicitly positions itself at the opposing side to everyone else, in a way being the underdog itself, the only one capable of fighting for the ordinary people (or the ultimate underdog).

---

[7] ... и това, което е казал, ме вцепени .... Добре, бе хора - какъв човек трябва да си, за да кажеш нещо подобно?! Първо, какъв човек трябва да си, за да си го помислиш, а след това и да го кажеш?

[8] ... И сега какво? Сега какво, а? Какво ще стане? Ще ги накажат ли тия, които са взели парите?

[9] Суверенът (Oct. 15/1).

[10] Сами срещу всички. Заедно с вас.

Moral outrage is directed towards the former prime minister, Boyko Borisov. The speaker goes to great lengths to remind the audience of old gaffes which may have shocked the public, and to reveal other politicians as immoral, indecent people who are allegedly so blatant in their immorality that only an ignorant person cannot see it. The moral outrage porn has a very peculiar strategic goal: by claiming kinship (as the underdog of the political scene who alone is capable of understanding the plight of ordinary people, who are decent, as opposed to the elites), the speaker claims legitimisation on the basis of that kinship. This strategy deflects from questions about policy and concrete measures which the party would seek to implement once in power. Political changes or policy are not discussed in the posts of the dataset, even though such issues would usually be at the forefront in political communications during an election campaign. As moral outrage porn leads its consumers to form simplified moral representations of the world, instrumentalising it leads to consumers aligning with the proposed moral stance in order to increase their sense of 'moral self-confidence without adequate epistemic justification' (Nguyen and Williams 2020: 162). The use of such populist strategies encourages consumers to prefer morally gratifying sources. In particular, Nguyen and Williams (2020) identify problems of a moral nature along with epistemic problems. In the context of the dataset, the audience is discouraged from questioning both the moral representations and the validity of the judgements proposed to them.

4 Frames and the social actor

Often as part of the strategic goals, the speaker works to construct and project a social image of themselves to the audience: this image will be referred to as the 'social actor', namely, the constructed persona who is endorsing a particular role in the frame and who is adjusted in the various possible keyings in the actual realisation of discourse. The term 'social actor' is crafted upon Goffman's frame analysis (1974): the social actor is any participant in social interaction who engages with fellow interlocutors, takes responsibilities, commitments and engagements upon herself, who is accountable for her own social choices, and who endorses qualities, stances, beliefs and commitments in the course of interaction. The term is intended to capture the agency of both the speaker who engages in intentional communication and the performer of illocutionary acts – conventional social acts which alter social and interpersonal relations.[11] The construction of the social actor can be intentional and unintentional: interlocutors can infer large quantities of information about each other during interaction from

---

[11] For a detailed discussion of illocutionary acts and social actor projections in political discourse, see Chankova (2019).

particular word choices, styles of talking, general demeanour, tone of voice and illocutionary acts attempted by the speaker, all of which may potentially carry relevant information. Depending on their own attention span, degree of involvement in the interaction, their own agenda and communicative and strategic goals, people construct an image of their interlocutors, which they will activate (contingent upon their memory, the needs of the interaction, and other factors) in subsequent interactions. This is the basis upon which speakers in strategic interaction contexts will calculate their own moves and anticipate their interlocutors' subsequent moves.

The question of how the social actor is constructed in political discourse disseminated in the new media depends on the defining characteristics of the new medium. The social actor is performed rather than told: in offline interactions, every detail of the surroundings, sartorial choices, objects, props, body positions and body language, eye contact or tone of voice (and so on) can play a role in the performance (see Goffman 1969). Online performances, such as the ones under discussion, are quite unlike offline performances because of the different affordances of the medium. Fragmentation, the dependence on offline events and discourses (which leads to an erosion of context), the format of the message (written post, video, gifs or pictures), and sometimes the lack of identifiable other player(s) who will constitute the target of the strategies at play are some of the particularities which require the written post to be self-sufficient for enacting the social actor. Thus, discursive choices will be contingent upon conveying more or less explicitly the qualities the speaker wishes to claim for herself, and the moral or ideological statements the speaker makes will provide grounds for the moral or ideological stances she endorses. The production of moral outrage content described in the previous section constitutes a performance of the social actor, projecting an image of a person of high moral values, which is shared with the audience. This is found in studies which look at Facebook as performances (Hendriks et al. 2016), or as self-branding, which consists in constructing a platform-specific online persona (Duffy et al. 2017).

Goffman takes frames to be basic identifiable units of organising human experience (1974: 10–11). What frames mainly carry are structures of expectation (Tannen 1993), which subsequently leave linguistic traces in the produced discourse, as well as in the interpretative process carried out by the audience, revealing the cultural and sociological underpinning of this notion (Hymes 1974; Fillmore 1977; Tannen 1993). The frames embody the structure of the expectations, and the interpretation of speech events (as well as non-verbal events) relies on matching 'the internal representation of particular events and individuals with internally represented prototypes' (Chafe 1977: 42, quoted in Tannen 1993). Along with interactional frames, people build knowledge schemas, described by Tannen and Wallat (1987: 207) as the 'participants' expectations about people, objects, events and settings' which are being constantly 'checked against experience and revised'.

Interlocutors may include elements that function as frame cues in the discourse stretches. This is all the more valid for Facebook posts, which can suffer from contextual void: if the post is not framed as a response to a physically occurring stretch of discourse in the same medium, the speaker will need to include contextual elements to anchor the interpretation. These elements also function as framing devices, as they help to set the frame in which the speaker operates:

(4) (Oct. 15/1) I have just watched on the news Kiril Petkov declare that he is negotiating with *'Ima Takav Narod'*. This is not true ... Besides, *'Ima Takav Narod'* is not in the habit of pre-emptive negotiations with any political power. This is not a sign of our being unwilling to negotiate. We believe that after it becomes clear how the people have voted, it will be much simpler and much more logical to do the sovereign's will.[12]

(5) (Oct. 15/2) I have watched an interview by Mirolyuba Benatova with the Bulgarian presidential candidate Prof. Atanas Gerdzhikov.[13]

(6) (Oct. 5) Boyko Borisov is in Slovenia – I have no idea why he is there and I do not care.[14]

(7) (Sept. 27) *'Ima Takav Narod'* have just registered for the upcoming election. It is the third election that we have registered for this year.[15]

Examples (4) to (7) feature opening sentences of Facebook posts which depict the events which cause the intervention: offline events, for which commentary is provided. They also serve to point to the primary frame of interpretation – often the 'regular citizen' reacting to news, which blends in with the frame of the 'aspiring politician', bringing in correction or perspective on some aspects of those news stories. Example (4) provides a short factual correction concerning political negotiations. The two frames have distinct linguistic elements which can be associated with them. The 'politician' frame can be

---

[12] Току-що гледах по новините как Кирил Петков заяви, че води разговори с 'Има такъв народ'. Това не е вярно. ... Освен това, 'Има Такъв Народ' не води предварителни разговори с нито една политическа сила. Това не е израз на нежелание. Ние смятаме, че след като стане ясно как е гласувал суверенът, ще бъде много по-просто и логично да се постъпи правилно именно в интерес на суверена.
[13] Гледах едно интервю на Миролюба Бенатова с кандидата за президент на България проф. Анастас Герджиков.
[14] Бойко Борисов е в Словения - нямам представа защо е там, а и въобще не ме интересува.
[15] Току-що „Има такъв народ" подаде документи за участие в предстоящите избори. За трети път отиваме на избори тази година.

Political discourse and the new media 111

recognised by the use of the deictic 'we', which refers to the party leadership and not to Trifonov personally; formal elements which are absent from other frames, such as the full spelling of the party name; the declaratory style and slogan-like phrasing. To illustrate these linguistic elements:

(8) (Aug. 16) The Ministry of Internal Affairs and the Ministry of Defence must work in absolute coordination in order to deploy police and army forces on the border and to defend selflessly the Bulgarian territory and citizens. We from *'Ima Takav Narod'* will do everything in our power to support both as citizens and as a political party the government and the president in their effort to overcome the upcoming crisis.[16]

Example (5) takes up the presidential candidates' race in a noticeably long post, in which the speaker exposes those he considers to be unworthy of the presidential institution, without explicitly naming the candidate he supports, taking issue at the same time with the interviewing journalist's questions. In it, Trifonov writes that even though the questions were moderate, the lack of integrity of the presidential candidate was so glaring that it prevented him from answering those questions. The post also included the contrast between the mainstream media on the one hand, and smaller, private television stations and alternative media propagated via the Internet on the other, which are praised as the only place where one can speak one's mind without (self-)censorship. Such an observation is aligned with the idea of democratisation of people's voices; however, put forth by the owner of a private television channel, it is tinged with ambiguity. This ambiguity is due to the oscillating frames: it is no longer the 'politician' frame, nor the 'ordinary citizen' frame, but the 'popular entertainer' frame which enters into play. As an entertainer, the speaker has enjoyed great discursive liberties, since entertainers produce content which is not considered to be serious, in terms of Austin's (1962) distinction between serious and etiolated uses, and thus not subject to the same restrictions.[17]

Example (6) takes up a comment by former prime minister Boyko Borisov directed at the President, in an effort to mobilise moral outrage, as detailed in the previous section. For context, at a press conference and in relation to COVID-19 deaths for that day, former prime minister Borisov had said

---

[16] Министерството на вътрешните работи и Министерството на отбраната трябва да работят в абсолютна координация, за да разположат полицаи и военни на границата и с всички сили самоотвержено да защитят територията и гражданите на България. Ние от „Има Такъв Народ" ще направим всичко необходимо да подкрепим и като граждани, и като политическа сила, правителството и президента на републиката, за са се справим на всяка цена със задаващата се криза.
[17] The adjacent problems of responsibility for etiolated uses of language and the freedom of expression in Bulgaria will not be addressed in this paper.

that 178 people had passed on to a better world than the one of Bulgarian president Rumen Radev (Sega 2021). The frame of the ordinary citizen, reacting to events on the political scene, is invoked here. The speaker invites the readers to align themselves with the moral judgement, launching into rhetorical questions such as 'What kind of a person do you have to be to say a thing like that?!', 'What do you think of that?' and 'Who is to blame?' The 'politician' frame would call for the scrutiny of Boyko Borisov's position and policy towards COVID-19 management, resulting in inconsistent confinement measures in the early months of the epidemic, as well as severe vaccine shortages. Instead, Trifonov focuses on his outrage at the callousness of using human tragedy to attack a political opponent. The 'ordinary citizen' frame also has specific discursive elements which can be seen in (6), such as the displayed indifference for the political actions of opponents (in this case, former prime minister Borisov), which underlines the speaker's detachment from the political scene.

Resorting to moral outrage seeks to blend the 'ordinary citizen' frame with the 'politician' frame, as moral values are used as a legitimisation strategy. Example (7) equally blends the 'politician' frame with the 'ordinary citizen' frame, combining the rallying call (with the crux of the announcement being that the party registered for the election) with an ordinary-citizen commentary of the political system:

(9) (Sept. 27) You must not think very highly of Bulgarian politics. Me neither. Especially when I used to look at it from the outside. Now I am looking at it from the inside and I'll tell you what I see . . . . Actually, Bulgarian politics is the reflection of ourselves . . . Just as the people who live in an apartment building . . . have difficulties to come to an agreement, the MPs in the Bulgarian Parliament have the same difficulties.[18]

The comments where the speaker frames himself as a political outsider in tune with the ordinary citizens are combined with the viewpoint of the politician. They offer common-sense wisdom in terms of describing political life as a reflection of ordinary life, with all its imperfections, complete with the simplified comparison of MPs as defenders of one's own personal self-interest, instead of treating them realistically as elected representatives of large communities who pledge to take responsibility for defending public interests.

The oscillation between frames is not unnoticed by the speaker himself: the switch from 'I' to 'we' to underline a party line or position, the great

---

[18] Сигурно си мислите не особено приятни неща за българския политически живот. И аз така. Особено когато го гледах отвън. Сега го гледам отвътре и ще ви кажа какво виждам . . . .Всъщност, българският политически живот е отражение на самите нас . . . . Точно колкото могат да се разберат хората, живеещи в един блок . . ., толкова могат да се разберат и депутатите в българския парламент.

emphasis on common notions of decency and consistency in one's beliefs, and adherence to truth. All of these serve to project the image of the champion of the ordinary people, of the politician who is outside of the political system. Ambiguity between the frames serves a very important strategic purpose: if it is not entirely clear how the audience should be reading a particular intervention, it becomes very difficult for that audience to be able to efficiently judge the value of the intervention, its veracity, and the speaker's benevolence and trustworthiness. This disturbs the uptake of the speaker's message. Example (4) is more or less clear, as questioning the veracity of a claim on the part of a political opponent seems to be the primary strategic purpose of the piece. In second place comes the social actor work: by allegedly bringing Petkov's claim into question, the speaker wishes to imply that he himself would be truthful. The political work done in the segment concerns, first, the implication that if an opponent has misled on something that is easily verifiable, he may not be dependable for more serious things, and, second, the clear moral divide between the speaker and his opponents. Example (5) receives quite different interpretations in the different frames: the 'ordinary citizen' frame calls for a recommendation of something seen on other media; passing moral judgement on the character of the presidential candidate is not inconsistent with this frame. However, the 'politician' frame yields another reading, that of an agitprop[19] move, in which several presidential candidates are branded as unsuitable for office, the emphasis being on the aforementioned professor, who appeared to be the only serious competition to the then sitting president. Furthermore, the 'politician' frame is compatible with yet another reading, a veiled advertisement for the cable television channel owned by the speaker, described (by extension) as the space in which one can ask important questions without censorship.

In some cases, the ambiguity between frames allows the speaker to avoid addressing important issues. Consider (10):

(10) (Aug. 28) I see that Boyko Borisov after my interview from last night is quite concerned for my health. This is so nice of him. I am touched. During the last election Tatyana Doncheva was also concerned for my health. She too, the sweet lady, is such an empathetic person . . . Rest assured, people, I am fine, I manage to get along, and if I get sick even a little, I will inform you right away, so that you do not worry.[20]

---

[19] Agitprop is defined here as propagating political information and ideas, especially with the intention of influencing the public.
[20] Виждам, че Бойко Борисов в коментара си за снощното ми интервю е загрижен за моето здравословно състояние. Това е толкова мило. Така се разчувствах. На миналите избори Татяна Дончева беше загрижена за моето здравословно състояние. И тя, милата, е толкова състрадателен човек . . . . Спокойно бе, хора, добре съм, справям се и дори леко да настина, веднага ще ви информирам, за да не се притеснявате.

The frame of the politician blends with the performer frame, thereby allowing for the use of sarcastic comments which effectively deflect the main point of the criticisms levelled at the speaker, namely his unwillingness to engage with journalists and other politicians, and his prolonged absence from the public scene. Political actors cannot afford to reject the checks and balances provided by the press (however corrupted or imperfect they may believe them to be), or to reject participation in public debates with other politicians, and the speaker seems to be aware of this. This partial emancipation from public constraint appears to be strategically motivated, underlining his own and his party's stand as asystemic candidates who refuse to play political games, while at the same time they conduct their political activities via their own media outlets, which fall outside of the system of checks and balances. Notwithstanding the echo chamber effect, the Internet platforms, praised by the speaker (see example (11) below) do not guarantee the support of the people who visit them, even though the proliferation of media outlets heightens visibility (in this case, Facebook pages for different media products and political purposes). All of these media environments rally different audiences, who do not necessarily align with the political agenda of the party, but who may be interested in the performer or the entertainer. A comparison of the Facebook page followers and the electorate who voted for the party in November confirms the nuanced story about digital following: Trifonov's personal page under study here lists approximately 648,000 followers as of September 2022, the Facebook page of *7/8 TV* lists approximately 150,000 followers, while the number of people who voted for the party in November 2021 was 249,743 (Centralna Izbiratelna Komisia 2021).[21] Consequently, popularity and entertainer politicians are not guaranteed political success. The large number of people who visit the page under study produce many thousands of comments, which cannot all be read or engaged with by the speaker. The reliance appears to be on pre-existing sympathy for the figure of the performer-entertainer, as well as his support for the popular protests against former prime minister Borisov,[22] which excludes actual engagement with people's attitudes or ideas.

Switching between the frames allows for work on the social actor projections, which ultimately aim to achieve legitimisation for the political figure, and will later serve to collect political dividends. The projections of the social actor are intrinsically connected with the kind of expectations that both speaker and audience have about a particular frame. Throughout his various roles on the public scene, as a performer and a talk show host who has (almost) daily prime time television exposure, Trifonov has had a prominent presence on television for a large proportion of the

---

[21] In the 2022 elections, Slavi Trifonov's party did not pass the 4% barrier in order to enter Parliament. It received 97,071 votes.
[22] An overview of the 2020–1 protests against Borisov can be consulted on Wikipedia (Wikipedia 2023).

Political discourse and the new media

Bulgarian population. As a talk show host, the speaker has a particular role to play, both entertaining and, to a certain extent, mirroring some of the contentions the audience might have with public figures. In this sense, the audience feels a particular kind of alignment with the show host, whose comments are not taken seriously – and they cannot be, given that the host does not share the economic situation that most of his audience experience.

In one of the Facebook posts, Slavi Trifonov states that the election campaign effort of the party was limited to the Internet. We quote the post in its entirety:

(11) (Nov. 11) Here comes the end of a disgusting and stupid election campaign, from which it is doubtful that the electorate would be able to make a serious choice about who to vote for in the upcoming election. My opinion is that neither the parties, nor the media, or the sociologists or political analysts have drawn any conclusions about their own behaviours. Once again, most of those important election participants have adopted the role of referees beyond reproach in this campaign. This is why we took part in this campaign by not taking active part in the media. Our campaign field was personal contacts and the Internet, the only completely free environment in the contemporary media. Was that a successful strategy? Who can tell what success is in today's situation? To come first in the election and not to be able to form a government or to come in last and to be the one whom the constitution of the government depends on. I am referring to the last election when we were first and could not form a government, while 'Get up BG! We are coming!' were last and the formation of the government depended on them. So you tell me what success is. For me, success is to be consistent, to act with dignity and to put the common good before your own personal interest. Tomorrow evening, I will be answering all of your questions, together with Iva Miteva, former chairperson of the General Assembly in two parliaments, and Lyubomir Karimanski, former chairperson of the Budget Committee in the last General Assembly. And we will be answering them live.[23]

---

[23] Идва края на една отвратителна и глупава предизборна кампания, от която избирателите едва ли могат да направят по-сериозни изводи за кого да гласуват на предстоящите избори. Моето мнение е, че нито голямата част от партиите са си направили сериозни изводи за своето поведение, нито медиите, нито социолозите, нито политолозите. За пореден път повечето от тези важни за изборите участници се вживяха в ролята си на безпогрешни рефери на предизборната ситуация. Затова ние участвахме в тази кампания, неучаствайки активно медийно. Полето за изява за нас са личните контакти и интернет, единственото напълно свободно пространство в сегашната медийна среда. Дали това е било успешен ход? Кой може да ми каже кое е успех в

There are several points made by Trifonov in (11). This post demonstrates Trifonov's uneven attitude towards the media and their role in political campaigning, as his evaluation of the campaign as being 'disgusting and stupid' presupposes that he had followed the media campaign; in other posts there are references to televised interventions, interviews and press conferences, as illustrated in (4–6). All participants in the election campaign – the entire political and media establishment – are described as displaying unsuitable types of behaviour, namely assuming the role of 'referees beyond reproach' in (11). The choice of isolating the party from the public forum is explained by the refusal to abide by the media's self-ascribed role of 'referees'. Glossing over the question of media and political commentators playing the role of checks and balances,[24] Trifonov reflects on the question of whether confining the party's presence to the Internet was a successful strategy. The absence of any discussion of policies or political actions in the dataset is offset by the focus on personal qualities mentioned in the previous section, which are reiterated in (11): acting in a consistent manner, behaving with dignity and prioritising the common interest. Trifonov does not provide details about his party's political intentions or programme, and removing the party from the public scene spares them any questions about that. The definition of success, as well as the vision of the role of political parties, as described in this post, paired with the retreat from public discussion, conforms to the political strategy outlined in the previous section. For many different reasons, populists consider the establishment incapable of upholding the will of the people, so they seek political power because they believe they are the ones who can act according to the will of the people (Pasquino 2008; De Cleen 2017). Defining political success as being consistent, and acting with dignity for the common good, the speaker reiterates the image of the underdog who shares the values of ordinary people. His bid for legitimisation rests upon those shared values, as no concrete political aims are articulated in this or the other posts in the dataset. Finally, the live question session is advertised to be broadcast on Trifonov's private television channel and

---

сегашната ситуация? Да си първи и да не можеш да съставиш правителство или да си последен и от теб да зависи съставянето на правителство. Имам предвид резултатите от последните избори, на които ние бяхме първи и не можахме да съставим правителство, а „Изправи се БГ! Ние идваме!" бяха последни и от тях зависеше дали ще се състави правителство. Така че – вие ми отговорете кое е успех. За мен успех е да си последователен, да се държиш достойно и да поставяш обществените интереси над личните. А иначе утре вечер аз ще отговарям на всички ваши въпроси, заедно с Ива Митева, бивш председател на Народното събрание в два парламента, и Любомир Каримански, бивш председател на бюджетната комисия в предишното Народно събрание. И ще отговаряме на живо.

[24] This means that a system is put in place on behalf of the people, aiming to subject politicians to scrutiny and ensuring a fair and balanced representation of views.

on Facebook, and people are invited to post their questions on the channel's website.[25] Advertising with a vested interest exposes this outlet to the shortcomings of mainstream media, namely that they appear to present a particular story (or narrative) in a top-down manner, without taking into consideration the media consumers. The organisers retain a significant amount of agency over the choice of the questions which are addressed; and given the venue, there is very little incentive for genuine debate, as the participants have not left their comfort zone or epistemic bubble. Users may actively engage with the Facebook posts by posting reactions themselves, but the dataset does not provide any ostensible evidence for how far Trifonov takes those reactions into consideration.

The praise of the Internet which provided the campaign platform is due to some distinguishing characteristics: the freedom that is provided by a platform which does not constrain the user to answer specific questions, and on which users are free to post their contributions as they see fit. The opportunities for both asynchronous and synchronous types of interaction leave users free to select the types of interaction and the timing of their own contributions. Equally, there is no one acting as a referee, setting questions or demanding answers – in short, providing checks and balances which may be unwanted by Trifonov. The Facebook posts of the speaker rarely address matters of importance. This happens twice in the dataset: a post about the fraud and embezzlement charges against construction firms made public by the Ministry of Interior (12), and a post on possible Afghan migrants after the retreat of the United States from the country (13):

(12) (Nov. 5) The information released by the MI about the construction of one lot of the Hemus highway is not scandalous, it is mind-boggling. According to this information, 60 million of the 84 million levs transferred before the construction of even one millimetre of the highway had been taken out in bags and sacks ... Arrogant people whom we have entrusted to govern our money just take some of it when they feel like it.[26]

(13) (Aug. 16) One million migrants are ready to leave Afghanistan in order to flee the Taliban regime that has conquered the country.[27]

---

[25] The media have reported this to be the first live political intervention by Trifonov in the November 2021 campaign (Standartnews 2021).
[26] Изнесената информация от МВР за строителството на само един лот от магистрала „Хемус" не е скандална, а е умопомрачителна. Според тази информация, от преведените предварително 84 милиона лева, без да е построен и един милиметър магистрала, 60 милиона са изнесени с чували и сакове .... Самозабравили се хора, на които сме се доверили да управляват нашите пари, просто си взимат от тях, когато им скимне.
[27] Един милион мигранти са готови да тръгнат от Афганистан, за да избягат от режима на талибаните, който завладя страната.

In both cases, the posts do not engage with these issues substantially. In (12), the information is used to elicit moral outrage; in (13), the comment makes Trifonov's position on border control explicit. Even though the platform allows users to publish longer pieces which address in depth a particular question, this is not the default type of post. The 'reaction' type of post, compatible in spirit with the characteristics of citizen journalism, puts forth the personal story, the life experience side, the validation of a unique lived experience, which is subjective and not to be judged in the same way one judges other information sources (Jandura and Friedrich 2014).

5 Conclusion: Some epistemic questions for alternative media

In order to sketch out admittedly partial answers to the question about the new architectures of post-digital political communication, it is important to take into consideration the (virtual) reality of digitally based platforms. Political communication was affected by the changes in public service broadcasting which had to adapt to the realities brought about by the democratisation of the Internet, and especially so the Participative Web 2.0, and became dependent upon digital platforms for exposure and participation (Steensen and Westlund 2021). Peer-to-peer content-sharing platforms allowed for the emergence of what researchers call citizen journalism, emphasising first-person accounts and subjective experiences (Allan 2009). Circumventing traditional media outlets carries the presupposition that the information put forward by citizen journalism is hidden or else unavailable by other means (Allan 2009). This tendency in information dissemination operates a qualitative shift in our approach to gauging information. On the one hand, this includes the optimistic and affirming premise that those platforms allow the voices of ordinary citizens to be heard and valued. On the other hand, this shift includes the lack of any gatekeepers other than the somewhat arbitrary and often inconsistent moderation rules enforced by the private companies running those platforms, with traditional media hastening to remain relevant by featuring that content. This translates into a complete inability to rely on the veracity of the information provided because the very idea of veracity has been undermined.

The case study depicts an unusual political campaign on the Bulgarian political scene of a party which has opted to use the affordances of online platforms and subtract itself from traditional media. The personal page of the party leader, Trifonov, displays posts which are self-contained and do not necessarily combine together into a coherent story (however loosely conceptualised), which results in discourse fragmentation. Fragmentation is not exactly conducive to engaging seriously with the issues discussed – instead, events are utilised for eliciting moral outrage. The posts under study do not promote political communication, as the political actor exploits these platforms while switching between speaker frames. For all its claims of reach, the posts are not engaged with by a very large audience, and, most notably, they do not seem to reflect challenging or adverse ideas. Furthermore, the collective content production by all kinds of political actors and analysts amounts to hundreds of thousands of bytes per day; for perspective, Facebook users generate four petabytes of content daily (Wiener and Bronson 2014) for any curious citizen who would like to keep informed. This impossible situation is exacerbated by the epistemic bubble effect: bouncing off Nguyen's description of a common effect of online platforms, any particular user, regular citizen or politician alike has a very limited vision of what the other participants are talking about online, revolving around topics (people, discussion threads) which are of interest to themselves. This results in a distorted picture of the public debate.

Moreover, it appears that traditional media outlets, criticised and blamed for various shortcomings, are still relied upon for a semblance of common grounding of the political information shared in the common public space, as evidenced by the results. In fact, the role of traditional media is utilised in an attempt to promote a special image of the political actor, namely the outside-the-system underdog. This effect is notably dampened by the promotion of just as traditional a venue for conducting political advertising (in other words, private television). This uneven relationship with traditional venues for political dialogue further exacerbates the issues which can be observed in Bulgarian political communication. Legitimisation is sought by exploiting the affordances of the digital platform, in the case of Facebook – through the construction of an online image which does not have the same costs attached as the offline persona. As a tool for rallying support without really engaging in depth with the real implications of immoral deeds and discourse, moral outrage is equally devoid of consequence for the online persona. Nonetheless, it can be the source of moral satisfaction and feelings of moral justice, gratuitously mistaken for real moral stances. Finally, exploiting interpretative frames by switching between them or relying on frame confusion also diffuses responsibility. These aspects contribute to a particular, qualitatively different type of control over political discourse on the part of the political actor, which only upholds the illusion that every citizen can participate in the political conversation.

References

Allan, S. (2009). Histories of citizen. In: Allan, S. and Thorsen, E., eds, *Citizen Journalism: Global Perspectives*. New York: Peter Lang, pp. 17–31.

Austin, J. L. (1962). *How to Do Things with Words*. Cambridge, MA: Harvard University Press.

Camerer, C. (2003). *Behavioral Game Theory*. Princeton, NJ: Princeton University Press.

Cap, P. (2013). *Legitimisation in Political Discourse: A Cross-Disciplinary Perspective on the Modern US War Rhetoric*. 2nd edn. Newcastle upon Tyne: Cambridge Scholars Publishing.

Centralna Izbiratelna Komisia (2021). Obobshteni danni ot izbor na narodni predstaviteli, 14 noemvri 2021. [Summarised data from election of people's representatives, 14 November 2021.] Centralna Izbiratelna Komisia. Available from https://results.cik.bg/pvrns2021/tur1/rezultati/index.html [accessed 10 August 2022].

Chafe, W. (1977). Creativity in verbalization and its implications for the nature of stored knowledge. In: Freedle, R., ed., *Discourse Production and Comprehension*. Norwood, NJ: Ablex, pp. 41–55.

Chankova, M. (2019). Rejecting and challenging illocutionary acts. *Pragmatics*, 29 (1), pp. 33–56. doi: 10.1075/prag.17041.cha.

Chankova, M. (forthcoming). Political discourse strategies in online communication: A case study. In: Proceedings volume from the 21st International Conference of the Department of Linguistics of the University of Bucharest: *Current Trends in Theoretical and Applied Linguistics*, 19–20 November 2021. Pragmatics Workshop.

Chebib, N. K. and Sohail, R. M. (2011). The reasons social media contributed to the 2011 Egyptian revolution. *International Journal of Business Research and Management (IJBRM)*, 2 (3), pp. 139–62.

Chilton, P. (2004). *Analysing Political Discourse: Theory and Practice*. London: Routledge.

De Cleen, B. (2017). Populism and nationalism. In: Kaltwasser, C. R., Taggart, P., Ostiguy, P. and Ochoa Espejo, P., eds, *The Oxford Handbook of Populism*. Oxford: Oxford University Press, pp. 342–62.

Debray, R. (2007). Socialism and print. *New Left Review*, 46, pp. 5–28.

Desmurget, M. (2019). *La Fabrique du Crétin Digital*. Paris: Seuil.

Duffy, B. E., Pruchniewska, U. and Scolere, L. (2017). Platform-specific self-branding: Imagined affordances of the social media ecology. In: *#SMSociety17: Proceedings of the 8th International Conference on Social Media & Society*, SMSociety, pp. 1–9. doi: 10.1145/3097286.3097291.

Fillmore, C. J. (1977). Scenes-and-frames semantics. In: Zampolli, A., ed., *Linguistic Structures Processing. Fundamental Studies in Computer Science*. Amsterdam: North Holland Publishing. pp. 55–81.

Goffman, E. (1969). *Strategic interaction*. Philadelphia: University of Pennsylvania Press.

Goffman, E. (1974). *Frame Analysis*. New York: Harper & Row.

Habermas, J. (2000). *On the Pragmatics of Communication: Studies in Contemporary German Social Thought*. Cambridge, MA: MIT Press.

Hendriks, C. M., Duus, S. and Ercan, S. A. (2016). Performing politics on social media: The dramaturgy of an environmental controversy on Facebook. *Environmental Politics*, 25 (6), pp. 1102–25. doi: 10.1080/09644016.2016.1196967.

Hymes, D. (1974). Ways of speaking. In: Bauman, R. and Sherzer, J., eds, *Explorations in the Ethnography of Speaking*. Cambridge: Cambridge University Press, pp. 433–51.

Jaeger, G. (2008). Applications of game theory in linguistics. *Language and Linguistics Compass*, 2 (3), pp. 406–21. Available from: https://psycnet.apa.org/doi/10.1111/j.1749-818X.2008.00053.x [accessed 22 June 2023].

Jandura, O. and Friedrich, K. (2014). The quality of political media coverage. In: Reinemann, C., ed., *Political Communication*. Berlin: Mouton de Gruyter, pp. 351–73.

Morozov, E. (2011). *The Net Delusion: How Not to Liberate the World*. London: Penguin.

Nguyen, C. T. (2020). Echo chambers and epistemic bubbles. *Episteme*, 17 (2), pp. 141–61. doi: 10.1017/epi.2018.32.

Nguyen, C. T. and Williams, B. (2020). Moral outrage porn. *Journal of Ethics and Social Philosophy*, 18 (2), pp. 147–72. doi: 10.26556/jesp.v18i2.990.

Pasquino, G. (2008). Populism and democracy. In: Albertazzi, D. and McDonnell, D., eds, *Twenty-First Century Populism*. London: Palgrave Macmillan, pp. 15–29. Available from: https://link.springer.com/chapter/10.1057/9780230592100_2 [accessed 22 June 2023].

Reyes, A. (2011). Strategies of legitimization in political discourse: From words to actions. *Discourse & Society*, 22 (6), pp. 781–807. doi: 10.1177/0957926511419927.

Sandvine (2022). *Phenomena: The Global Internet Phenomena Report*. January 2022. Available from: https://www.sandvine.com/hubfs/Sandvine_Redesign_2019/Downloads/2022/Phenomena%20Reports/GIPR%202022/Sandvine%20GIPR%20January%202022.pdf [accessed 22 June 2023].

Sega (2021). Borisov sreshtu Radev: koi e vinoven za Kovid katastrofata. [Borisov against Radev: whose fault is the COVID catastrophe.] 6 October. Available from: https://www.segabg.com/node/194732 [accessed 4 December 2022].

Shullenberger, G. (2020). The new net delusion. *The New Atlantis*, 62, pp. 46–52.

Standartnews (2021). Slavi progovarya. Eto kade mozhe da mu zadadete vapros. [Slavi breaks his silence. Here is where you can ask him your question.] 11 November. Available from: https://www.standartnews.com/izbori-2-v-1/slavi-progovarya-eto-kade-mozhe-da-mu-zadadete-vpros-476341.html [accessed 10 January 2023].

Statista (2021). Distribution of Facebook users in Bulgaria 2021. Available from: https://www.statista.com/statistics/805460/facebook-users-bulgaria/ [accessed 22 June 2023].

Steensen, S. and Westlund, O. (2021). *What is Digital Journalism Studies?* London: Routledge.

Taibbi, M. (2022). Thread 1. The Twitter Files. Twitter. Available from: https://www.twitter.com/mtaibbi/status/1598822959866683394 [accessed 22 June 2023].

Tannen, D. (1993). What's in a frame? Surface evidence for underlying expectations. *Framing in Discourse*, 14, p. 56.

Tannen, D. and Wallat, C. (1987). Interactive frames and knowledge schemas in interaction: Examples from a medical examination/ interview. *Social Psychology Quarterly*, 50 (2), pp. 205–16.

van Aelst, P., Strömbäck, J., Aalberg, T., Esser, F., De Vreese, C., Matthes, J., Hopmann, D., Salgado, S, Hubé, N., Stępińska, A. and Papathanassopoulos, S. (2017). Political communication in a high-choice media environment: A challenge for democracy? *Annals of the International Communication Association*, 41 (1), pp. 3–27.

van Leeuwen, T. (2007). Legitimation in discourse and communication. *Discourse & Communication*, 1 (1), pp. 91–112. doi: 10.1177/1750481307071986.

Wagner, K. and Swisher, K. (2017). Read Mar Zuckerberg's full 6,000-word letter on Facebook's global ambitions. *Vox*, 16 February. Available from: www.vox.com/2017/2/16/14640460/mark-zuckerberg-facebook-manifesto-letter [accessed 22 June 2023].

Wiener, J. and Bronson, N. (2014). Facebook's top open data problems. Meta, 21 October [blog post]. Available from: https://research.facebook.com/blog/2014/10/facebook-s-top-open-data-problems/ [accessed 22 June 2023].

Wikipedia (2022). *7/8 TV*. Available from: https://en.wikipedia.org/wiki/7/8_TV [accessed 22 June 2023].

Wikipedia (2023). *2020–2021 Bulgarian Protests*. Available from: https://en.wikipedia.org/wiki/2020–2021_Bulgarian_protests [accessed 22 June 2023].

Corpus

Facebook: https://www.facebook.com/STTrifonov/

CHAPTER 6

Meaning-making in Trump's anti-Biden political campaign commercials: Multimodal perspective

Tetiana Krysanova

1 Introduction

Important political events nowadays are accompanied by various media interpretations which have great potential to influence public opinion (Wodak et al. 2020). The growing role of video commercials in modern political campaigns generates interest in the context-based process of meaning-making through the synergy of various semiotic resources. A multimodal perspective paves the way for explaining the persuasive force of political discourse. This perspective takes into account the constructive integration of semiotic modes and resources in a given semiotic environment, in conjunction with the communicants' shared knowledge, as well as social and cultural factors.

The objective of this chapter is to provide an insight into the multimodal dimension of emerging meaning in Donald Trump's anti-Biden political campaign commercials. We focus on Trump's 2020 election campaign commercials with a twin aim. Theoretically, we intend to explain the mechanism of multimodal meaning-making in political campaign advertising. Empirically, we define the combining potential of each semiotic resource in meaning-making. Semiotics, as Deely (1990: 39) explains, investigates the action of signs in meaning-making, as signs communicate meanings. This research is less concerned with which meanings are constructed in the commercials, and, instead, focuses to a greater extent on the multimodal means employed to construct a particular meaning and the variables which add to the process of meaning-making. In order to reach this goal, we apply a combination of cognitive-pragmatic and cognitive-semiotic approaches to study multimodal meaning-making in commercials.

Both cognitive pragmatics and cognitive semiotics address meaning-making, although they focus on different aspects of this process. Cognitive-pragmatic accounts emphasise the intersubjective interaction of communicants in constructing and reconstructing meanings, as well as the interactive and embodied character of meaning-making (Schmid 2012; Foolen 2019). As Foolen (2019: 44) claims, 'pragmatics and cognitive studies recontextualize into each other's direction' and 'interactional-dynamic perspective on human communication should play a guiding role in this process'. The cognitive-semiotic vantage point stresses the dynamic character of meaning-making, which involves

> the internal cognitive structure of a thought, the way we construe a story, an argument, a description, an evaluation, a complex emotion, and the way we arrange the external expression of such a construal, which has its own semiotic communicative logic.
> (Brandt 2020: 9)

The cognitive-semiotic perspective in this study emphasises the meaning-making potential and integration of semiotic modes and resources in commercials, as well as the cognitive processes, which make the semiotic processes possible. As Brandt (2020: 9) argues, meaning 'refers, through semiosis, to the existence of a sphere of communicative networks in the world of intersubjective exchange and sociocultural discourse in a broad sense'. The semiotic and social aspects of meaning-making are interrelated, as 'meaning arises in social environments and in social interactions' (Kress 2010: 54). The use of the integrative cognitive-pragmatic and cognitive-semiotic framework will make it possible to explain meaning-making in political commercials as a dynamic, enactive and embodied process, which is the result of the intersubjective interaction of the candidate and the electorate in constructing 'meaning-in-context'. This integrative framework is underpinned by the theories of conceptual integration (Fauconnier and Turner 2003), blended classical joint attention (Turner 2017) and performativity (Fischer-Lichte 2008).

Political advertising is a form of campaigning which enables candidates to communicate indirectly with their voters and influence their choice. By running advertisements on television and on the Internet, candidates not only communicate important issues to the target audience, but also highlight the shortcomings of their opponents. Trump's anti-Biden political campaign commercials are short films (about thirty seconds) which aim to persuade viewers to vote against Biden by eliciting viewers' negative emotions, mainly of fear. They make up a brief story predicting a fearful future life for American citizens under a Biden presidency on the basis of shared patterns of verbal and non-verbal human behaviour. Commercials provide the dynamics of meaning-making through various multimodal means: language, dynamic images, the body movements of characters in commercials, music, light, camera movements, and so on. Consequently, meaning is constructed on the screen by a combination of multifarious semiotic resources, which, at the same time, represent the system of social values of a given society. This highlights the interplay between the material-perceptive and socio-semiotic aspects of meaning-making, and focuses on the interaction between the candidate and voters as participatory meaning-makers.

Although there is a significant amount of research on various aspects of commercials, including the lexical analysis of differences between winning and losing commercials (Lowry and Naser 2010), campaign advertising strategies (Denton et al. 2020), gender peculiarities (Williams 2019) and functional differentiation of political commercials (Airne and Benoit 2005), there are very few multimodal accounts of meaning-making in political campaign commercials. Among them, Meade and Robles (2017) explore how language and communication are linked with historical narratives through the use of multimodal stories in political commercials in the United States (US). Arnold-Murray (2021) examines a variety of semiotic resources used to construct dialogues multimodally in political commercials. Moreover, Horst (2018) studies multimodal metaphorical and metonymical meaning-making processes in German and Polish commercials.

In this chapter, we will first explain the rationale of the integrative approach applied to the study of meaning-making in Trump's anti-Biden political campaign commercials. Next, we will discuss various semiotic resources which are specific to the construction of fear in Trump's anti-Biden commercials, then identify their potential for the construction of meaning, and finally, single out typical multisemiotic patterns of meaning-making. We will subsequently elaborate on the interactional-dynamic view by highlighting the interaction between a candidate and electorate aimed at (re)constructing meanings. We will draw some tentative conclusions and make suggestions for broadening the multimodal analysis of meaning-making in commercials.

2 Analysing meaning-making in political campaign commercials: Method and data

In this section, we will specify the corpus of the study and explain the applied methodology. We will then clarify the multimodal and multisemiotic features of political commercials which allow us to consider them as a cinematic phenomenon, where meanings can be constructed not only by verbal means, but also through the use of dynamic images and specific technical devices peculiar to cinematography. Finally, we address the expressive nature of commercials aimed at eliciting some of the viewers' emotions in particular.

2.1 Method and data

The corpus of the study comprises seventeen of Trump's anti-Biden political campaign commercials which aired during the 2020 United States presidential election. In order to illustrate the multimodal issues of meaning-making in political commercials, we employ the case study of videos titled *Cards* (2020) and *Break In* (2020), which demonstrate the typical semiotic resources in meaning-making involved in Trump's anti-Biden commercials. The examples given in this chapter are accompanied by screenshots of corresponding video fragments released on the Internet.

Both commercials address criminal justice and economic issues, while constructing meanings which are related to the fears of ordinary American citizens regarding a future Biden presidency. *Break In* depicts a scared elderly woman who becomes a victim of a home burglary attack allegedly due to the defunding of the police and is attributed to Biden's future policy. Having noticed the burglar, she dials 911 and hears a voice recording which states that there is no one to answer her emergency call. A voice-over confirms that due to a decrease in funding there has been a reduction in the number of police officers. At the end of the video, the woman is shown to be severely attacked by the intruder.

Cards is focused on the worries of a young Afro-American woman caused by economic and financial problems, which may be connected to Biden's policies. She is sitting silently on the edge of a bed displaying posters with messages in block text. Flipping through the posters, the woman mentions that she has four children and worries about Biden's plans to raise taxes and grant amnesty to illegal immigrants.

Trump's anti-Biden political campaign commercials are intended to influence the audience by eliciting fear associated with the Biden presidency and are directed to make voting for Biden impossible. Fear is a basic negative emotion, caused by a malefic action and aimed at mobilising efforts to prevent harm to the individual. Constructed fear in commercials is social in nature and is connected with real-life situations, which may appear to be frightening for voters. These include decreasing police funding (which will lead to higher crime rates), raising taxes, a deterioration in the standard of living, the immigration crisis, unemployment, and so on. In order to reduce the risk of becoming a victim and protect themselves from these situations, viewers are expected to vote against Biden.

As commercials are multimodal and multisemiotic by their very nature, meanings are constructed not only verbally, but also through other semiotic resources, namely non-verbal and cinematic ones. Emotions of characters on the screen are not real: they are constructed and embodied through physiological and sensory-perceptual manifestations, and behavioural patterns which characterise a certain emotion. On-screen emotions are viewed as the 'construction of signs, formed after a model of a general human emotion, to create a believable and convincing illusion of the emotion as we know it in daily life' (Konijn 2000: 60). Accordingly, actors' body movements, facial expressions and dialogues should refer to the components of real life in order to construct the imitated emotion on screen. The main 'tools' for the implementation of constructed emotions include the combination of verbal and non-verbal means, as well as specific technical cinematic devices aimed at intensifying filmic emotion. The constructed meaning is viewed as a semantic whole, which is the result of the multisemiotic integration.

However, the role of the various semiotic resources in meaning-making is different. While the verbal component in Trump's anti-Biden political campaign commercials mostly combines emotional and rational aspects, non-verbal and cinematic means are predominantly connected with emotional perception. Therefore, in order to explain the mechanism of meaning-making, we analyse the meaning-making potential of each semiotic resource separately and then explain how the integration of multisemiotic elements serves to construct the meaning.

The integrative approach applied in this research comprises several stages of the procedure. First, we determine the elements of verbal, non-verbal and cinematic semiotic resources specific to constructing on-screen fear in commercials. Next, we highlight the meaning-making potential of multisemiotic elements and the different configurations possible. We then single out typical multisemiotic combinations on the basis of cognitive and functional parameters. Finally, we explain cognitive-pragmatic aspects of emerging meaning in political commercials.

2.2 Political campaign commercial as a cinematic phenomenon

The issue of constructing meanings in political campaign commercials focuses attention on the cinematic features of this type of video. They are created in order to have an impact on voters and to ensure that voters will interpret a candidate's message through the combination of various semiotic means in the commercial. Meaning-making in commercials emerges as a dynamic process of mediated interaction between the candidate and voters. The communicative nature of political campaign commercials is rooted in reality, as it unites the 'worlds' of politicians and voters on the basis of shared knowledge. Their interaction emphasises the role of communication as a dynamic, situationally dependent process of constructing social values and social relations which highlights the interpretive and constructed character of meanings. This interaction is mediated by the camera, which guides and directs the audience's attention in the meaning-making process. Meanings emerge as a result of the ongoing and enactive joint interpretative activity of politicians and voters, who appear to be participatory meaning-makers. As Foolen (2019: 44) states:

> the mind is not seen as something isolated from the rest of the world ... but as connected to body, the environment, and other minds; or, in a popular phrasing in this approach, it is embodied, embedded, extended, and enactive.

The interactive character of meaning-making in commercials is due to the active role of filmmakers and viewers in (re)constructing meanings.

All participants involved in constructing on-screen meanings in commercials may be considered filmmakers. They include a candidate, namely Donald Trump, his public relations team members who create meaning, and those directly involved in the filmmaking process – the director, the cameraman and actors, among others – who construct the intended meaning on screen. The target audience of political commercials are viewers: they are remote in space and time with different ethnic, socio-cultural and gender characteristics. They do not take part directly in creating meaning; their participation is indirect. However, filmmakers take into account their world knowledge, including social and cultural characteristics.

Political campaign commercials are multimodal and multisemiotic in nature, since a synergistic combination of verbal, non-verbal and cinematic semiotic systems constructs the meaning in commercials through audial and visual modes. The concept of mode, as Bateman and Schmidt (2012) argue, is associated with sensory modality, as it is related to the way an individual hears, sees or perceives material objects. The audial mode in commercials is realised through speech, music, voice and sound effects, while the visual mode is represented by the screen image – mimics, body movements, visual effects, drawings and so on. Every mode contains semiotic resources – socially conditioned meaning-making resources which construct social, individual and affective meanings according to the needs of a particular community (van Leeuwen 2006). In section 3.1, we will describe the semiotic resources typically required for meaning-making in commercials.

Meaning emerges as the result of the integration of verbal, non-verbal and cinematic semiotic resources implemented through audial and visual modes. Each semiotic resource is presented in both modes employing specific semiotic means: verbal resource involves lexical, syntactic and discursive means represented in the form of oral speech or in written form on the screen; non-verbal resource encompasses facial expressions, gestures, voice changes and body movements; and cinematic resource includes camera shot, camera angle, sound and light effects. The synergistic effect gives rise to meaning-making, which is grounded in bodily experience associated with emotional perception.

Emotions are crucial for most people's cinematic experience and are therefore widely constructed in commercials. Commercials are emotively pre-focused, and as Lakoff argues, 'emotion is both central and legitimate in political persuasion' (Lakoff 2008: 8). Consequently, meanings constructed in commercials should be viewed through the prism of their emotionality. Emotions, as Barrett et al. (2007: 374) claim, are 'entailed or instantiated by physical processes in the brain or body and thus can be explained by events in the physical world'. Their representation in social interaction is immanent and they are dynamic, interactive and socially constructed. According to Tan (1999: 50), film is an 'emotion machine' where 'the visual image of a film character is capable of producing direct appeal'. The constructing of emotive meaning in commercials is closely related to social contexts, namely specific communicative situations. These situations reflect the real-life experience of viewers, which is emotionally conditioned.

Emotions in commercials have a significant motivational potential, which has a twofold impact on viewers. On the one hand, filmic emotions activate viewers' perceptual and cognitive spheres involved in the reconstruction of meaning and associated with their world knowledge. On the other hand, they elicit viewers' feelings and emotions grounded in their 'identification with character' (Grodal 1999: 131), which is at the heart of empathy (Tan 1999). Filmmakers are able to predict the emotional reactions of viewers by taking on board social and cultural aspects and speculating on them in order to fulfil their pragmatic aim, namely to persuade viewers to vote against Biden. Therefore, it is essential to explain the mechanism of meaning-making through the semiotic strata as well as to analyse the role of filmmakers and viewers in (re)constructing meanings.

3 Results and discussion

A multimodal analysis of the semiotic resources used for constructing fear in commercials makes it possible to determine their meaning-making potential and systematise the ways in which they are integrated. This section addresses the cognitive, semiotic and pragmatic issues of meaning-making which are underpinned by the theories of conceptual integration, blended classical joint attention, and performativity.

3.1 Semiotic resources for constructing fear in political commercials

The multimodal perspective of political commercials focuses on the interplay between modes and semiotic resources in constructing meaning. These semiotically heterogeneous resources are blended to construct emotive meaning and the configurations of semiotic elements determine the contextual properties of emotive meanings. In order to explain how meaning emerges in commercials, it is necessary to establish the role of each semiotic resource in meaning-making. The meaning of fear in the political commercials under analysis is constructed by specific components of verbal, non-verbal and cinematic semiotic resources through audial and visual modes.

The verbal semiotic resource is represented in oral and written forms and comprises lexical and syntactic means. The combination of rational and emotional aspects in the verbal semiotic resource is realised through the use of appropriate lexical and syntactic means. For instance, *Break In* contains the verbal component represented by the over-the-screen voice, on-screen text messages and on-screen posters with slogans, which prove the employment of audial and visual modes for meaning-making. The negative meaning is constructed mostly by action verbs: 'defund' refers to withdrawing financial support in the legislative sphere, 'reduce' to decreasing funding, and 'remove' to taking away subjects from the occupied position. They appeal to the reasons connected to the increase in the crime rate and to the loss of life security indirectly constructing fear. The ability of these lexical units to construct fear is context dependent and tied to a particular communicative situation. Portch et al. (2015) claim that action verbs are capable of evoking knowledge relevant to certain emotional states. We argue that the action verbs used to refer to real-life situations are sensitive to societal issues and serve to attribute a negative connotation to the facts, namely the meaning of fear in the analysed commercials. Example (1) illustrates the use of the lexemes 'defund' and 'remove' referring to the reasons for the increasing crime rate. The elderly woman is listening to the TV news anchor and reacts unhappily to this message:

(1) Seattle's pledge to defund its police department by 50 percent, even including a proposal to remove 911 dispatchers from police control. (*Break In.* 00.00.10)

The commercial *Cards* employs the verbal semiotic resource only through the visual mode and contains the emotion-laden words 'scared', 'afraid' and 'worry', which explicitly realise fear, and action verbs 'raise', 'embrace', 'empty' and 'risk', which acquire a negative meaning in the context. The use of the adjective 'weak' in relation to Biden negatively characterises him and directly reveals the attitude towards him as a future president (example 2):

(2) Joe Biden worries me. He is weak. (*Cards.* 00.00.05)

Moreover, the use of statistical data in commercials is perceived by viewers as facts which influence their logic and rational perception, thereby contributing to meaning-making. Factual information is used in both commercials, dealing with the 50% reduction in funding in *Break In* (example 1), and illegal immigrants in *Cards* (example 3):

(3) Give amnesty to 11 million immigrants. (*Cards.* 00.00.13)

Syntax performs an expressive function with the implicit realisation of fear. It is represented by imperative sentences (example 4), incomplete sentences (example 5) and negative sentences (example 6) refuting the ability of the Biden presidency to guarantee the safety of American citizens. Imperative sentences on posters represent the slogans 'Defund the police' and 'Defund NYPD', which became popular during the George Floyd protests in 2020, and support removing funds from police departments. These expressive forms are directed to affect the viewers by evoking the speaker's negative psychological state of mind as a reaction to the fact:

(4) Defund the police. (*Break In.* 00.00.03)

Meaning-making in political campaign commercials 131

(5) I'm afraid to say this out loud . . . (*Cards*. 00.00.21)

(6) I won't risk my children's future with Biden. (*Cards*. 00.00.23)

Non-verbal semiotic resource is an integral part of meaning-making in political commercials and is represented through bodily signs represented by actors' mimic, prosodic and gestural actions. The human body appears to be phenomenal and semiotic, since it expresses the emotion as well as serves as its sign. While the elements of the verbal resource combine rational and emotional aspects, the non-verbal elements are inherently emotional. The connection of emotions with the body lies in the fact that emotion, as Damasio (2003: 86) explains, 'is the perception of a certain state of the body along with the perception of a certain mode of thinking'. In Zlatev's parlance (2008: 228), embodiment involves a cross-modal mapping between the perception of the surroundings and the perception of the body; it corresponds to a certain action, object or event. A bodily sign in commercials is used communicatively and is therefore apt to be meaningful.

Bodily signs used to construct fear in the analysed commercials correspond to those described by psychologists (Izard 2013: 364) as relevant to the expression of fear. The meaning of fear both in *Break In* and *Cards* is constructed through facial expressions and body movements. Wide eyes, a look of panic, compressed lips and a tense face are common features in both commercials. In *Break In*, the elderly woman realises the impending danger and her mouth twitches. Her body movements become uncontrolled, she starts swinging her arms, and a grimace of horror appears on her face at the moment of assault. In *Cards*, however, the woman's body movements are characterised by the head shaking up, down and sideways, which may be viewed as a muscle tremor caused by fear or anxiety (Izard 2013: 366).

Cinematic semiotic resource, which includes camera shots, camera angles, light, and sound techniques, and so on, also have meaning-making potential in commercials. Cinematic means create the mimetic effect which entails imitating reality. It may complement and intensify the emotive meaning constructed by verbal and non-verbal means. As Heimann et al. (2014) claim, viewers are bodily engaged while observing both the movement of cinematic devices and the emotions of on-screen characters. Moreover, the sensory-motor areas of the human brain are able to change their activity due to the camera position, which makes viewers feel emotions.

Close-up or middle-up camera images are a mandatory component for constructing fear in *Break In* and *Cards*, thereby emphasising different aspects of emotions. While a close-up is mostly effective at highlighting primarily the facial expression, the middle-up stresses the activity connected with body movements.

A camera angle focuses on the dynamics of character's actions which indicate the emotional state of fear. This requires a wide use of various angle types in analysed commercials. In *Break In*, side, back and Dutch angles and a point-of-view (POV) shot are used. They emphasise different aspects of the emotion. For instance, POV is represented by the camera position, which makes it possible to see reality represented through the eyes or mind of the character, thus forcing the audience to experience fear at the same time as him or her. The Dutch angle is achieved by tilting the camera when vertical lines are at an angle to the side of the frame and the horizon line is not parallel with the base of the frame. Its use generates an atmosphere of uneasiness, fright and ominousness. The Dutch angle is employed as a means of constructing the meaning of fear in the scenes where the elderly woman realises there is a danger and hears the sound of a person breaking in. The use of camera angles in *Cards* is less variable and is limited to a low angle (where a camera angle is positioned below the average eye line), which gives viewers a subtle psychological nudge to see a weak and vulnerable character as a victim in danger.

Sound effects are frequently used in commercials for constructing fear. They include non-diegetic music, the use of voice-overs and diegetic sounds. While diegesis refers to the fictional world of the commercial, non-diegetic music is not part of the narrative and is directed to the audience in order to create a certain emotional effect. The prevalent use of non-diegetic music proves the hypothesis that all events in the commercials aim to affect viewers. Non-diegetic music is applied in both videos to construct the fearful emotional state of the characters. Emotions caused by music arise as a result of the complex interaction between music, viewers and the situation (Juslin 2001: 7) and emerge independently of the viewers' consciousness (Cohen 2011: 264). While music is able to express and cause emotions, the screen represents the object to which this emotion is directed. The music employed in commercials may be described as sharp, discontinuous, non-linear and disturbing, with a preference for stringed instruments, which is fear-inducing (Cohen 2011).

Voice-over is an effective 'tool' in meaning-making, since it serves to objectify and intensify the meaning constructed visually on the screen, as is the case in *Break In*. Voice-over is used here to represent the TV news narrative which comments on defunding of the police (example 1). We then hear the well-known voice of Fox News' Sean Hannity claiming over the screen:

(7) Joe Biden said he's absolutely on board with defunding the police. (*Break In*. 00.00.15)

This statement is followed by the voice-over of Biden saying:

(8) Yes, absolutely. (*Break In*. 00.00.20)

Voice-over, combined with the verbal component, provides intertextual clues connecting the defunding of the police with the Biden presidency

Meaning-making in political campaign commercials 133

and the meaning of fear constructed in the commercial. Consequently, this technique attracts the viewers' attention by engaging them with the narrative, delivering the verbal component, and highlighting the particular emotion visualised on the screen through the woman's bodily signs.

The diegetic sounds employed in *Break In* make the events of the commercial more realistic by emphasising the emotional state of the character and creating tension for the viewers. The sounds of dialling, a phone beep without a dispatcher's answer and the crack of the door broken by the intruder all serve as symbols of approaching danger and the development of fear.

The light effects which are requisite for constructing fear in commercials include dim light, shadowing and combinations of black and white light. Such effects create oppressiveness, highlighting the mood of characters and evoking viewers' emotions. Women in both commercials are highlighted in white, while their surroundings are dim. The events of *Break In* take place in a dark room, but a table lamp shines on the elderly woman's face, which contrasts with the dark figure of the intruder.

Figure 6.1 illustrates the construction of fear non-verbally and cinematically in the commercial *Break In*. The fragment under analysis depicts an elderly woman who experiences a burglary while she is at home. While watching a televised news story about defunding the police, she notices

Figure 6.1 Break In *(00.00.05)*

someone breaking into her house and experiences fear. The non-verbal dimension contains indicators of fear such as a tense face, contoured lips, and a look of panic. Cinematic devices clarify and intensify the emotive meaning. While the middle-up stresses the woman's immobile body, the Dutch angle depicts her state of unease for the benefit of the viewers. The sound effects employed in this commercial are slow in tempo but sharp and disturbing in tone, with non-diegetic music accompanied by a voice-over which reports cuts to police funding. The combination of a black and white light creates an ominous atmosphere.

Although verbal, non-verbal and cinematic resources have different levels of potential for constructing meaning, the meaning cannot be constructed through the elements of a separate semiotic resource. They may be singled out for the purpose of analysing their meaning-making potential and specifying their role in creating meaning. Neither of them may construct the meaning independently. Only the integration of semiotic resources can serve to achieve meaning-making. The multifaceted analysis of political commercials shows how the meaning of fear in commercials is a multimodal dynamic construct, which occurs as the result of multisemiotic integration.

3.2 Multisemiotic integration in political campaign commercials

The mechanism of meaning-making may be explained through the analysis of the ways in which the elements of semiotic resources integrate. These shed light on the multimodal dimension of meaning-making in political commercials. As Bateman and Schmidt (2012: 91) argue, 'This is the central issue for a theory of multimodality in a nutshell: just what are the ways in which semiotic modes can be brought together and what does the combination achieve?' The different semiotic resources applied in political commercials interact with one another, thereby making sequences which can be analysed only in terms of their dynamics. The synergy of this integration creates multisemiotic blends.

From a cognitive-semiotic perspective, meaning-making in political commercials may be viewed as the result of conceptual integration. Applying the theory of conceptual integration (Fauconnier and Turner 2003), each semiotic resource – verbal, non-verbal and cinematic – is treated as a separate mental input space, since the meanings constructed in each mental space are interpreted and processed in different ways (Krysanova and Shevchenko 2021: 362). This involves the activation of the generic mental space, which contains information about communicants' shared knowledge about the emotion of fear. The meanings which are relevant to each input space are projected into a mixed space, where they intersect and cross-map, thus giving rise to the creation of a blend. The meaning constructed in the blended space is emergent, as it is only partially motivated by the meanings in input spaces. The specificity of the emergent meaning lies in its novelty. Therefore, emergent blends tend to be dynamic integrated entities which appear to maintain their own meaning-making identity, despite being created by the integration of semiotic components. The formation of emergent blends of emotive meanings is a continual process as any change of a semiotic element provokes the formation of a new blend with the modified meaning.

The process of conceptual integration underlies the formation of multi-semiotic combinations which, in turn, can be reduced to certain patterns based on static and dynamic criteria. The static criterion makes it possible to single out patterns caused by quantitative (two- or three-component), qualitative (convergent or divergent) and salient (parity or non-parity) issues, while the dynamic criterion highlights the synchronous or consecutive patterns (Krysanova 2019; Krysanova and Shevchenko 2022).

The elements of three semiotic resources form a three-component pattern which constructs the meaning of fear in *Break In* and *Cards* – and this pattern forms the quantitative dimension. The verbal component, represented orally or in writing, supports the image, which, in turn, reinforces the verbal text, while the cinematic elements specify and intensify the emotive meaning. This pattern includes multifarious configurations of semiotic elements which are the cause of unstable combinations. The most typical combination for *Break In* is the meaning-making combination of the verbal component as represented by lexemes with the negative meaning, the non-verbal component – woman's facial expression, and the cinematic component – the middle-up, non-diegetic music, and voice-over (Figure 6.2). In *Cards*, the peculiar three-component pattern is represented by the combination of emotion-laden words, facial expressions, the middle-up, and non-diegetic music.

The qualitative dimension is associated with the ability of multisemiotic elements to construct unidirectional or multidirectional meanings (Krysanova 2019; Krysanova and Shevchenko 2022). As the components of all the semiotic resources in commercials are directed to construct fear, they create a convergent pattern. The elements of all these semiotic resources complement one another and reinforce the same meaning in constructing fear, which can be interpreted when combined as a whole. Consider example (9), which represents three-component and convergent patterns. The verbal component is comprised of the lexeme 'defunding', negatively characterising the future of Biden's policy regarding safety issues. This may implicitly contribute to the construction of fear, and the meaning becomes evident when the viewers see the woman's tense face and her worried look; these elements form the non-verbal component. The cinematic component generates emotive meaning and intensifies it through the use of the close-up and the side angle. These make it possible to observe the woman's facial expression, with diegetic beeping sounds engaging viewers in the narrative, disturbing non-diegetic music affecting viewers and creating the alarming atmosphere, and voice-over, which links the woman's worries with the Biden presidency. As the voice-over states:

Figure 6.2 Break In *(00.00.13)*

(9) Joe Biden said he's absolutely on board with defunding the police. (*Break In.* 00.00.15)

The elements of three semiotic systems integrate to construct the meaning of fear experienced by the elderly woman, which is caused by the breaking into her house and is implicitly connected with the future Biden presidency.

In terms of the salience of multisemiotic elements within the semantic combination, parity and non-parity patterns can be determined (Krysanova 2019; Krysanova and Shevchenko 2022). In *Break In* and *Cards*, the parity pattern, which involves the equivalent use of multisemiotic elements equally participating in constructing fear, is the most typical pattern. It demonstrates the significant meaning-making potential of all semiotic resources in commercials. For instance, in *Cards* (Figure 6.3), the parity pattern is constituted by the verbal component represented by the emotion-laden lexeme 'afraid' and the expressive incomplete statement, while the non-verbal component is represented by a woman's tense face and her frightened look. This is the cinematic component – the middle-up and disturbing non-diegetic music. As a result, the semiotic elements of three resources equally participate in meaning-making, therefore demonstrating their equal ability to construct meanings.

The dynamic criterion makes it possible to distinguish between synchronous or consecutive patterns through the simultaneous or sequential use

Meaning-making in political campaign commercials 137

Figure 6.3 Cards *(00.00.20)*

of multisemiotic devices. The semiotic elements within the synchronous pattern simultaneously generate emotive meaning-making, while the components of the consecutive pattern are consistently involved in the construction of fear. The analysis shows that both patterns are represented in commercials by almost the same ratio, which indicates a tendency towards the dynamic construction of fear in the analysed commercials. The synchronous pattern is typical for constructing meaning in *Cards*, while *Break In* employs the consecutive pattern.

Consider Figures 6.4 and 6.5, which illustrate the use of the consecutive pattern in *Break In* and show the sequence of the illegal break-in. Initially, the woman is alarmed and frightened by the burglar's attack and the lack of a response to her emergency call. Her scared look and tense face, combined with the middle-up, diegetic sounds – the tone of the phone beeping, and non-diegetic disturbing music – contribute to meaning-making. We then see the moment of the assault: her face becomes distorted, her mouth is wide open, and her movements aimed at self-protection are uncontrolled. The middle-up and the side angle are combined with the voice-over stating the absence of dispatchers to answer the call, with alarming non-diegetic music and dim lighting. The verbal semiotic resource indicates the probable cause of the burglar's attack, as indicated by the negative sentence on the screen, which negates any chance of living in safety during a Biden presidency. The consecutive chain of semantic combinations gives the episode more dynamism and intensifies the construction of fear.

Therefore, the typical patterns of meaning-making in Trump's anti-Biden political commercials *Break In* and *Cards* contain three components and parity, and are convergent, synchronous and consecutive. They show that

Figure 6.4 Break In *(00.00.21)*

Figure 6.5 Break In *(00.00.24)*

semiotic resources are able to integrate different meaning-making combinations depending on the filmmaker's intentions. This becomes possible, as any element in the multimodal discourse is semiotic and may be used to communicate. Although multisemiotic combinations may be characterised by the volatility of their elements, they can be organised according to particular conventions, which are connected with the cognitive, semiotic and pragmatic aspects of multimodal meaning-making.

The analysis of the mechanism of meaning-making requires the explanation of the interaction of filmmakers and viewers in (re)constructing meanings in political commercials.

3.3 Meaning-making as the joint participation of candidates and voters

In this analysis of the emergence of meaning in political campaign commercials, we proceed from the claim that meaning-making is the dynamic process of intersubjective interaction between filmmakers and viewers (Krysanova 2019), who can be viewed as participatory meaning-makers. Their interaction is socially related, since they co-participate in this process through the implementation of social values within the framework of social practice. Meaning-making appears to be intersubjective and results from the human desire to interact, which is achieved through the sharing of feelings, emotions and thoughts. Political campaign commercials as a cinematic phenomenon are the 'environment' for meaning-making in the communication process between candidates and voters. Filmmakers and viewers interactively take part in this process as co-participants in the constructing and reconstructing of meanings through their shared knowledge.

Although the communication between filmmakers and viewers is delayed in time and is remote in space, these speakers are able to jointly identify the same object on screen in the reconstructing of meanings. The joint participation of filmmakers and viewers is grounded in the understanding that communicants who exist in different spatial and temporal environments are attending the same event, even if they do not know of each other's existence (Turner 2017: 3). In political commercials, filmmakers' and viewers' joint attention is bidirectional, as 'each agent is aware of the other's experiences – even if they are not mutually aware of sharing experiences' (Brinck 2008: 121). According to the theory of blended classical joint attention (Turner 2017), filmmakers and viewers are able to create the emergent multimodal blend in order to construct the same meaning.

In the case of political commercials, convergent meaning is possible due to the ways in which viewers (as potential voters) evaluate these commercials, in addition to how commercials affect the willingness of viewers to vote for or against a particular candidate. To illustrate these claims, we address the results of the poll conducted on 30 July 2020 by YouGov, a well-known international Internet-based data analytics firm. They demonstrate that two-thirds of registered voters (67%) classified the tone of *Break In* as negative. The commercial slightly dampened the positive opinion of Biden held by Democrats and Independents. After viewing *Break In*, positive opinion of Biden dropped among registered voters (49% before; 45% after), Independents (46% before; 40% after) and Democrats (86% before; 78% after) (Sanders 2020).

Since the commercial is made for viewers and is directed to a particular social group of viewers, it brings the performative aspect of interaction between filmmakers and viewers to the fore. We claim that the performative aspect emphasises how viewers perceive and reconstruct on-screen meanings, as well as how filmmakers take the social, national or gender characteristics of viewers into account. Applying the theory of performativity (Fischer-Lichte 2008), we view meaning-making in political commercials as a performative act grounded in the dynamic intersubjective interaction of communicants. As viewers are involved in on-screen events through their identification with the characters, they experience the same emotions. Everything that happens on the screen, namely the terrifying music, crying, screaming, pleas for help and so on, triggers unpleasant emotions (mostly fear and despair), thus engaging viewers to jointly participate in the meaning-making process. The on-screen events constructed by various semiotic resources turn out to be real. This makes their experience liminal, as 'generating emotions and inducing a liminal state go side by side and cannot be separated from one another' (Fischer-Lichte 2008: 177). This is evidenced by the viewers' and writers' reactions to the analysed videos when mentioned in media publications. Commentators note the generally negative tone of the commercials directed against Biden, defining them as 'frenetic, angry and negative' (McManus 2020). Moreover, in their analysis of *Break In*, the authors reconstruct the meaning of the commercial in a fearful tone, comparing it with the horror or thriller film genre and emphasising the target audience, as in the following examples:

(10) This commercial plays more like a horror film, which could be the desired effect, especially if it can effectively stoke the fears of the elderly. (Martinez 2020)

(11) "Break In," a mini-thriller that shows an older woman telephoning 911 to report an intruder, but all she gets is a recording. (McManus 2020)

Consequently, in political commercials, intersubjective, performative and semiotic aspects are interwoven. While the intersubjective aspect stresses the interaction of communicants in meaning-making, the performative aspect emphasises the active role of viewers in reconstructing meanings, and the semiotic aspect focuses on the materiality of signs and their combinations involved in the construction of meanings.

4 Conclusion

This paper provides a multimodal perspective on the emergence of meaning in political commercials. Drawing on the theories of blended classic joint attention, performativity and conceptual integration, we have applied the integrative cognitive-pragmatic and cognitive-semiotic approaches to explain how the meaning of fear is constructed in Trump's ant-Biden political campaign commercials.

Meaning-making in political commercials is a dynamic process which entails the enactment of social relations between a candidate and the electorate through the use of multimodal semiotic resources. The candidate constructs meanings in commercials and the electorate reconstruct them on the basis of their shared knowledge. Commercials are viewed as a communicative event through which social relations between filmmakers and viewers are established.

The multimodal nature of political commercials highlights the decisive role of modes and semiotic resources in constructing meaning. Accordingly, emotive meaning in commercials appears as an emergent dynamic construct – the result of the multisemiotic integration of verbal, non-verbal and cinematic elements, all of which possess a significant meaning-making potential. The multisemiotic components which characterise the construction of fear comprise verbal means, which explicitly and implicitly express the emotion; specific facial expressions and body movements; and cinematic devices – the close-up and the middle-up, various angle types, non-diegetic music and noises, and voice-over.

The combinations of multisemiotic elements are subject to static and dynamic criteria which enable constructive patterns to be isolated. This demonstrates the paradigmatic relationship between the semiotic elements. The typical requisites for constructing fear in commercials are three-component, convergent, parity and synchronous or consecutive patterns.

We hope that the suggested integrative approach will contribute to deepening our comprehension of meaning-making and shed light on the ways that different modes and semiotic resources create semantic sequences in political commercials.

References

Airne, D. and Benoit, W. L. (2005). Political television advertising in campaign 2000. *Communication Quarterly*, 53 (4), pp. 473–92. doi: 10.1080/01463370500168765.

Arnold-Murray, K. (2021). Multimodally constructed dialogue in political campaign commercials. *Journal of Pragmatics*, 173, pp. 15–27. doi: 10.1016/j.pragma.2020.11.014.

Barrett, L., Mesquita, B., Ochsner, K. N. and Gross, J. J. (2007). The experience of emotion. *Annual Review of Psychology*, 58 (1), pp. 373–403. doi: 10.1146/annurev.psych.58.110405.085709.

Bateman, J. and Schmidt, K. H. (2012). *Multimodal Film Analysis: How Films Mean.* London and New York: Routledge.

Brandt, P. A. (2020). *Cognitive Semiotics. Signs, Mind, and Meaning.* London: Bloomsbury Academic.

Brinck, I. (2008). The role of intersubjectivity in the development of intentional communication. In: Zlatev, J., Racine, T. P., Sinha, C. and Itkonen E., eds, *The Shared Mind: Perspectives on Intersubjectivity.* Amsterdam: John Benjamins, pp. 115–40.

Cohen, A. (2011). Music as a source of emotion in film. In: Sloboda, J. A. and Juslin, P. N., eds, *Handbook of Music and Emotion: Theory, Research, Applications.* Oxford: Oxford University Press, pp. 249–72.

Damasio, A. (2003). *Looking for Spinoza: Joy, Sorrow, and the Feeling Brain.* New York: Harcourt.

Deely, J. (1990). *Basics of Semiotics.* Bloomington and Indianapolis: Indiana University Press.

Denton, R. E., Trent, J. S. and Friedenberg, R. V. (2020). *Political Campaign Communication: Principles and Practices.* Lanham, MD: Rowman & Littlefield.

Fauconnier, G. and Turner, M. (2003). *The Way We Think: Conceptual Blending and the Mind's Hidden Complexities.* New York: Basic Books.

Fischer-Lichte, E. (2008). *The Transformative Power of Performance: A New Aesthetics.* London and New York: Routledge.

Foolen, A. (2019). Quo vadis pragmatics? From adaptation to participatory sensemaking. *Journal of Pragmatics*, 145, pp. 39–46. doi: 10.1016/j.pragma.2019.03.008.

Grodal, T. (1999). Emotions, cognitions, and narrative patterns in film. In: Plantinga, C. and Smith, G. M., eds, *Passionate View: Film, Cognition and Emotion.* Baltimore, MD and London: Johns Hopkins University Press, pp. 127–45.

Heimann, K. S., Umiltà, M. A., Guerra, M. and Gallese, V. (2014). Moving mirrors: A high density EEG study investigating the effects of camera movements on motor cortex activation during action observation. *Journal of Cognitive Neuroscience*, 26 (9), pp. 2087–101.

Horst, D. (2018). *Meaning-making and Political Campaign Advertising: A Cognitive-Linguistic and Film-Analytical Perspective on Audiovisual Figurativity.* Berlin: Mouton de Gruyter.

Izard, C. (2013). *Human Emotions.* New York: Springer.

Juslin, P. N. (2011). Music and emotion: Seven questions, seven answers. In: Deliege, I. and Davidson, J., eds, *Music and the Mind: Essays in Honour of John Sloboda.* New York: Oxford University Press, pp. 113–35.

Konijn, E. A. (2000). *Acting Emotions: Shaping Emotions on Stage.* Amsterdam: Amsterdam University Press.

Kress, G. (2010). *Multimodality: A Social Semiotic Approach to Contemporary Communication.* London: Routledge.

Krysanova, T. (2019). Constructing negative emotions in cinematic discourse: A cognitive-pragmatic perspective. *Cognition, Communication, Discourse*, 19, pp. 55–77. doi: 10.26565/2218-2926-2019-19-04.

Krysanova, T. and Shevchenko, I. (2021). Conceptual blending in multimodal construction of negative emotions in film. In: Pawelec, A., Shaw, A. and Szpila, G., eds, *Text-Image-Music: Crossing the Borders. Intermedial Conversations on the Poetics of Verbal, Visual and Musical Texts. In Honour of Prof. Elzbieta Chrzanowska-Kluczewska. Series: Text – Meaning – Context: Cracow Studies in English Language, Literature and Culture*, vol. 19. Berlin: Peter Lang, pp. 357–71. doi: 10.3726/b18012.

Krysanova, T. and Shevchenko, I. (2022). Multisemiotic patterns of emotive meaning-making in film. *Alfred Nobel University Journal of Philology / Visnyk Universitetu imeni Alfreda Nobelya. Seriya: Filologicni Nauki*, 2 (24), pp. 238–48. doi: 10.32342/2523-4463-2022-2-24-20.

Lakoff, G. (2008). *The Political Mind: A Cognitive Scientist's Guide to your Brain and its Politics*. London: Penguin.

Lowry, D. T. and Naser, M. A. (2010). From Eisenhower to Obama: Lexical characteristics of winning versus losing presidential campaign commercials. *Journalism and Mass Communication Quarterly*, 87 (3–4), pp. 530–47. doi: 10.1177/107769901008700306.

Martinez, J. (2020). Audit finds two-thirds of Trump's campaign TV ads contain misleading claims. *Complex*, 16 August 2020. Available from: https://www.complex.com/life/2020/08/audit-finds-two-thirds-of-trump-campaign-tv-ads-contain-misleading-claims [accessed 23 June 2023].

McManus, D. (2020). Column: This year's political ads: The good, the bad and the deceptive. *Los Angeles Times*, 25 October 2020. Available from: https://www.latimes.com/politics/story/2020-10-25/doyle-column-political-ads-2020-biden-trump [accessed 23 June 2023].

Meade, M. R. and Robles, J. S. (2017). Historical and existential coherence in political commercials. *Discourse and Communication*, 11 (4), pp. 404–32. doi: 10.1177/1750481317707560.

Portch, E., Havelka, J., Brown, C. and Giner-Sorolla, R. (2015). Using affective knowledge to generate and validate a set of emotion-related, action words. *PeerJ*, 3: e1100. doi: 10.7717/peerj.1100.

Sanders, L. (2020). How voters view Donald Trump's political advertisement, 'Break In'. *YouGovAmerica*, 4 August 2020. Available from: https://today.yougov.com/topics/politics/articles-reports/2020/08/04/trump-advertisement-break-in-poll [accessed 23 June 2023].

Schmid, H.-J. (2012). Generalizing the apparently ungeneralizable. Basic ingredients of a cognitive-pragmatic approach to the construal of meaning-in-context. In: Schmid, H.-J., ed., *Cognitive Pragmatics: Handbooks of Pragmatics*, vol. 4. Berlin: Mouton de Gruyter, pp. 3–22.

Tan, E. S. (1999). Sentiment in film viewing. In: Plantinga, C. and Smith, G. M., eds, *Passionate View: Film, Cognition and Emotion*. Baltimore, MD and London: Johns Hopkins University Press, pp. 48–64.

Turner, M. (2017). Multimodal form-meaning pairs for blended classic joint attention. *Linguistics Vanguard*, 3, pp. 1–7. doi: 10.1515/lingvan-2016-0043.

van Leeuwen, T. (2006). *Introducing Social Semiotics*. London: Routledge.

Williams, L. (2019). Political advertising in the 'Year of the Woman': Did X mark the spot? In: Cook, E. A., Thomas, S. and Wilcox, C., eds, *The Year of the Woman*. New York: Routledge, pp. 185–203.

Wodak, R., Culpeper, J. and Semino, E. (2020). Shameless normalisation of impoliteness: Berlusconi's and Trump's press conferences. *Discourse and Society*, pp. 1–25. doi: 10.1177/0957926520977217.

Zlatev, J. (2008). The co-evolution of intersubjectivity and bodily mimesis. In: Zlatev, J., Racine, T.P., Sinha, C. and Itkonen, E., eds, *The Shared Mind: Perspectives of Intersubjectivity*. Amsterdam: John Benjamins, pp. 215–44.

Corpus

Break In (2020). Video commercial. Available from: https://www.youtube.com/watch?v=moZOrq0qL3Q [accessed 23 June 2023].

Cards (2020). Video commercial. Available from: https://www.youtube.com/watch?v=FucY0Tm6XO0 [accessed 23 June 2023].

Part III

Legitimisation strategies and conceptualisation

CHAPTER 7

A critical analysis of figurative language in the political discourse of conflict in Africa

Issa Kanté

1 Introduction

This corpus-based study investigates discourses of conflict delivered by political leaders in six West and Central African countries. It focuses on how metaphor and metonymy interact with syntax, lexicalisation and ideologies of glorification in such discourses to handle new forms of conflicts. We postulate that such discursive constructions aim at shaping the opinions and (re)actions of recipients with regard to conflicts. The study of 'local meanings' in texts (van Dijk 2001: 103–6), such as the lexicon and the structures of propositions, can reveal underlying subjective representations and the personal fragility of political leaders. Adopting a cognitive and critical discourse approach (see van Dijk 1995a, 2001, 2009; Lakoff and Johnson 2003 [1980]; Chilton 2004; Musolff 2016, 2018, for example), our goal is, on the one hand, to point out the manipulative and mind-controlling nature of such discourses. On the other hand, it is to uncover underlying meanings and purposes of figurative constructions within the speaker's strategies and attempts to convince the recipients. Thus, sections 3.2–3.4 examine the interplay between figurative language, sentence structures, lexical collocations and glorification ideology, which are combined not only to background the atrocities of the conflicts, but also to foreground the positive aspects of leaders and the negative ones of adversaries. Going further, section 3.5 proposes a brief socio-cognitive analysis to illustrate how figurative language is used as a foregrounding construction to perform both persuasion and mental manipulation functions in political discourses of conflict. Finally, section 3.6 demonstrates to what extent such discourses are characterised by purposive omissions of the crises' main causes and solutions from the text.

2 Context and theoretical framework

2.1 Corpus and context of the conflicts

The corpus is composed of fifteen speeches (35,283 words) delivered by presidents in contexts of armed conflict and socio-political turmoil in six French-speaking African countries: Burkina Faso, the Central African Republic (CAR), Chad, Ivory Coast, Mali and Niger – see corpus details following the references. These countries have in common the collision between different forms of conflicts, which include political instability, ethnic issues, rebellions, military coups and, since the 2010s, armed terrorist groups. Although each country has its socio-political specificities, states such as Burkina Faso, Mali and Niger have been facing violence and insecurity rooted in similar internal turmoil and in the same Islamist terrorism in the so-called Three Borders Area. External factors, among which are the war in Libya, the intervention by the North Atlantic Treaty Organization (NATO) (Igwe et al. 2017) and the fall of Muammar Gaddafi's regime in 2011, have also engulfed the region and accelerated the destabilisation of northern Mali by rebel groups and their alliance with terrorist groups in 2012. The crisis became multidimensional when President Amadou Toumani Touré was overthrown by a military coup in March 2012, which gave more opportunity to rebel and terrorist groups to seize the main northern cities. In January 2013, the French President, François Hollande, through Operation Serval, sent troops to stop the advance of insurgents aiming to take over the whole country. Yet terrorist attacks have occurred repeatedly in the region. For example, the corpus includes a speech given by Burkina Faso's president, Roch Marc Christian Kaboré, in reaction to a terrorist attack on the village of Solhan (in the north-east of the country) that killed more than 160 people in June 2021. Neighbouring Niger and Mali have also been facing similar terrorist attacks on soldiers and civilians. In addition, because of the state leaders' failure to tackle terrorism, among other reasons, waves of military coups have occurred in the region: in Mali in August 2020 and May 2021 (Jeune Afrique 2021) and in Burkina Faso in January and September 2022 (Kappès-Grangé and Roger 2022).

Similarly, although the crises in Ivory Coast, the CAR and Chad have their own defining characteristics, they have all been triggered or exacerbated by rebellions and attempts to take power by military force. In Ivory Coast, President Laurent Gbagbo gave his 2000 inaugural speech in the context of a controversial election in which President Henri Konan Bédié (who was overthrown in December 1999) and former Prime Minister Alassane Ouattara were not allowed to run for the presidency. During the process of vote counting, in which Laurent Gbagbo was leading over the military ruler, General Robert Gueï, the latter stopped the process and declared himself the winner of the election. Popular protests and soldiers loyal to Laurent Gbagbo forced General Gueï to leave power. In September 2002, rebels from the north attacked the country down into Abidjan, beginning a long-term violent conflict in the country (see Dozon 2011 and Notin 2013, among others). Likewise, the CAR has been facing a series of rebellions, among which François Bozizé's military coup against President Ange-Felix Patassé in March 2003. Ten years later, President Bozizé was overthrown by Seleka rebels, whose leader, Michel Djotodia, seized power but had to resign in January 2014 after months of manipulated religious and ethnic violence (IPIS 2018). In January 2021, former President Bozizé contested President Faustin Archange Touadera's re-election, and launched a rebellion under an alliance called 'Coalition of Patriots for Change – CPC' (Losh 2021; Olivier 2021). In neighbouring Chad, President Idriss Déby Itno, who took power in 1990 after a rebellion and a coup, faced many rebellions and uprisings. In August 2020, the National Assembly appointed him Field Marshal of Chad to honour his military offensive against terrorist group Boko Haram in the Lake Chad region. In April 2021, Idriss Déby was killed during a military operation against Libya-based rebels who called themselves the 'Front for Change and Concord in Chad – FACT'. His son, General Mahamat Idriss Déby, has since been appointed head of the Transitional Military Council to run the country (BBC News 2021). This brief socio-historical outline shows to what extent the conflicts in these countries are multidimensional and share many triggering and exacerbating features, all of which have given rise to new challenges and discourses within and outside of each country.

2.2 Theoretical framework

This chapter relies on both Critical Discourse Studies (CDS) and analyses in Cognitive Linguistics (Fairclough 1992; van Dijk 2001, 2009; Chilton and Schäffner 2002; Lakoff and Johnson 2003 [1980]; Chilton 2004; Musolff 2018, among others). Although van Dijk (2001: 97–8) mainly focuses on 'sociocognitive discourse analysis', he also advocates 'a broad, diverse, multidisciplinary and problem-oriented' Critical Discourse Analysis (CDA) which involves the theoretical triangle of discourse–cognition–society. The main principle is that in carrying out a critical discursive study, a direct connection has to be established between discourse realisations, cognitive representations and their relations to society. As cognitive studies have shown, our experiences in society are often represented metaphorically, 'by mapping well-understood source domains of experience onto more schematic ones' (Chilton 2004: 51–2). The aim is to better understand one concept in terms of another (Chilton and Lakoff 1995; Lakoff and Johnson 2003 [1980]). Metaphorical mappings are usually subconscious and are often used in politics for reasoning about 'target' domains which are ill understood, vague or controversial (Chilton 2004: 52). The fact that the 'source' domain is, in general, intuitively understood and has a holistic structure entails an easier understanding of its 'target' referent. Consequently, in order to comprehend certain abstract concepts more clearly, metaphors are useful for making sense of certain concepts through others which are more familiar to the reader or the hearer. Chilton and Lakoff (1995: 38–9) demonstrate how, in foreign policy, but also in politics in general, THE NATION IS A PERSON metaphor is frequently used to transfer the mode of reasoning about human beings to issues about nations. This metaphor and others are used to make one's message more accessible to the recipients; see examples (1), (2) and (11). Beyond the use of metaphor itself, the crucial effects are that these conceptualisations can form the basis for positive or negative (re)actions in society. If nations are considered as individuals, they are then construable as having personal identities and social relationships with other nations, which will be seen as friends, enemies, neighbours, strong, weak, and so on. Hence Musolff's remark that the use and elaboration of the NATION-AS-PERSON metaphor, or 'nation-personifications', are useful in political discourse 'to create an image of a unified social collective that is able to *speak with one voice* and *act* as a singular, independent *agent*' (2018: 261, original italics).

Another key theoretical concept in this study is metonymy, which is viewed in cognitive linguistics as a 'reference point' (or a 'source') which activates a 'target' meaning within the same cognitive (matrix) domain (Lakoff and Johnson 2003 [1980]; Panther and Thornburg 2004, among others). To put it simply, conceptual metonymy is the substitution of one entity for another, both belonging to the same matrix domain. In political discourse, metonymy can be utilised for various discursive functions and purposes, among which are positive or negative evaluations of the 'target' referent and foregrounding or backgrounding of one aspect of a concept – for the sake of objectivity, euphemism and vagueness; for a comprehensive account on these issues, see Littlemore (2015: 99–104). This is in line with the conclusions of Ruiz de Mendoza and Díez Velasco (2004) and Ruiz de Mendoza and Galera-Masegosa (2011). In their analyses, the mapping in metonymic conceptualisations involves 'domain expansion' when the 'source' is a sub-domain of the 'target' domain ('source-in-target' metonymy). Conversely, this entails 'domain reduction' when the 'target' is a sub-domain of the 'source' domain ('target-in-source' metonymy).

The last theoretical framework (employed in section 3.2) deals with the syntactic manipulations of 'thematic proto-roles' in discourses of conflict. The notion of 'theta-roles – thematic role (type)' is defined by Dowty (1991: 552) as 'a set of entailments of a group of predicates with respect to one of the arguments of each'. To put it differently: 'a thematic role type is a kind of second-order property, a property of multi-place predicates indexed by their argument positions.' Dowty (1991: 551, 571–5) deals with theta-roles in terms of PROTO-ROLES based on two cluster-concepts: Proto-Agent (P-Agent) and Proto-Patient (P-Patient)[1] – each characterised by a set of verbal entailments. For example, the subject arguments of these predicates (*x murders y* or *x nominates y*) share the entailments:

---

[1] Generally, in semantic studies, more familiar categories are used: *agent, goal, source, patient, experiencer* (cf. Dixon 2005).

that *x* does a volitional act, that *x* moreover intends this to be the kind of act named by the verb, that *x* causes some event to take place involving *y* (i.e. *y* dies or *y* acquires a nomination), and that *x* moves or changes externally (i.e. not just mentally).

(Dowty 1991: 552)

Considering Dowty's concept of 'entailment clusters', Chilton (2004: 53–4) explains that the notion of a 'set of entailments' is significant for social and political interactions where issues of volition, sentience and causation are salient. Going further, Chilton (2004: 53) argues that 'prototypical categories are embedded in human cognition as a result of interaction with the physical environment'. This means that discourse can be analysed as coherent chains of propositions which establish a 'discourse world' about 'the "reality" that is entertained by the speaker, or meta-represented by the speaker as being someone else's believed reality' (Chilton 2004: 54).

3 Corpus findings and discussion

3.1 Method and data sample

In order to identify metaphorical and metonymic conceptualisations in the corpus, we used, first, the software AntConc (Anthony 2020) to extract a word frequency list, from which potentially metonymical and metaphorical candidates were isolated. Second, we applied a 'word sketch' search, using Sketch Engine (Kilgarriff et al. 2014), to our list of potential figurative candidates, which enabled us to extend the list to other less frequent but potentially metaphorical words in the corpus, among which are *family*, *body parts* and *building* metaphors. Then, an AntConc concordance query was carried out to visualise the most frequent potential candidates in context. At this stage, each lexical unit in context was manually validated as metaphoric as a result of applying step 3c of Metaphor Identification Procedure (MIP): 'If the lexical unit has a more basic current–contemporary meaning in other contexts than the given context, decide whether the contextual meaning contrasts with the basic meaning but can be understood in comparison with it' (Pragglejaz Group 2007: 3).

As for metonymic mappings, we applied Biernacka's (2013: 117) adaptation of MIP during the manual validation process. The dot chart shown in Figure 7.1,[2] based on a dataset of a sample of lexical units, contrasts their metonymic and metaphoric uses in the corpus with their non-figurative

---

[2] To create the graph, we used the *dot chart* function in R, which is 'a free software environment for statistical computing and graphics'. R Core Team 2022, https://www.r-project.org/ [accessed November 2022]. The dot chart or plot is also called Cleveland's dot plot: https://uc-r.github.io/cleveland-dot-plots [accessed November 2022].

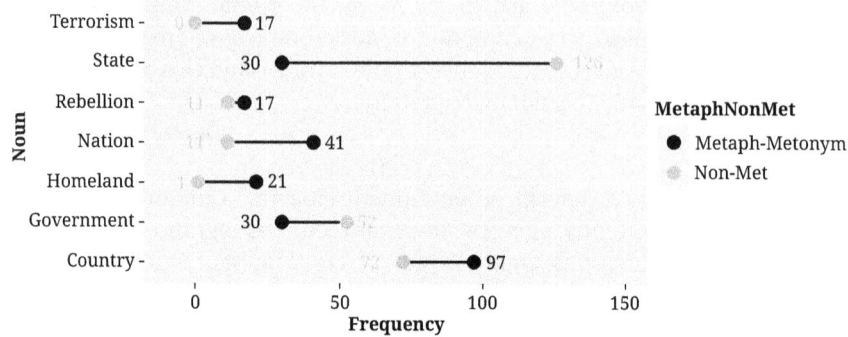

Figure 7.1 *(Non-)metaphoric and metonymic uses of some key concepts*

ones. The black dots indicate the number of metaphoric and metonymic uses of each concept, while the grey dots represent their non-metaphoric and non-metonymic occurrences. Among the seven nouns in the dataset, only two have more non-figurative uses than figurative ones, with their grey dot figures appearing at the end of the line on the right: *state* (30 versus 126 occurrences), and *government* (30 versus 52).

The analysis of the lexical units in context has enabled us to extend the list to other less frequent words in the corpus, but which are potentially metaphorical, such as FAMILY metaphors (*the Nation's brothers, sisters, daughters, sons, father*, among others) and the figurative use of BODY PARTS and the BUILDING scenario[3] as shown in the example below:

(1) The Homeland will remember their sacrifice. No will is too much in helping the State, the Country and the Nation to overcome the serious hardship of this moment. Each **hand is useful to rebuild brick by brick the common edifice** of which we were so proud and **which proved to be so fragile!** (President Dioncounda Traoré, Mali, 2012; author's translation)[4]

Firstly, in the corpus, metaphoric and metonymic mappings are often intertwined, as demonstrated in the example above which expresses the NATION-AS-BUILDING metaphor and the HAND FOR PERSON[5] (MEANS FOR AGENT)

---

[3] For the definition of this concept, see Musolff (2004: 17, 126–41) for a detailed analysis of ARCHITECTURE–HOUSE-BUILDING scenarios.
[4] 'La Patrie se souviendra de leur sacrifice. Aucune volonté n'est de trop pour amener l'Etat, le Pays et la Nation à surmonter les graves épreuves de l'heure. Chaque main est utile pour reconstruire brique après brique l'édifice commun dont nous étions si fiers et qui s'est révélé si fragile!'
[5] For a detailed analysis of 'hand' used in metonymical and metaphorical conceptualisations, see Billioti de Gage (2012).

Table 7.1 *Metaphoric and metonymic uses of* Homeland, State, Country *and* Nation

Concepts	Metaphoric and metonymic occurrences		Non-figurative occurrences		Total
State	30	19%	126	81%	156
Country	97	57%	72	43%	169
Nation	41	79%	11	21%	52
Homeland	21	95%	1	5%	22

metonymy. Secondly, the extract is particularly illustrative of the lexical co-occurrence, as well as the alternation of the following four concepts: Homeland (*Patrie*), State (*État*), Country (*Pays*) and Nation (*Nation*), as represented in the above dot chart. Of these terms, *country* and *state* are the most frequent ones in the corpus, but *nation* and *homeland* have the highest figurative conceptualisation rates, as illustrated in Table 7.1.

Although these terms are semantically different, in this study we generically use the NATION-AS-PERSON metaphor to refer to the figurative occurrences of *State, Country* and *Nation*.[6] The term Homeland (*Patrie*) occurs especially in certain types of political speeches. Therefore, in sections 3.3 and 3.4, specific analyses are carried out on its metaphoric conceptualisation in terms of HOMELAND-AS-PERSON, while the next section examines the interplay between thematic roles and the figurative constructions.

3.2 Figurative language and theta-roles in discourse

Based on Dowty's (1991) and Chilton's (2004) studies discussed in the theoretical framework (section 2.2), we can argue that the syntactic manipulation of thematic proto-roles is crucial in discourses of conflict, since the issues of responsibility, intention, martyrdom and victimhood – in the sense of military heroism and other forms of self-sacrifice – are central to the arguments. As Chilton (2004: 54) observes, the main discourse referents are 'who does what to whom, when and where', to which the speaker assigns different theta-roles regarding the relations they have and through the lexical and syntactic patterns he or she chooses. Furthermore, syntactic sentence structures can have ideological implications in discourse (van Dijk 1995b: 24): for example, the association of responsible agency with the grammatical subject. In this connection, our corpus analysis reveals a frequent interplay between figurative language and the theta-roles held by certain nouns in the discourse. P-Agent and P-Patient, through simple or complex nominals (such as *sons and daughters of the country*), are used metonymically or metaphorically in such a way that the hearer or

---

[6] For reasons of space, this chapter does not discuss the distinctive semantic features of each concept and its particular figurative use.

reader can perceive who acts how and towards what goals, as illustrated by example (2) below. When construed metonymically or metaphorically, entities like *country, government, rebellion* and *terrorism* are assigned a particular theta-role in the discourse (P-Agent or P-Patient). This makes the positive or negative properties of referents more salient through various syntactic[7] and lexical patterns:

(2) That is why, in order **to put back our country on its feet**, I shall **count on all the valiant sons and daughters of this country**. (General François Bozizé, CAR, 2003, proclaiming himself president; author's translation)[8]

In this extract from General Bozizé's self-proclamation in 2003 as head of state, he metaphorically refers to the P-Patient, 'our country', as a person or physical entity which needs *to be stood up*, and to do so the P-Agent is the 'sons and daughters of the country'. The utterances rely not only on the metaphor of THE NATION IS A MOTHER/FATHER but also on the presupposition that it has fallen down, which derives from 'in order to put the country on its feet'. This metaphoric conceptualisation also leads to others such as THE NATION/HOMELAND IS A HOUSE(HOLD), as shown in examples (1) and (2). Similarly, as illustrated in the examples below, there is a clear tendency in the corpus to use metonymic conceptualisations. For example, 57% of the occurrences of GOVERNMENT FOR PRESIDENT/MINISTERS (17/30) appear in P-Agent positions as the 'doers' of **positive** actions:

(3) **The Government of Mali will not tolerate** abuses and amalgams. Besides, **it has ordered an investigation** from which we will draw all the implications. (President Dioncounda Traoré, Mali, 2013; author's translation)[9]

(4) **The government pays particular attention** to the schooling of young girls, which is a fundamental condition for the emancipation of women. (President Mahamadou Issoufou, Niger, 2017; author's translation)[10]

---

[7] We observe that passive and cleft constructions are also used in the corpus to foreground or background entities, as shown in this extract: Dear friends, make no mistake, **it is Ivory Coast that is attacked! My country is attacked!** (our translation) / 'Chers amis, ne vous y trompez pas, **c'est la Côte d'Ivoire qui est attaquée! Mon pays est attaqué!**' (President Laurent Gbagbo, Ivory Coast, 2002). These constructions are examined in this study.
[8] 'C'est pourquoi, afin de **mettre debout notre pays**, je crois devoir **compter sur tous les vaillants fils et filles de ce pays**.'
[9] 'Le Gouvernement du Mali ne tolérera les exactions et les amalgames. Du reste **il a ordonné une enquête** dont nous tirerons toutes les implications.'
[10] 'Le gouvernement porte une attention particulière à la scolarisation des jeunes filles, condition essentielle à l'émancipation de la femme.'

In these examples, *government* has a metonymic reading in the sense that it stands as the 'source' domain (also called the 'vehicle') referring to the 'target' which is the country's authorities. The frequent topicalisation of this metonymic concept aims at activating the perception of the government in the recipients' minds as a personified agent who (re)acts positively – expressed by verbs such as *tolerate, order, pay (attention)* – as displayed in examples (3) and (4).

Another type of interplay between thematic proto-roles and metonymy is the negative depiction of opponents as P-Patient or Agent. For example, in the metonymic conceptualisation of TERRORISM FOR TERRORISTS, 76% of the occurrences (13/17) are in P-Patient position, and are negatively or adversely depicted. The four occurrences in the P-Agent role also appear in negative contexts. These are illustrated by the following utterance:

(5) **Terrorism has already caused tens of thousands of victims**, most of them Muslims. (President Mahamadou Issoufou, Niger, 2019; author's translation)[11]

In this example, Muslims, as P-Patient, are highlighted as the main victims of terrorists who pretend to fight for Islam. An analogous metonymic mapping is REBELLION FOR REBELS: nine of out 17 of its uses occur as the P-Patient who is *condemned* or is required to *disarm, accept discussion*, and so on. The other eight occurrences appear as the P-Agent with negative attitudes: *jeopardising peace, lacking willingness to negotiate*, among others. In addition to the interplay between agentive roles and metonymy, the next section examines another rhetorical strategy which associates metaphor with aggressive and emotive lexicon in discourses of conflict, for greater cognitive impact on recipients.

3.3 Metaphor and lexical collocations

In discourse studies, lexical choices have often been presented as a major strategy of ideological expression and persuasion (van Dijk 1995b, 2001). This section demonstrates that lexical items and metaphors are a key persuasion strategy in discourses of conflict too. As Lakoff and Johnson (2003) and Chilton and Lakoff (1995) argue, metaphors are one of our primary means for conceptualising the world, as in THE NATION IS A MOTHER/FATHER and THE NATION/HOMELAND IS A HOUSE(HOLD). The cognitive interpretation of this chain of generalisation and entailment in a discourse of conflict is that if you 'attack' or defend the nation or homeland, you are attacking or defending not only our common mother or father, but also our house(hold),

---

[11] '**Le terrorisme a fait déjà des dizaines de milliers de victimes**, pour la plupart des musulmans.'

encoded in examples (1), (2) and (6). To give more impact to this entailment, various lexical concepts are used by the speakers, including the notion of PATRIE (*homeland, motherland* and *fatherland*), which occurs 22 times in our corpus – 21 occurrences are figurative. Etymologically, the term *patrie* means 'fatherland' or 'land of ancestors or fathers'). It derives from the Latin adjective *patrius* (*paternal*, '*to/of the father*'), itself a derivative of the noun *pater* (*father*).[12] Although *patrie* originally means *fatherland*, grammatically it is a feminine word in French – probably because of its original feminine declension. Therefore, in political discourse in French, this word is sometimes associated with *mother* in the expression *la mère-patrie*, meaning *the motherland* or literally '*the mother-homeland*', as in the example below from President Kaboré's address to the Nation on the terrorist attack in Solhan, Burkina Faso (see section 2.1):

(6) In these difficult times when we are suffering these setbacks, our salvation must lie in the unity, cohesion and the strong commitment of the daughters and sons of our country to defend the **Motherland** or **Mother-Homeland**. (President Roch Marc Christian Kaboré, Burkina Faso, 2021; author's translation)[13]

The analysis of the term *patrie* (*homeland*) shows that, on the one hand, it frequently occurs in inaugural speeches and during ceremonies to pay tribute to soldiers or civilians killed by the enemy. On the other hand, it is generally associated with specific collocations to glorify the defence of the nation and keep people mobilised for the fight, as illustrated in examples (6) to (10) with the author's highlighting:

(7) I have decided to come in person to express the gratitude of the HOMELAND, **inconsolable** but not at all defeated, to these men **torn from the affection of their loved ones, in the prime of their lives**, for what they are for us: our **heroes**, our **martyrs**. (President Mahamadou Issoufou, Niger, 2019; author's translation)[14]

(8) Lieutenant-Colonel Hassane Anoutab, you and your 70 soldiers have **acted courageously**; that is why **your death is glorious**. **Death in the service** of one's HOMELAND with arms in hand is one of the best ends. Your families are **mourning** today, but **your children will always be proud to have had parents of your stature**. Yes,

---

[12] Larousse Latin–French dictionary (Chabrier et al. 2013).
[13] 'En ces moments difficiles où nous subissons ces revers, notre salut doit résider dans l'unité, la cohésion et l'engagement déterminé des filles et fils de notre pays à défendre la **Mère-Patrie**.'
[14] 'J'ai décidé de venir, en personne, pour témoigner la **reconnaissance** de la PATRIE, **inconsolable** mais nullement vaincue, à ces hommes **arrachés à l'affection des leurs, à la fleur de l'âge**, pour ce qu'ils sont pour nous: nos **héros**, nos **martyrs**.'

Figurative language in the political discourse of conflict 157

>   your children will always be proud of you, because **you have left them courage as a legacy. The entire Nation is proud of you.**
>   (President Mahamadou Issoufou, Niger, 2019; author's translation)[15]

Notice that the commonly used metaphors of THE HOMELAND IS A MOTHER/ FATHER/OUR HOUSEHOLD is tightly related to strong emotional lexicons such as *glorious death, mourning, proud of dead soldiers, courage, legacy*, whose purpose is national glorification and mobilisation.

3.4 The ideology of glorification concealing the reality of the conflict

Van Dijk (2006: 738) defines national self-glorification as 'positive references to or praise for one's own country, its principles, history, and traditions'. The type of glorification we refer to here is the glorification of death and self-sacrifice for the nation. As Naqvi (2007: 89) demonstrates, 'a cult of heroism seeks to de-individualize death and in this way make possible death's glorification and transfiguration for the benefit of some greater collective such as the fatherland or the nation', and examples (6) to (10) illustrate this discursive construal:

(9) Since it is its very existence as a Nation, as a State, as a territory that is at stake. That is why I would like to spare a thought for **our soldiers who died at the front**, savagely murdered ... **The HOMELAND will remember their sacrifice.** (President Dioncounda Traoré, Mali, 2012; author's translation)[16]

(10) I need to have a **proud and emotional thought** for ... and so many other brave sons of Chad who **gave their lives to the HOMELAND** ... I also think of those martyrs who fell on the battlefields of Tiné, Bahai, Wadi Doum, Hadjar Marfaine, Ndjamena, Bohoma, and so on, **to defend the HOMELAND** and to protect the Chadian people. (President Idriss Déby Itno, Chad, 2020; author's translation)[17]

---

[15] 'Lieutenant-colonel Hassane Anoutab, tes 70 soldats et toi, avez fait **acte de courage**; c'est en cela que **votre mort est glorieuse**. La **mort** au **service** de sa **PATRIE** les armes à la main est **une des meilleures fins**. Vos familles sont aujourd'hui en pleurs mais **vos enfants seront toujours fiers d'être issus de parents de votre trempe**. Oui, vos enfants seront toujours fiers de vous car **vous leur laissez le courage en héritage. La Nation entière est fière de vous.**'
[16] 'Puisque c'est son existence même en tant que Nation, en tant qu'Etat, en tant que territoire qui est en jeu. C'est pourquoi je voudrais avoir une pensée émue à l'égard de **nos soldats morts au front, sauvagement assassinés**... La **PATRIE** se souviendra de leur **sacrifice**.'
[17] 'Je ne peux m'empêcher d'avoir **une pensée fière et émue**, à ... et tant d'autres **valeureux fils du Tchad qui ont donné leur vie à la PATRIE**... Je pense également à ces **martyrs tombés sur les champs de bataille** de Tiné, Bahai, Wadi Doum, Hadjar Marfaine, Ndjamena, Bohoma, etc., **pour défendre la PATRIE et pour protéger les Tchadiennes et les Tchadiens.**'

When referring to THE HOMELAND AS A PERSON in discourses of conflict, the following collocations are used: ***defence*** *of the homeland and territorial integrity;* ***love*** *and* ***dignity*** *of the homeland;* *the field of* ***honour***; *glorious* ***death***; *paid with their* ***lives***; *ultimate* ***sacrifice***; ***courage, determination, honour, dignity*** *and* ***gratitude*** *of the soldiers,* to name but a few. Although the explicit aim of these collocations is to glorify and highlight the defence and sacrifice for the nation, their implicit and manipulative goal is to background the true fate of the people who are killed or injured in the conflicts and the real impact on their families and beyond. To put it more bluntly, discourses of conflict can rely on figurative language and ideology to hide the actual causes and atrocities of the crisis, and to background the authorities' failure or weakness to settle the conflict. In this regard, the appealing conceptualisations of THE NATION/HOMELAND IS A MOTHER/ FATHER/OUR HOUSEHOLD are not only a way to keep the military and the population mobilised, but also a powerful strategy to hide the crucial and often gruesome reality of the conflicts. If the ideology of glorification can be viewed as an important way for state leaders to hold the country together in order to fight against the 'enemy', it is inevitably a powerful strategy to conceal the crucial causes and wide-ranging consequences of violence. In conjunction with this, the next section proposes a concise socio-cognitive analysis. This will help to explain how figurative language is used manipulatively to foreground opponents' negative aspects and highlight one's own positive attitudes in order to shape recipients' opinions and (re)actions in the conflict.

3.5 A socio-cognitive analysis of metaphor and metonymy in a discourse of conflict

When the rebellion began in Ivory Coast in 2002, in his plea to call the country's armed forces and the population for a general mobilisation, President Laurent Gbagbo used strong war rhetoric through figurative language as follows:

(11) Against all our good will, they declare war. **Against our good faith, they declare war.** Well, let me tell you this today: **whoever comes to me with an olive branch in his hand, I will give him a kiss and embrace him. But whoever comes with a sword, I will take out a sword and we will fight.** (President Laurent Gbagbo, Ivory Coast, 2002; author's translation)[18]

---

[18] 'Malgré toute notre bonne volonté, on engage la guerre. **Contre notre bonne foi, on engage la guerre.** Eh bien, je vous le dis aujourd'hui: **quiconque vient vers moi avec un rameau d'oliviers à la main, je lui donnerai un baiser et je l'embrasserai. Mais quiconque vient avec une épée, je sortirai une épée et nous nous battrons.**'

In this extract, President Gbagbo relies on the combination of different types of repetitions:

- Anaphora: illustrated by the repetition of *'whoever comes'* at the beginning of the last two sentences of extract (11).
- Epistrophe: through the double occurrence of *'they declare war'* at the end of the first two sentences of the extract.
- Parallelism combined with antithesis, which enables the speaker to oppose *an olive* branch versus *a sword* paired with *to kiss* or *embrace* versus *to fight*.

He also uses word and clause orders such as left dislocation (*Against all our good will, they declare war. Against our good faith, they declare war*) and pronominal relations and oppositions *I* versus *whoever* and *they*. More importantly, the speaker mainly uses extended metaphor (allegory) and, to a lesser extent, metonymy. As Gibbs (2020: 13) explains, the literary term 'allegory' derives from the Latin word 'allegoria' indicating 'veiled language'. It refers 'to discourse that conveys meaning which is hidden or beneath the overt understanding of the words presented'. As a literary device, allegories are usually construed through symbolic figures, actions or imagery to express moral, spiritual or political messages. In general, 'allegorical messages are expressed through extended metaphors in which an entire narrative introduces and elaborates upon a metaphorical source domain' (Gibbs 2020: 13). The analysis below shows how President Gbagbo used these devices to convince the recipients.

3.5.1 Metaphor and its cognitive effects
Using the OLIVE BRANCH and the SWORD metaphors, President Gbagbo symmetrically aligns them with the act of *kissing* and *embracing*, and *fighting*. The aim of this discursive construction is to emphasise the speaker's own positive attitude and state of mind versus the rebels' negative aspect and aggressiveness. The underlying cognitive aim of these conceptualisations (with various underlying concepts, such as *peaceful man, reconciliation, aggression, courage, self-defence*) is to activate multiple cognitive representation models in the recipient's mind. On the one hand, the constructions insist on the peaceful and conciliatory attitudes of the leader and at the same time on his fearlessness. On the other hand, they point out the aggressive and violent attitudes of the adversary who is presented as a person brandishing a sword. The cognitive activation of the 'attacking frame' suggests that it is then legitimate to defend oneself and fight that kind of person. We can summarise the schematic mapping of the two symmetrical metaphors and their cognitive entailments as follows:

- an *olive branch* equals *peace* and *reconciliation*, so the person deserves in return *kissing* and *embracing* – implying peace not war;

- a *sword* equals *aggression, violence*, so the violent person *has to be fought against with a sword* too, which evokes *courage* and *legitimacy*.

Here, the connection between 'discourse', 'cognition' and 'society' (see van Dijk 1995a, 2001, 2009) is carried out through mental representations of the allegorical construction. The *olive branch* and *sword* metaphors facilitate the realisation of abstract concepts such as *aggression, violence, rebellion, peace, reconciliation* and *courage*. To put it differently, through metaphor and allegory the speaker makes abstract concepts more tangible, which cognitively help the recipients to construe their own mental representations and map them on the discourse situation involving people, attitudes, events, locations, causes and so on. Furthermore, the allegory has the advantage of activating an ancient Christian symbolism of the *olive leaf* or *branch* from the Genesis flood narrative of Noah's Ark.[19]

3.5.2 Metonymy and its cognitive effects

In the extract, in addition to the use of metaphor and allegory President Gbagbo also has recourse to metonymy to create another polarisation when he declares: '*Against our good faith, they declare war.*' The notion of 'good faith' is metonymically expressed, even personified, as something on which one can wage war – FAITH FOR PERSON metonymy. A non-metonymic and non-dislocated form of the utterance could be: 'They wage war on us despite our good faith.' The difference between the metonymic left dislocation form and this non-metonymic sentence is that they do not encode the same discursive and cognitive impacts. Saying that 'someone waged war on you' has a lesser cognitive effect than saying 'they waged war on your good faith'. The former activates only the *aggression* frame, while the latter highlights both the *good faith* and *aggression* frames, with a particular foregrounding of the *good faith* frame. The aim of such metonymy in an antagonistic context is to create a polarisation between 'a peaceful and good faith person' and 'an aggressive person'. The cognitive representation which the speaker seeks to impose on the recipients is that 'although he and his people are peaceful and sincere, rebels are not sparing them'. Syntactically, the left dislocation of the P-Patient (*our good faith*) emphasises it more, implying that rebels are of 'bad faith' in acting this way. To go further, the last section raises the issue of the real causes of the conflicts and examines to what extent responsibilities are actually mentioned in the discourses.

---

[19] This reference appears in Genesis: 'He waited seven more days and again sent out the dove from the ark. When the dove returned to him in the evening, there in its beak was a freshly plucked olive leaf! Then Noah knew that the water had receded from the earth.' Genesis 8: 10. *Holy Bible*. New International Version, https://www.christianity.com/bible/niv/genesis/8 [accessed 31 March 2023].

3.6 Absences from the discourse concealing the leaders' fragilities

In the corpus, the real causes of the multidimensional conflicts in these countries are rarely, if ever, mentioned in state leaders' speeches. The six countries have either rebellions or military coups, which have common causes, such as: *corruption, despotism, nepotism, prejudice against some populations, the polarisation of ethnic issues* and *poverty*. Those are just some of the countries' fragilities triggering conflicts; yet they are scarcely expressed in state leaders' speeches, probably because they seek to conceal their own responsibilities and accountability. Likewise, regarding possible solutions, the discourses are organised in such a way that true solutions are not foregrounded, since they may curtail the leaders' own privileges. For example, the term *corruption* occurs only seven times in a corpus of 35,283 words (with 15 speeches) – in other words, a ratio of 19.8 per 100,000 words, on the basis that acts of corruption[20] are among the frequent power abuses in these countries. Interestingly, when *corruption* is mentioned in the corpus, it is only in inaugural or international meeting opening speeches. This includes one in President Dioncounda Traoré's inaugural speech, three in President Touadera's (where the term *embezzlement* [*détournement*] is also used twice), one in President Déby's Field Marshal ceremony and two in Mahamadou Issoufou's speech at the 60th Session on Human and People's Rights. Another unfair use of power in these countries is *nepotism*, which is used once in Mahamadou Issoufou's speech in conjunction with *corruption* as issues to be tackled in Africa:

(12) It is this dimension of the moral authority of the State that led us to sign the declaration of the 'Mountain of the Table' ensuring total freedom of the press. That is what leads us to promote a relentless fight against **corruption**; to support efforts to build a modern State, that is to say an impartial state which is above **nepotism** and things such communitarianism. (President Mahamadou Issoufou, Niger, 2017; author's translation)[21]

The term *poverty* occurs twice, while *despotism* is not used at all in any of the speeches. Ironically, the discourses are construed in such a way that the discursive backgrounding or concealment of the main causes and real

---

[20] For example, in the 2021 worldwide Corruption Perceptions Index (CPI), of 180 ranked countries and territories, the CPI of the six countries in question is as follows: Burkina Faso 78th, Ivory Coast 105th, Niger 124th, Mali 136th, CAR 154th and Chad 164th (Transparency International 2021).
[21] 'C'est cette dimension de l'autorité morale de l'Etat qui nous a amené à signer la déclaration de la 'Montagne de la Table' assurant une totale liberté de la presse. C'est elle qui nous conduit à promouvoir une lutte implacable contre la **corruption**; à soutenir les efforts de construction d'un Etat moderne, c'est-à-dire impartial donc au-dessus du **népotisme** et autre communautarisme.'

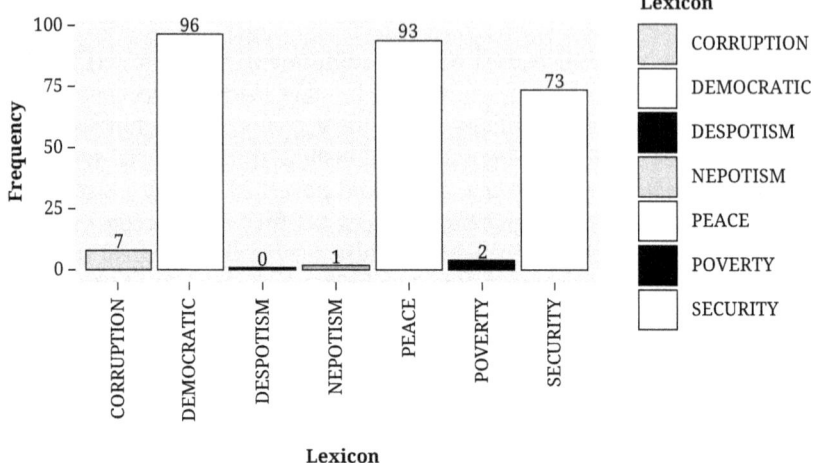

Figure 7.2 *Bar plot of lexical foregrounding and backgrounding in the corpus*

solutions of the conflicts are counterbalanced by the frequent use of other appealing terms. These include *democracy, democratic, democratically* and *democratisation*, which occur 96 times in the corpus. Similarly, *peace* is used 93 times (including three occurrences about *rest in peace*), while *security* occurs 73 times – nine of which refer to the United Nations Security Council. The bar graph shown in Figure 7.2 (R Core Team 2022), from our second dataset, provides an enhanced visualisation of the huge discrepancy between the real causes of the crises and the leaders' discursive foregrounding of some consensual values and norms. On the one hand, this chart reflects the foregrounding of words in the discourse which favour state authorities, and on the other hand, it shows how they background aspects that may reveal their own accountability or fragility.

4 Conclusion

This corpus-based study has investigated recurrent foregrounding and backgrounding strategies combined with figurative language to achieve specific goals in discourses of conflict. It has shown that there is a significant interplay between figurative language (metaphor and metonymy in particular) and some collocations aligned with the speakers' propensity to assign specific thematic roles to certain concepts. Thus, the discursive organisation of theta-roles and the agentive foregrounding or backgrounding enable the political leaders in conflict to insist on their own positive attitudes and their adversaries' negative standpoints. The study also pinpoints the crucial role played by the combination of metonymy, metaphor, allegory and repetition with the ideology of glorification and the lexicon and syntax when the speaker seeks to impose his perspective on the audience or hide certain realities of the conflict. In this regard, the critical socio-cognitive approach and analyses in cognitive linguistics enhance the understanding of the underlying cognitive meanings and purposes of these discursive constructions. More specifically, among the focalisation strategies, the speakers use rhetorical repetitions (including anaphora, epistrophe and parallelism) with allegory and syntactic dislocation, as foregrounding and backgrounding devices, to convince or even manipulate the recipients, as demonstrated in subsections 3.5.1 and 3.5.2. In this regard, the deliberate absences from the discourses aim at hiding the leaders' political fragilities and responsibilities in conflicts. Further studies are needed for a more comprehensive understanding of this issue. Similarly, we need to carry out a specific study to know how these kinds of discourses of conflict cognitively affect audiences, either in generating support or provoking forms of counter-discourse. Such a study can also examine how the recipients react to the narrative and perspective that the speaker seeks to impose on them. The counter-discourses, the media coverage and the socio-political (re)actions which were subsequent to the leaders' speeches in the six countries can be relevant data for analysis in order to measure the cognitive effects of the discourses.

References

Anthony, L. (2020). 'AntConc' (Version 3.5.9) [Computer Software]. Waseda University, Tokyo.
BBC News (2021). Chad's President Idriss Déby dies after clashes with rebels. *BBC News*, 20 April 2021. Available from: https://www.bbc.com/news/world-africa-56815708 [accessed November 2022].
Biernacka, E. (2013). The role of metonymy in political discourse. PhD thesis. The Open University, Milton Keynes.
Billioti de Gage, C. (2012). Hands and manipulations in the grammar and cognitive systems of English. Linguistics. PhD thesis, Université Michel de Montaigne, Bordeaux. https://theses.hal.science/tel-00734308/document [accessed 28 March 2023].
Chabrier, M., Assaf, B. and Prissette A., eds. (2013). *Dictionnaire Latin–Français / Français–Latin*. [Dictionary] Paris: Larousse.
Chilton, P. (2004). *Analysing Political Discourse: Theory and Practice*. London: Routledge.
Chilton, P. and Lakoff, G. (1995). 'Foreign policy by metaphor.' In Schäffner, C. and Wenden, A. L., eds, *Language and Peace*. Amsterdam: Harwood Academic Publishers, pp. 37–59.
Chilton, P. and Schäffner, C. (2002). *Politics as Text and Talk: Analytic Approaches to Political Discourse*. Amsterdam: John Benjamins.
Dixon, R. M. (2005). *A Semantic Approach to English Grammar*. Oxford: Oxford University Press.
Dowty, D. (1991). Thematic proto-roles and agreement selection. *Language*, 67 (3), pp. 547–619.

Dozon, J. P. (2011). *Les Clefs de la Crise Ivoirienne*. Paris: KARTHALA.
Fairclough, N. (1992). *Discourse and Social Change*. Cambridge: Polity.
Gibbs, R. W. (2020) Allegory in Literature and Life. In: Čubrović, B., ed., *BELLS90 Proceedings: International Conference to Mark the 90th Anniversary of the English Department*. Vol. 1, pp. 13–31. Belgrade: University of Belgrade. doi: 10.18485/bells90.2020.1.ch1.
Igwe, S. C., Abdullah, M. A., Kirmanj, S., Fage, K. S. and Bello, I. (2017). An assessment of the motivations for the 2011 NATO intervention in Libya and its implications for Africa. *Canadian Social Science*, 13 (4), pp. 1–12. doi: 10.3968/9470.
IPIS (2018). Central African Republic: A conflict mapping. *The International Peace Information Service (IPIS)*, Antwerp: International Peace Information Service (IPIS).
Jeune Afrique (2021). Mali: Assimi Goïta démet le président Bah N'Daw et le Premier ministre Moctar Ouane. *Jeune Afrique*, 25 May. Available from: https://www.jeuneafrique.com/1177652/politique/mali-assimi-goita-demet-le-president-bah-ndaw-et-le-premier-ministre-moctar-ouane/ [accessed 26 June 2023].
Kappès-Grangé, A. and Roger, B. (2022). Burkina: Paul-Henri Sandaogo Damiba contraint à la démission. *Jeune Afrique*, 2 October. Available from: https://www.jeuneafrique.com/1381713/politique/burkina-paul-henri-sandaogo-damiba-contraint-a-la-demission/ [accessed 26 June 2023].
Kilgarriff, A., Baisa, V., Bušta, J., Jakubíček, M., Kovář, V., Michelfeit, J., Rychlý, P. and Suchomel, V. (2014). The Sketch Engine: Ten years on. *Lexicography*, 1, pp. 7–36. doi: 10.1007/s40607-014-0009-9.
Lakoff, G. and Johnson, M. (2003) [1980]. *Metaphors We Live by*. Chicago: University of Chicago Press.
Littlemore, J. (2015). *Metonymy: Hidden Shortcuts in Language, Thought and Communication*. Cambridge: Cambridge University Press.
Losh, J. (2021). Central African Republic: A disputed election and a strange rebel alliance. *BBC News*, 7 January 2021. Available from: https://www.bbc.com/news/world-africa-55558642 [accessed 26 June 2023].
Musolff, A. (2004). *Metaphor and Political Discourse. Analogical Reasoning in Debates about Europe*. Basingstoke: Palgrave Macmillan.
Musolff, A. (2016). Metaphor and persuasion in politics. In: Semino, E. and Demjén, Z., eds, *The Routledge Handbook of Metaphor and Language*. London: Routledge, pp. 309–22.
Musolff, A. (2018). Nations as persons: Collective identities in conflict. In: Bös, B., Kleinke, S., Mollin, S. and Hernández, N., eds, *The Discursive Construction of Identities On- and Offline: Personal - Group – Collective*. Amsterdam: John Benjamins, pp. 249–66.
Naqvi, F. (2007). *The Literary and Cultural Rhetoric of Victimhood: Western Europe, 1970–2005*. New York: Palgrave Macmillan.
Notin, J. C. (2013). *Le Crocodile et le Scorpion: La France et la Côte d'Ivoire (1999–2013)*. Monaco: Editions du Rocher.
Olivier, M. (2021). Centrafrique: François Bozizé, jusqu'à la dernière balle? *Jeune Afrique*, 23 April. Available from: https://www.jeuneafrique.com/1157004/politique/centrafrique-francois-bozize-jusqua-la-derniere-balle/ [accessed 26 June 2023].
Panther, K-U. and Thornburg, L. L. (2004). The role of conceptual metonymy in meaning construction. *Metaphorik.de*, 6, pp. 91–116.
Pragglejaz Group (2007). MIP: A method for identifying metaphorically used words in discourse. *Metaphor and Symbol*, 22 (1), pp.1–39. doi: 10.1080/10926480709336752.

R Core Team (2022). *R: A language and environment for statistical computing.* Vienna: R Foundation for Statistical Computing. Available from: https://www.R-project.org [accessed 26 June 2023].

Ruiz de Mendoza, F. J. and Díez Velasco, O. (2004). Metonymic types and anaphoric reference. In: Radden, G. and Panther, K. U., eds, *Studies in Linguistic Motivation.* Berlin and New York: Mouton de Gruyter, pp. 293–320.

Ruiz de Mendoza, F. J. and Galera-Masegosa, A. (2011). Going beyond metaphtonymy: Metaphoric and metonymic complexes in phrasal verb interpretation. *Language Value,* 3 (1) pp. 1–29. doi: 10.6035/LanguageV.2011.3.2.

Sketch Engine (2022). Available from: http://www.sketchengine.eu [accessed 26 June 2023].

Transparency International (2021). *Corruption Perceptions Index 2021.* Transparency International. Available from: https://www.transparency.org/en/cpi/2021 [accessed 26 June 2023].

van Dijk, T. A. (1995a). On macrostructures, mental models, and other inventions: A brief personal history of the Kintsch-van Dijk theory. In: Weaver, C. A., Mannes, S. and Fletcher, C. R., eds, *Discourse Comprehension: Essays in Honor of Walter Kintsch.* Hillsdale, NJ: Lawrence Erlbaum, pp. 383–410.

van Dijk, T. A. (1995b). Discourse analysis as ideology analysis. In: Schäffner, C. and Wenden, A. L., eds, *Language and Peace.* Amsterdam: Harwood Academic, pp. 17–33.

van Dijk, T. A. (2001). Multidisciplinary CDA: A plea for diversity. In: Wodak, R. and Meyer, M., eds, *Methods of Critical Discourse Analysis.* London: Sage, pp. 95–120.

van Dijk, T. A. (2006). Politics, ideology, and discourse. In: Brown, K., ed., *The Encyclopedia of Language and Linguistics.* Vol. 9. Oxford and New York: Pergamon Press, pp. 728–40.

van Dijk, T. A. (2009). Critical Discourse Studies: a sociocognitive approach. In: Wodak, R. and Meyer, M., eds, *Methods of Critical Discourse Analysis.* 2nd edn. London: Sage, pp. 62–86.

Corpus

Burkina Faso

Kaboré, R. M. C. (2015). Inauguration, 29 December. 2,464 words.
Kaboré, R. M. C. (2021). Address to the Nation (terrorist attack in Solhan), 27 June. 833 words.

Central African Republic

General Bozizé, F. (2003). Address to the Nation (taking power in a coup), 16 March. 644 words.
Touadera, F. A. (2021). Re-election speech, 18 January. 2,192 words.
Touadera, F. A. (2021). Inauguration, 30 March. 4,911 words.

Chad

Marshal Déby, I. I. (2020). Field Marshal ceremony, 11 August. 2,339 words.
General Déby, M. I. (2021). Address to the Nation (rebellion and killing of President Idriss Déby Itno), 27 April. 1,564 words.

Ivory Coast

Gbagbo, L. (2000). Inauguration, 26 October. 1,794 words.
Gbagbo, L. (2002). Address to the Nation (rebel attacks), 20 September. 1,824 words.
Gbagbo, L. (2006). ECOWAS Summit in Abuja, Nigeria, 6 October. 9,256 words.

Mali

Touré, A. T. (2012). Address to the Nation (rebel and terrorist attacks in the North), 1 February. 640 words.
Traoré, D. (2012). Inauguration as interim president, 12 April. 1,334 words.
Traoré, D. (2013). African Union summit in Addis Ababa, Ethiopia, 28 January. 2,419 words.

Niger

Issoufou, M. (2017). 60th session of African Commission on Human and Peoples' Rights, Niamey, Niger, 8 May. 2,159 words.
Issoufou, M. (2019). Address to the Nation (Inatès terrorist attack), 13 December. 910 words.

CHAPTER 8

The CARD metaphor 'play the X card' as a social practice and its pragmatic functions

Yuuki Tomoshige

1 Introduction

This chapter aims to show that the CARD metaphor 'play the X card' is a social practice where X prototypically refers to a social member or identity in the metaphorical domain SOCIETY AS A PLAYGROUND. This study aims to answer the issue of why one's identity is prototypically inserted in the slot X and how the metaphor is used in society via the Corpus of Contemporary American English (COCA).[1] The study is based on metaphor analysis in cognitive linguistics (see, for example, Lakoff and Johnson 1980) and a corpus-based approach (Stefanowitsch and Gries 2007). The research questions are: (1) What kinds of nouns or adjectives are embedded in the slot of 'play the X card' in contemporary American English? (2) What are the functions related to a legitimatisation strategy of the CARD metaphor? The methods of analysis are as follows: (1) identifying nouns and adjectives in the slot via the COCA to find prototypes of this metaphor; (2) categorising them into a particular group based on the social structure retrieved from MetaNet Metaphor Wiki (MMW);[2] (3) analysing a specific context to identify how and why the CARD metaphor is used.

Our assertion is that the CARD metaphor has a function of legitimising people's arguments and actions. This characterisation is not limited to political actors. Depending on the social structure, social actors set out to legitimise

---

[1] According to the COCA, 'the corpus contains more than one billion words of text (over 25 million words each year between 1990 and 2019) from eight genres: spoken, fiction, popular magazines, newspapers, academic texts, and (with the update in March 2020): TV and Movie subtitles, blogs, and other web pages' (COCA). This database is useful for observing the frequency of words, phrases, expressions and collocations.

[2] According to MMW (n.d.), this database has 'a system that makes use of a repository of formalized frames and metaphors to automatically detect, categorize, and analyze expressions of metaphor in large-scale text corpora'. In order to identify the link between metaphors, frames, and society, this database has been used.

their arguments in times of crisis, either in the political domain or in other areas of society. This study seeks to reveal how CARD metaphor players typically use their literal social status or identify as social practice to achieve their purpose. The metaphor can also function as an illocutionary act, such as blaming and persuading, which is linked to metonymy in CAUSE FOR EFFECT (Herrero-Ruiz 2018). In what follows, section 2 discusses the general meanings of 'play the X card'; section 3 covers a literature review; section 4 focuses on the data; and in section 5, we will observe concrete examples of the metaphor based on social structure. We will present the conditions and the generalisation of the CARD metaphor in the final section.

2 The basic meaning of 'play the X card' in the OED and the MW

The following definitions show the features of the CARD metaphor as defined in the *Oxford English Dictionary*[3] (OED) and the *Merriam Webster*[4] (MW) dictionary. They present certain historical perceptions underlying the schema 'play the X card':

- sure card (*Oxford English Dictionary*)
  (Compounds 2)[5] An expedient certain to attain its object; a person whose agency, or the use of whose name, will ensure success. Similarly with other adjectives, as good, safe, likely, doubtful, etc., (*Oxford English Dictionary*)
- to play the Orange card (*Oxford English Dictionary*)
  (Phrases 4. c.)[6]. To appeal to Northern Irish Protestant sentiment for political advantage. (*Oxford English Dictionary*)
  1886[7] R. Churchill *Let.* 16 Feb. in R. R. James *Ld. Randolph Churchill* (1959) viii. 233: I decided some time ago that if the G.O.M. went for Home Rule, the Orange card would be the one to play. (*Oxford English Dictionary*)
- (Phrase 4. c.) to play (also use) the —— card (*Oxford English Dictionary*)

---

[3] OED online retrieved from: https://www.oed.com [accessed 26 June 2023].
[4] *Merriam-Webster* online retrieved from https://www.merriam-webster.com [accessed 26 June 2023].
[5] The section entitled 'Compounds' consists of two parts: C1 and C2. Retrieved from: https://www.oed.com.kwansei.remotexs.co/view/Entry/194868?redirectedFrom=sure+card#eid1328814090 [accessed 20 February 2023].
[6] When we input the noun 'card' in the search box, there are five entries: card, n1, cardn2, cardn3, cardv1, cardv2. Since the first entry does not include examples of card metaphors, we view the second entry, in which we can find the section PHRASES. This section has 8 entries from P1 to P8. In Phrases 4, there are subsections: a, b, and c. Retrieved from: https://www.oed.com.kwansei.remotexs.co/view/Entry/27830?rskey=bc0D5y&result=2&isAdvanced=false#eid [accessed 20 February 2023].
[7] 1886 refers to the year when the example was used.

The CARD metaphor as social practice and pragmatic function 169

to play (also use) the —— card and variants: (originally) to introduce a specified issue or topic in the hope of gaining sympathy or political advantage, by appealing to the sentiments or prejudices of one's audience; (in later use also) to exploit one's membership of a specified minority or marginalized group as a means of gaining sympathy or an unfair advantage (depreciative, and chiefly used in accusations of others). Frequently as to play the race card.

1885[8] *Times* 22 May 10/1 It is said that the change of intention on the part of the Cabinet is due to pressure brought to bear upon them by their Liberal friends in Ulster, who wish to play the land purchase card at the elections.

According to the *OED*, the adjective 'sure' was originally filled in the slot; the expression dates back to the sixteenth century. Other adjectives such as 'good', 'safe', 'likely' and 'doubtful' were also brought into play. It is noteworthy that none of the adjectives described here are found in the COCA. It may be considered that this absence is the result of the changing nature of language due to the socio-economic conditions wherein different adjectives are used in contemporary English.

In accordance with a section[9] entitled 'Playing the — Race card? Woman card? The history of political card-playing' in the *MW*, some modifiers are directly taken from card games such as bridge. The 'trump card' refers to a card used in the game if we interpret it literally; the phrase figuratively signifies giving someone an advantage. In 1886, Randolph Churchill, an English journalist, writer, soldier and politician, initially devised the idiomatic expression 'play the Orange card', whose meaning is 'to appeal to Northern Irish Ulster Unionists in order to gain political advantage' (*MW*).[10] Against this backdrop, politicians and critics came to broaden the metaphorical phrasing applied to 'political advantage' (*OED*). In addition, the fact that the 'race card' and 'gender' are relatively present-day expressions is of particular interest. According to the *MW*, it was only in 1974 that the phrase 'play the race card' came into use and the 'gender card' followed sixteen years later, in the 1990s. The *MW*[11] also states that the gender card is 'the act of using one's status as a woman to achieve a desired end (such as a campaign victory)'. Overall, the *OED*[12] states that the schema 'play the X card' originally meant 'to introduce a specified issue or topic in the hope of

---

[8] 1885 refers to the year when the example was used.
[9] Retrieved from: https://www.merriam-webster.com/words-at-play/playing-the-card [accessed 20 February 2023].
[10] Retrieved from: https://www.merriam-webster.com/words-at-play/playing-the-card [accessed 20 February 2023].
[11] Retrieved from: https://www.merriam-webster.com/words-at-play/playing-the-card [accessed 20 February 2023].
[12] Retrieved from: https://www.oed.com.kwansei.remotexs.co/view/Entry/27830?rskey=EL4R3d&result=2&isAdvanced=false#eid [accessed 20 February 2023].

gaining sympathy or political advantage'. In the following section, we will explore how this original meaning extends to other fields, reviewing the current theories on the CARD metaphor.

3 Literature review

In cognitive linguistics, Lakoff and Johnson (1980) are the pioneers in developing a theory of metaphor from a cognitive perspective. In the extensive literature based on their studies there has been a growing body of research on metaphor in cognitive linguistics (Charteris-Black 2004; Gibbs 2017; Kövecses 2019). Lakoff and Johnson (1980: 3) present and establish a detailed portrait of the 'conceptual metaphor theory' (CMT), arguing that 'metaphor is pervasive in everyday life, not just in language but in thought and action'. In their theory, if we have an abstract concept A (target), it is common to use the 'A is B' format to grasp the concept A (target) in terms of B (source), and this is proposed as the conceptual mapping between A and B (Lakoff 1993: 206–7). This study also applies their theory and the image schema in considering the relationship between the CARD metaphor and society. The image schema has to do with spatial orientations, such as up–down, in–out, front–back, on–off, deep–shallow, and central–peripheral (Lakoff and Johnson 1980). In this study, society is regarded as a container with these spatial orientations, and we suggest that there is a metaphor entitled SOCIETY IS A PLAYGROUND, where people can play their identity cards like business cards or card games. In addition, studies have yielded important insights into a link between the CARD metaphor and society regarding its metaphoricity (Howe 1988; Ching 1993; Semino and Demjén 2017; Harp 2019).

Drawing on the CMT approach, Ching (1993) investigates how metaphors of games and play pervade American cultural discourse, adopting Caillois's (1979) typology of games. He posits that one metaphor, LIFE IS PLAYING A GAME, is the most well-known metaphor in the United States of America (USA) which produces expressions like 'X is still a player' and 'Xs are still players' (Ching 1993: 47). The fixed phrases depict typically ideal American men from the point of view of a game or sport, and by 'ideal'; Ching (1993) explains that the metaphor user represents their own dominance and leadership. He also argues that these traits are compatible with the masculinity ingrained in American culture. According to Ching (1993), positive masculine traits such as 'daring', 'adventure', 'activeness' and 'willingness to take risk' stem from football or card games, and among them are phrases such as 'high cards', 'winning chips' and 'raising the ante,' as in the case in (1):

(1) Both sides [American and Iraqi] have some 'high cards to play,' but most entail risks that are probably unacceptable ... 'We might gain a military chip but lose the political war' a Western diplomat said. (Ching 1993: 49)

Example (1) describes USA–Iraq diplomatic relations, and the expression 'high cards to play' elucidates the strength or power behind the metaphor. The second phrase, 'gain a military chip', emphasises the game element, implying military force. From this, the power structure, as well as the entertainment factor, may be the criteria of the CARD metaphor. This rhetoric also demonstrates the game's broader meaning, including tempering power or de-emphasising conquest and winning (Ching 1993). Furthermore, Ching (1993: 50) states that 'football metaphors can also expand to stress group cooperation in carrying out a "game plan"'. Regardless of any kind of games, however, winning requires 'team effort' (Ching 1993: 50).

Leaving aside the political arena, Semino and Demjén (2017) analyse the CARD metaphor as used in an online forum for cancer patients. See the following examples:[13]

(2a) I threw a strop and **played a cancer card** today and came home early ... impressed? (Semino and Demjén 2017: 195)

(2b) [NB: in response to (31)] You have such a busy schedule, i'm [sic] glad **you played a card** and opted out of the meeting. (Semino and Demjén 2017: 196)

The online conversation given above shows that the referent of 'I' played the cancer card in order to go home early, and (2b) indicates that 'I' was able to get out of the meeting with the help of the CARD metaphor. With respect to its function, Semino and Demjén (2017: 197) argue that '[the] cancer (card) is used humorously to recount and justify the many different ways in which having cancer can be exploited to the person's advantage, not just by getting special treatment but also by excusing potentially unacceptable behaviors'.

Moreover, the study conducted by Semino and Demjén (2017) reveals how the metaphor forges bonds between cancer patients by creating an exclusive community to share their feelings and experiences. They explore the effects of the CARD metaphor in a specific discourse community, known as 'Warped'[14] (Semino and Demjén 2017: 182). Consequently, interaction between people who have a life-threatening illness can overcome the mental burden via compelling rhetoric.

In addition, their study allows us to reconsider the distinction between the literal and metaphorical use. Given that the verb 'play' co-occurs with the noun 'card', the collocation elicits the card game scenario. The phrase 'I've got cancer ... here's my card ... run away' (Semino and Demjén

---

[13] (2a) and (2b) are originally retrieved from: HoneyBee, date='2011-11-01 20:18:00' and Sue2, date='2012-01-12 20:42:00'.

[14] The open community forum of a UK-based cancer charity; it is entitled 'For those with a warped sense of humor WARNING – no punches pulled here' (Semino and Demjén 2017: 182).

2017: 190),[15] however, enables us to speculate on the different kinds of cards: business cards, green cards and so on. They unambiguously provide a new insight into the figurative expression, as it provides us with an understanding of the cards' nature. We may therefore reasonably summarise the main points of the CARD metaphor:

1. The CARD metaphor can show power or authority.
2. The nouns describing the socially vulnerable groups can be embedded in the slot.
3. Third parties occasionally criticise users due to their intentions.
4. Used by a particular community, there is a possibility that the CARD metaphor helps people build a sense of unity which generates humour or other effects.

While all of the above points provide insight, there is room for further research into the CARD metaphor, as there is currently a lack of detail on its general usage. This brings us to four additional areas of study:

1. The kinds of nouns and adjectives in the slot are not thoroughly examined.
2. Ching (1993) does not differentiate between the card game and the cards used in society.
3. Semino and Demjén (2017) only deal with identity in relation to cancer sufferers and do not reveal the other identities which appear in the slot.
4. Previous studies do not fully explain the feature of the CARD metaphor, or even its generalisation and conditions.

As described in this section, Ching (1993) specifies the conceptual metaphor, LIFE IS PLAYING A GAME, stating that the vehicle–tenor relation generates the subordinate metaphors. Based on an actual game played in our everyday life, it is plausible to examine the CARD metaphor more thoroughly. This issue will be addressed through analyses of the data retrieved from the COCA. This will be achieved by investigating its pragmatic functions and lexical categories in the slot 'play the X card'. We suggest that the metaphor LIFE AS A GAME should be replaced by SOCIETY AS A PLAYGROUND. In terms of the schematic meaning of 'play the X card', the MetaNet Metaphor Wiki (MMW) provides us with a detailed frame of the CARD metaphor. It is important to observe such frames to show why the metaphor SOCIETY AS A PLAYGROUND is more plausible than LIFE IS PLAYING A GAME. A search was conducted for the noun 'game' in MMW,[16] and the frame given in (3) yields the schematic connotation:

---

[15] Originally featured in HoneyBee, 19 August 2011 (6:43 pm).
[16] Retrieved from: https://metaphor.icsi.berkeley.edu/pub/en/index.php/Frame:Game [accessed 20 February 2023].

(3) playing x-schema = Recreational competition.activity_x-schema

'Playing x-schema' indicates that a participant is playing a game within the frame of 'recreational competition'. Semino and Demjén (2017) also point out that the 'play frame' includes 'group bonding', 'solidarity' and 'intimacy'. These are the underpinnings of the CARD metaphor in terms of its nature which can be formulated as follows. The image schema 'container' (Lakoff and Johnson 1980) generates the schematic metaphor – SPACE IS A CONTAINER – and it yields the metaphor SOCIETY AS A PLAYGROUND. The verb 'play' itself evokes the recreational element, as in (3), and the fact that the verb is employed metaphorically in that domain triggers the frame of the metaphor: social activities are equal to playing games. This final stage is where its functions (such as criticising or cooperating) are observable in context.

The problem accompanying the previous approach to the CARD metaphor will be resolved by splitting the investigation into two types, which we will henceforth call the card game metaphor (CGM) and the identity card metaphor (ICM). Furthermore, it is essential to consider the social stratification when investigating the CARD metaphor due to a wide variety of nouns and adjectives which can be found in the slot. Concerning the distinction between literal and metaphorical usage, as long as one's identity is inserted in the slot, it can be considered metaphorical. However, it is necessary to establish whether 'play the X card' is used as a metaphor when a card game-related lexical item is inserted in the slot. If CGM is used in a card game genre, it is very likely that 'play the X card' is literal; otherwise, we need to consider the context and situation to determine whether it is used as a metaphor (Pragglejaz Group 2007). The following section discusses the data retrieved from the COCA.

4 The data

4.1 Nouns and adjectives in the slot

Keywords such as the lemma *play the [n*] card*, *play the [j*] card* were derived from the COCA to provide a concise analysis of the nouns and adjectives inserted in the slot. Table 8.1 shows the token and type of CARD metaphor.

The result of our research for the total token and type (nouns and adjectives) contains 857 tokens and 328 tokens respectively. The progressive (V-ing) is regularly used among the other grammatical forms, accounting for about 43% (n = 369). The second most utilised form is the present tense that comprises around 36% (n = 414). A few cases of the past perfect and the present or past perfect progressive are also present. Table 8.2 demonstrates the nominal variety in the top five in the slot and reveals that the most frequently occurring token is filled by 'race', as a nominal citation which accounts for about 60% of all tokens on average. Significantly, similar

Table 8.1 *Nouns and adjectives in the slot (COCA)*

	Noun		Adjective	
	Token	Type	Token	Type
Present tense	262	91	52	41
Progressive	332	82	37	34
Past tense	123	44	27	25
Present perfect	15	4	4	4
Past perfect	0	0	1	1
Perfect progressive	4	2	0	0
Total	736	223	121	105

kinds of nouns were collected from the COCA, and the data is helpful for contextualising our discussion, with the argument that nouns such as 'race' and 'gender' can represent the #MeToo movement and #BlackLivesMatter. This noticeable feature makes it possible to ascertain the link with identity politics (IP) and the distance from the card game metaphor (CGM) because of the types of nouns. IP[17] means 'the adherence by a group of people of a particular religion, race, social background, etc., to political beliefs or goals specific to the group concerned, as opposed to conforming to traditional broad-based party politics' (*OED*). In summary, the unit 'play the [noun] card' evokes one's identity more transparently.

The adjectives in the top ranking are nationalist (present tense/n = 5), ethnic/religious top (present progressive/(n = 2), highest/black (past tense/(n = 2), and lucky/Christian/anti-Washington/Islamist/lack-of-respect (perfect (present + past) n = 1). In CGM, the present tense (42.9% (n = 52)) tends to be used more frequently than the present progressive, and neither the present perfect progressive nor the past perfect progressive was found. As adjectives are assigned to X, the most commonly used adjectives, excluding the perfect form, account for 13.5% of all occurrences of the token. Only the CGM is involved with the game-related adjectives, such as 'winning', 'wild', 'ace' and 'highest'. The next subsection covers the CGM with reference to how they are used in the COCA.

4.2 Game-related terminology in the slot

In this section, we will provide an analysis of the card game metaphor (CGM), and the examples in (4) indicate the manner in which the CGM is construed in context:

---

[17] Searching for the keyword 'identity politics', we found a section entitled 'Compounds'. 'Compounds 4' provides us with the definition of IP. The first instance of IP in the *OED* appeared in 1973. Retrieved from: https://www.oed.com.kwansei.remotexs.co/view/Entry/91004?redirectedFrom=identity+politics#eid140722645 [accessed 20 February 2023].

The CARD metaphor as social practice and pragmatic function 175

Table 8.2 *Nouns in the slot (COCA)*

	Present	Present progressive	Past	Present perfect	Perfect progressive
1.	race (n = 120)	race (n = 190)	race (n = 67)	race (n = 11)	race (n = 3)
2.	victim (n = 22)	gender (n = 18)	victim (n = 6)	gender (n = 2)	proximity (n = 1)
3.	gender (n = 9)	victim (n = 17)	gender (n = 4)	orphan (n = 1)/ catastrophe (n = 1)	
4.	cancer (n = 7)	woman (n = 8)	China (n = 3)		
5.	religion (n = 3) China (n = 3)	China (n = 5)	trump (n = 2)		
%	62.5% (n = 164)	71.6% (n = 238)	66.6% (n = 82)	100% (n = 15)	100% (n = 4)

(4a) I'm just trying to **play the winning card**. And I understand very well that people are not attacking me because I'm a woman. They're attacking because I'm ahead. (COCA: spoken: NBC_Today, 2007)

(4b) If we **play the ace card**, which is the military, then our options will be limited at a time when undoubtedly a massive attack is going to result in some civilian causalities. (COCA: spoken: NPR_Saturday, 1998)

(4c) Arafat came under considerable criticism from Palestinian 'radicals' in the PFLP for **playing the trump card** of PLO recognition of Israel without firm guarantees. (COCA: academic: Gerner, Deborah J. 'Arab Studies Quarterly', 1991)

In (4a), the metaphor 'play the winning card' is used in remarks made by Hillary Clinton when she was blamed for referring to her gender to gain support. The adjective in the slot in (4a) illustrates the difference between the card game metaphor (CGM) and the identity card metaphor (ICM), and (4a) is classified as CGM. Although the adjective 'winning' is used in the slot, this does not mean that the CGM fails to maintain the core meaning of the general card game metaphor. In other words, regardless of the types – CGM and ICM – here is a shared meaning or schematic meaning of the metaphor, namely, giving someone 'an advantage'. In the case of Hillary Clinton, 'an advantage' refers to the fact that being a woman can be her political strategy to legitimise her claims. We will return to this issue in section 5.

The patterns in (4a) and (4b) are alike in terms of their functions. In (4b), the context presents the tension between the USA and Iraq which might lead to conflict. As the relative clause denotes, the 'ace card' indicates the military operation of the USA. This perception cannot be deduced from the dictionary definition because the interpretation is contingent on its context. The same holds for 'playing the trump card' in (4c): for the original meaning, 'a special advantage to produce a decisive effect' fluctuates depending on

4.3 The CARD metaphor and social structure

This subsection provides an overview of the available official data on the ICM. As social beings, people interact on different levels in society. In this respect, MetaNet Metaphor Wiki (MMW) enables us to examine the different layers in the social structure. These social groups primarily consist of 'community', 'disorderly group', 'economic status', 'family', 'organisation', 'social status' and 'society'. The events or functions which affect our lives fall more specifically into the categories of the economy, social status, race, gender, human relationships, life and death, crime, and catastrophe (see Appendix). The CARD metaphor is distributed into the ICM insofar as the nouns and adjectives with reference to these constituents are put into the slot. In this paper, the socially vulnerable include women,[18] minorities (including lesbian, gay, bisexual, transsexual and queer [LGBTQ] groups and African Americans), patients, the financially challenged, and so on.

It seems that speakers assess whether their position in society or a particular social situation justifies the use of the 'card' metaphor. Those who belong to a higher echelon of society may use their status or authority to obtain what they pursue. In contrast, the socially vulnerable groups require a different strategy by appealing to the sympathy of others. There are two patterns: first, when these groups are in a lower position; second, their lower position is not de facto as such, but a situation forces them into a position, where, for example, the power balance might change depending on the situation, as shown in (6). Originally defined as 'political advantage' in the *OED*, the CARD metaphor is customarily used in politics, and the pragmatic hallmark extends to other micro-domains, social groups, and their respective branches as exemplified in (5):

(5a) China's leaders will very probably continue to **play the nationalism card**. (COCA: news Jeffrey Wasserstrom, *Two big China stories you missed this year*, 2008)

(5b) A few Hollywood types do own homes in Big Mountain country, but **playing the celebrity card** just isn't Whitefish's style. (COCA: magazine: Peter Oliver, *The big time*, 1999)

---

[18] Harp (2019) and Ching (1993) argue that hegemonic masculinity shapes American political discourse.

(5c) Nathaniel, as your boss, I demand you take me to the Waverider. Gonna **play the boss card** again? (COCA: series: *DC's Legends of Tomorrow*, 2017)

Example (5a) is used prototypically because the fact that China's leaders are playing their 'nationalism card' implies that the leaders can exercise power in the political or the diplomatic arena. In (5b), the occurrence sheds light on a higher class in society which is part of the whole: a country. Celebrities are sometimes regarded as successful figures based on their achievement, although the extent to which celebrities are treated as achieved can vary (Stewart and Giles 2020: 5). The 'celebrity card' can be construed as using celebrity status to gain superiority over other people. The author of (5b), however, challenges the effectiveness of 'celebrity card,' arguing the card does not conform to Whitefish's style. The same is true for a figure of authority or power, as exemplified by (5c), in the sense that the 'boss' has a prerogative right over colleagues. However, in this case, the perspective shifts from the whole to the specific field, and (5c) stresses the human relationship on the basis of social hierarchy. The examples in (5) show that it is necessary to pay attention to the relationship between subordinates and those who are in control, based on the social hierarchy.

Not all CARD metaphors, however, function like the examples in (5). Even those who may be regarded as socially weak can benefit from CARD metaphors, depending on the situation. Positions which society views as vulnerable ('race', 'woman' or 'cancer') are well suited to capturing this type of metaphor, as in (2). For example, a cancer is considered to be unhealthy and weak, but cancer patients can use 'the cancer card' to obtain what they want without using 'power'. Most significantly, the third type – non-involvement of the power structure (romance, friendship or family) – rises to the surface. Consider the following example:

(6) A mother of three children, Ahrendts,[19] was based for many years in New York, at Donna Karan and Liz Claiborne, before moving her whole family to London. Asked about this upheaval, she joked: 'It's fun when you have kids because you get to **play the kids card**'. In persuading her husband to relocate, she recalled how she enthused, 'This will be so good for the kids!' (COCA: magazine: Olivia Cole, *Angela Ahrendts Talks Fashion*, 2011)

---

[19] Angela Ahrendts was born and raised in New Palestine, Indiana, eventually became the CEO of Burberry in 2006, and is well known for her leadership and her contribution to the company, which multiplied its annual revenue. Before working as the CEO in London, Ahrendts and her family were based in New York. As she was looking to move to London to further her career, she had to convince her husband. Retrieved from: Wikipedia (n.d.), https://en.wikipedia.org/wiki/Angela_Ahrendts [accessed 20 February 2023].

In the above context, Ahrendts uses the 'kids card' to persuade her husband that they should move to London. It seems that she did not wish for her husband to see her as a self-centred woman who prioritises her career over her family. In addition, the choice of the word 'kids card' gives more force to her statement because the CARD metaphor can mitigate her wishes, instead emphasising the children in (6). Note that in this example it is not so much societal hierarchy as persuasion which counts. Consider the following examples:

(7a) We went back to her place and started fooling around, but when I reached for a condom, she put on the brakes. I really wanted to get laid that night, so I decided to **play the pity card**. I lied and told her that ever since my ex-fiancée broke off our engagement, I hadn't wanted to have sex with anyone . . . until her. (COCA: magazine: Jennifer Benjamin, *Cosmopolitan*, 2003, vol. 234, iss. 3, p. 36)

(7b) You think **playing the friend card** while Barbara's marriage is on the rocks is gonna pay off? Big time! She's moving to Divorceville where I happen to own a motel on the corner of hot and desperate. (COCA: fiction. Rules of Engagement: Engagement Party, 2007)[20]

In (7a), the man uses 'the pity card' to spend the night with the woman. Again, the card is not used to exercise power based on the social hierarchy but to persuade the woman to sleep with him. He attempts to make her feel sympathetic towards him so that he can accomplish the desired goal. The same logic is applicable for (7b) in that 'the friend card' does not indicate dominance or authority based on the social hierarchy, as is the case in (5), but neutrally balanced power between friends; becoming friends with someone does not pre-define the social hierarchy. The *Urban Dictionary*'s[21] definition of 'the friend card' openly acknowledges its function as follows: firstly, 'the request of a favour from a friend; as to "play the friend card" like a playing card'; secondly, 'the request of a favour from a friend; as to use your credit with a friend, like a credit card promising repayment' (Jonah45 2008). In (7), the primary task is to convince people by using emotions, such as 'the emotion

---

[20] According to the gist of the episode, 'Adam and Jennifer come up with a scam to get more wedding shower gifts. Meanwhile, Russell falls in love with Audrey's sister, but he has no idea that she does not feel the same way.' In the case of (7b), the 'friend card' refers to Russell's game plan to go on a date with Audrey's sister, in the hope that he may sleep with her: his strategy is to hit on her, as if he is a friend, without her noticing he has romantic feelings.

[21] The *OED* and the *MW* do not provide a definition for 'the friend card'. *Urban Dictionary* 'was intended as a dictionary of slang or cultural words and phrases, not typically found in standard English dictionaries, but it is now used to define any word, event, or phrase (including sexually explicit content)'. Retrieved from: https://en.wikipedia.org/wiki/Urban_Dictionary [accessed 20 February 2023].

The CARD metaphor as social practice and pragmatic function   179

(sympathy) card', rather than exercising power. In other words, the power relation confirmed in (5) does not apply to (7). In summary, the following four features can be deduced from the data retrieved from the COCA:

1. Influential people in society prototypically use a CARD metaphor to persuade subordinates and people in workplaces, communities and domestic politics as well as for diplomacy.
2. People of socially low status and vulnerable groups need to make listeners sympathetic to them, thereby fulfilling their purpose.
3. In criticising a person or challenging their perceptions, the following attributes are the targets: their social position, gender and race.
4. Almost all the CARD metaphors in (1) to (3) above presuppose social class. However, this stratification does not come into play so long as the user's purpose is simply to persuade a listener; see examples (5) and (6).

5 The CARD metaphor, a legitimisation strategy and identity politics

Firstly, let us consider the CARD metaphor employed in the American political landscape, because it is the prototypical field, according to the COCA and the dictionary definitions:

(8a) You know **she's playing the woman's card. If she didn't play the woman's card** she would have no chance, I mean zero, of winning. (Khalid 2016)[22]

(8b) Mr. Trump accused me of **playing the woman card**. Well, if fighting for women's health care and paid family leave and equal pay is 'playing the woman card', then deal me in. (Harp 2019: 48)[23]

(8c) Dems always **play the race card** when they are unable to win with facts. (Factba.se n.d.)[24]

Both (8a) and (8b) are examples from the 2016 American presidential election. As for Donald Trump's use of the metaphor 'play the woman card' in (8a), Khalid (2016) states that it was a verbal attack on Hillary Clinton,

---

[22] Example (8a) is a remark made by Donald Trump at a rally in Spokane, Washington in May, 2016 (Khalid 2016; Harp 2019).
[23] During the 2016 presidential campaign, Donald Trump verbally attacked Hillary Clinton with the insult that she was playing the woman's card to win a US presidential election. (8b) is retrieved from: *The Washington Post* (Sargent 2016).
[24] Donald Trump used the phrase in (8c) on 27 July 2019. This example originally featured on Twitter.

who became the de facto presidential nominee for the Democratic Party. In response to (8a), Clinton launched a counter-attack, saying that she just wanted to promote 'health care', 'paid family leave' and 'equal pay'. Harp (2019: 48) holds that the statement in (8b) was 'a significant gender moment'. The researcher also argues that misogyny appeared in public discourse throughout the presidential campaign (Harp 2019: 110).

While (8a) and (8b) shed light on sexism, (8c) highlights Donald Trump's inclination for a racial issue, pointing the finger at Democrats. When used by a third party, the CARD metaphor implies that this third party is criticising someone who uses their identity to gain support from a particular group of people, or takes advantage of their status. There are two patterns when such criticism is linked to a legitimisation strategy: (1) criticism in itself as a strategy; (2) the opponent's criticism as a legitimisation strategy. For the first pattern, Trump's metaphor, 'play the woman('s) card', criticises Clinton while simultaneously uniting his support base. According to Khalid (2016), his metaphor is a message directed at male supporters, implying that all the women band together to vote for Hillary Clinton. Consequently, not only did Trump lambast Clinton, but he also attempted to unite men. If the criticism sounds fair for the male supporters, the metaphor no longer only criticises the opponent; rather, it can create a political reality in which women are not supposed to take the initiative.

Nonetheless, Clinton turned the disadvantage into an advantage (Khalid 2016). She dared to use Trump's accusation for a successful fundraiser by selling pink 'woman cards' and 'deal me in' T-shirts. According to Khalid (2016), 'Her campaign brought in $2.4 million in just a few days'. Moreover, Harp (2019: 48) points out that:

> Clinton's official campaign Twitter account tweeted an image of a bright pink card resembling a credit card with the message: 'Lower wage! No paid family leave! Limited access to health care! Just some of the perks of your #Woman Card.'
>
> (@HillaryClinton 2016)

In this way, Trump's criticism became Clinton's political strategy. These characteristics of the metaphor illustrate how the CARD metaphor – 'play the X card' – works in parallel with identity politics (IP).

As we saw in the preceding sections, the CARD metaphor is tightly associated with the concepts of 'power', 'authority', 'the socially vulnerable' and 'weakness' allegedly ingrained in society. Nonetheless, the question remains as to why it is filled in the slot prototypically. The reasoning for this is twofold: first, the schema 'play the X card' has coercive effects due to its socially schematic connotations or conditions. Second, social movements, such as the #MeToo movement since 2006 and #BlackLivesMatter since 2013, have gained a certain momentum (Edrington 2022). The social trend emerged around the early and mid-1960s (McWilliams 2000) before the recent social groups' protests finally had the intended effect (*Stanford Encyclopaedia of*

Philosophy n.d.). From this vantage point, the Corpus of Historical American English (COHA) provides us with the historical evidence: of all the citations (14 tokens), 12 of them 'play the race card', all of which were used in the 2000s. (A search for the schema 'play (lemma) the race card' and 'play (lemma) the woman card' did not reveal any instances of the latter.) These facts support the idea that the influence of identity politics should not be ignored when considering the link between society and the CARD metaphor.

One of the reasons why IP stood out in the 2000s is by virtue of the vast generation gap. As Fisher (2018) claims, the Millennial Generation is more diverse than older generations, such as the Baby Boomers and the Silent Generation, in terms of racial and ethnic diversity. According to Fisher (2018: 36), 'Millennials have voted significantly more Democratic for president than any other generation'. The new agitators are more open to multilayered social issues than the Silent Generation: gay marriage, defence spending, immigration, government services, global warming, aid to the poor, and abortion (Fisher 2018: 40). This characterisation demonstrates that Generation Z and the Millennials use their voices to push the boundaries of acceptability, the new frame of mind consistent with their self-identification which goes hand in hand with identity politics.

As the examples in (8) show, President Trump made no secret of his aversion to the IP approach, condemning the Democrats and Hillary Clinton for using their race or gender through the formulation of 'someone is playing the X card'. This schema thus has the effect of criticising people: their strength, weakness, societal status or race may unite a particular group and exclude other social groups.

6 The main characteristics of the CARD metaphor

Regardless of the types – the card game metaphor (CGM) and the identity card metaphor (ICM) – major characteristics of the CARD metaphor can be summarised as follows:

1. *Generalisation*: When A and B belong to a field, and there is a relationship between them in a game (competition), A tries to use their position or trait X to achieve A's objective Y to gain an advantage over B. The field to which A and B belong is a place or a specific social group which reflects the social structure.
2. *Conditions*: A must be either the powerful one, the weak one, or identifying with those who have a purpose to persuade others.
3. *Prototypical nouns in the slot*: Race, gender (woman), religion (the high frequency in the COCA).
4. *Extension of the prototypical use*: Social class or context-bound situation (including the low frequency type).

5. *Basic features*:
    - Power and social status are confirmed not only at the national level but also at the micro level.
    - If no significant hierarchy is observed, A elicits the sympathy (mercy) of B or a third party.
    - A intends to achieve a certain goal.
    - B or a third party intends to blame or persuade an addressee.
6. *A metonymic relationship between X and Y*: Cause: X (position or trait) / effect: Y (purpose) (CAUSE FOR EFFECT) (Herrero-Ruiz 2018).

The most immediate insight to be gained from the above list is that one's identities can be recognised in the place where 'A and B belong to a field, and there is a relationship between them'. This part reflects the actual social structure of a particular group of people, therefore giving rise to conflicts among groups. The gender or race card indicates that there are supportive third parties outside of the card users. So intimate is the relationship between identity politics and the identity card metaphor that the two can scarcely be thought of apart.

The reasoning behind the CARD metaphor is another metaphor, namely SOCIETY AS A PLAYGROUND, which enables us to play the card to win the metaphorical game, thereby gaining sympathy from supporters. As we observed in the previous section, social groups consist of small groups which provide us with a sense of belonging, and this process helps to achieve purpose Y. The final stage, 'A tries to use their position or trait X to achieve A's objective Y to gain an advantage over B', relates X to Y vis-à-vis metonymy: CAUSE FOR EFFECT (Herrero-Ruiz 2018: 56). For example, in the case of (8a), Clinton's 'woman card' is the CAUSE, while the EFFECT unites her support groups. It is possible that Trump could have sensed or predicted the metonymic relationship and tried to interfere with the EFFECT, using the schema 'someone is playing the X card' in order to yield certain illocutionary acts: criticising the opponent and persuading his supporters to uphold him. One explanation of these illocutionary acts is the implicature which allows us to predict the outcome after a speaker uses the X card.

7 Conclusion

The purpose of this research was to demonstrate that the CARD metaphor 'play the X card' is a social practice (Fairclough 2001) where X prototypically refers to a social member or identity in the metaphor: SOCIETY AS A PLAYGROUND. This study asked why one's identity is prototypically inserted in the slot X and how the metaphor is used in society, while supplementing previous studies and addressing the following three points: (1) The kinds of nouns and adjectives in the slot were thoroughly examined via the COCA; (2) the types of the CARD metaphor were divided into the card game metaphor

(CGM) and the identity card metaphor (ICM); (3) the generalisation and conditions of the metaphor were clarified. The findings of this paper contribute to studies on CARD metaphors in general. In particular, the prototype 'play the race card' (ICM) is highly correlated with identity politics (IP), which is the basis of the prototypicality. This prototypicality ensures that the metaphor is frequently used in the American political arena and political actors 'play the X card' to legitimise their actions. For instance, Donald Trump used the phrase 'play the woman card' to criticise Hillary Clinton through the use of IP, which attempts to de-legitimise the quality of being a female. Not only does the CARD metaphor behave as such, but it also expands into peripheral use. A closer look at these CARD metaphors has revealed that CARD metaphor players typically resort to their literal social status or identity, whether it is in the political arena or everyday life. Moreover, metaphors can serve as illocutionary acts, such as persuading, criticising and sympathising, as the result of CAUSE FOR EFFECT. Further corpus research is undoubtedly required to gain quantitative data of the metaphor from all-encompassing English resources. This may help us determine whether the choice of words in the slot reflects the varying degrees of the speaker's conception of IP grounded in wider society and culture.

Appendix A

Table 8.3 *Nouns and adjectives in the slot of 'play the X card' (COCA)*

diplomacy/politics/economy
• *noun* Russia/CIA, China, Japan, Taiwan, Iran, Kosovo, Israel, Iraq, Afghanistan, patriotism, nationalism, patriot (politicians) GOP, Reagan, communism, PKK, Mubarak, bipartisanship, competence, flip-flop, peace, war, terrorism, hostage, holocaust, WMD, money, economy, quota, proximity, tourism, oil, north–south, national-emergency, birther, unity, Trump, age, Dayton, energy, Ferraro, security, hydrogen, defence, Baker, backlash, Amtrack, York, equivalency • *adjective* Syrian, Palestinian, Kurdish, Islamic, Iraqi, anti-American, Islamist, southern, small-town, Russian, Iranian, Greek, provincial nationalist, national, ultranationalist, nationalistic, liberal, democratic, authoritarian, populist, orange, Nazi, conservative, nuclear, military, boomer-as-investor, anti-immigration, political, geopolitical, foreign, anti-Washington, environmental-friendly, anti-government, right
religion
• *noun* faith, Jew, Pharisee, Allah, saviour, Mormon, religion, redemption, antisemitism, persecution, martyr • *adjective* Christian, religious, Muslim, Mormon, (Mormon) foreign, sectarian, antisemitic, schematic, communal

Table 8.3 *(continued)*

social status / race / gender / evaluation / emotion / thinking / human relationship / life and death / disease
• *noun*   class, identity, celebrity, qualification, teacher, boss, victor, sheriff, expert, nepotism, MIT, cop, Schwarzenegger, underdog, orphan, victimisation, victim, vermin, slavery, minority, race, racism, Caucasian ethnicity, recognition, ignorance, generosity, honesty, homeboy, hero, intolerance, disrespect, flattery, sensitivity, offence, prejudice, bias fanboy, literalist, hypocrite, bullying, geek, emotion, outrage, revenge, fear, guilt, depression, compassion, sympathy, pity, reassurance, logic, list, victimology, sexism, sex, man, misogyny, gender/victim, gender, woman, women, widow, girl, hoochie, rights, Trump, transgender, incest, infidelity, relationship, friend, friendship, girlfriend, mom, kids, daughter, daddy, family, baby, car, engagement, marriage, divorce, polygamy, injury/sickness, cripple, therapy, contagion, cancer, disability, pregnancy, death   • *adjective*   public, social, racial, black, ethnic, magnanimous lack-of-respect, fat, crazy, crazy-crazy, underrated, incomprehensible, (LGBTQ) gay, ex-lesbian, sexy, sexist, woman-as-victim, dumb-blonde, female, feminist, macho, psychological, sic, disable, immortal, dead, autistic, stranger, ad-hoc

catastrophe
• *noun*   catastrophe, flood

crime/law
• *noun*   theft, amnesty, gold, charge   • *adjective*   only, get-out-of-jail-for-free

vague meanings used in TV shows or movies
wesen, truth, jet-setter, Carol, balor, trap, ref, Gunther, species, boycott, dog, Carrington, defiance, Rand, Tony, big, normal, positive, tone, time, scoreboard

References

Caillois, R. (1979). *Man, Play, and Games*, trans. M. Barash. New York: Schocken.

Charteris-Black, J. (2004). *Corpus Approaches to Critical Metaphor Analysis*. London: Palgrave Macmillan.

Ching, M. K. (1993). Games and play: Pervasive metaphors in American life. *Metaphor and Symbol*, 8 (1), pp. 43–65.

Edrington, C. L. (2022). Social movements and identification: An examination of how Black Lives Matter and March For Our Lives use identification strategies on Twitter to build relationships. *Journalism & Mass Communication Quarterly*, 99 (3), pp. 643–59. doi: 10.1177/10776990221106994.

Fairclough, N. (2001). *Language and Power*. 2nd edn. London: Longman.

Fisher, P. (2018). A political outlier: The district politics of the millennial generation. *Society*, 55 (1), pp. 35–40. doi: 10.1007/s12115-017-0209-7.

Gibbs, R. W. (2017). *Metaphor Wars*. Cambridge: Cambridge University Press.

Harp, D. (2019). *Gender in the 2016 US Presidential Election: Trump, Clinton, and Media Discourse*. London: Routledge.

Herrero-Ruiz, J. (2018). Exaggerating and mitigating through metonymy: The case of situational and cause for effect/Effect for cause metonymies. *Language & Communication*, 62 (A), pp. 51–65. doi: 10.1016/j.langcom.2018.07.001.
Howe, N., (1988). Metaphor in contemporary American political discourse. *Metaphor and Symbol*, 3 (2), pp. 87–104.
Jonah45 (2008). 'friend card' [sic]. *Urban Dictionary*. 12 March. Available from: https://www.urbandictionary.com/define.php?term=friend%20card [accessed 26 June 2023].
Khalid, A. (2016). Is Donald Trump playing the 'Man Card'? National Public Radio (NPR), 10 May 2016. Available from: https://www.npr.org/2016/05/10/477423028/is-donald-trump-playing-the-man-card [accessed 26 June 2023].
Kövecses, Z. (2019). Some consequences of a multi-level view of metaphor. In: Navarro i Ferrando, I., ed., *Current Approaches to Metaphor Analysis in Discourse*. Berlin and Boston: Mouton de Gruyter, pp. 19–33.
Lakoff, G. (1993). The contemporary theory of metaphor. In: Ortony, A., ed., *Metaphor and Thought*. Cambridge: Cambridge University Press, pp. 202–51.
Lakoff, G. and Johnson, M. (1980). *Metaphors We Live By*. Chicago and London: The University of Chicago Press.
McWilliams, J. C. (2000). *The 1960s Cultural Revolution*. Westport, CT: Greenwood Press.
Merriam Webster (n.d.). Playing the — card: Race card? Woman card? The history of political card-playing. [Dictionary] https://www.merriam-webster.com/words-at-play/playing-the-card [accessed 20 February 2023].
Oxford English Dictionary (n.d.). [Dictionary] https://www.oed.com [accessed 20 February 2023].
Pragglejaz Group (2007). MIP: A method for identifying metaphorically used words in discourse. *Metaphor and Symbol*, 22 (1), pp.1–39. doi: 10.1080/10926480709336752.
Sargent, G. (2016). Donald Trump tries to project strength, but reveals his brittle glass jaw. *The Washington Post*, 27 April. Available from: https://www.washingtonpost.com/blogs/plum-line/wp/2016/04/27/donald-trump-tries-to-project-strength-but-reveals-his-brittle-glass-jaw/ [accessed 20 February 2023].
Semino, E. and Demjén, Z. (2017). The cancer card: Metaphor, intimacy, and humor in online interactions about the experience of cancer. In: Hampe, B., ed., *Metaphor: Embodied Cognition and Discourse*. Cambridge: Cambridge University Press, pp. 181–99. doi: 10.1017/9781108182324.011.
Stanford Encyclopaedia of Philosophy (n.d.). https://plato.stanford.edu [accessed 20 February 2023].
Stefanowitsch, A. and Gries, S. T. (2007). *Corpus-based Approaches to Metaphor and Metonymy*. Berlin and New York: Mouton de Gruyter.
Stewart, S. and Giles, D. (2020). Celebrity status and the attribution of value. *European Journal of Cultural Studies*, 23 (1), pp. 3–17. doi: 10.1177/1367549419861618.
Urban Dictionary (n.d.). https://www.urbandictionary.com/define.php?term=friends%20card [accessed 20 February 2023].
Wikipedia (n.d.). https://en.wikipedia.org/wiki/Main_Page [accessed 20 February 2023].
Wikipedia (n.d.). *Urban Dictionary*. https://en.wikipedia.org/wiki/Urban_Dictionary [accessed 20 February 2023].
Wikipedia (n.d.). *Angela Ahrendts*. https://en.wikipedia.org/wiki/Angela_Ahrendts [accessed 20 February 2023].

Corpus

Corpus of Contemporary American English (COCA) (n.d.). https://www.english-corpora.org/coca/ [accessed 20 February 2023].

Corpus of Historical American English (COHA) (n.d.). https://www.english-corpora.org/coha/ [accessed 20 February 2023].

Factba.se (n.d.). *Donald Trump Unabridged – Speeches, Tweets, Interviews*. https://factba.se [accessed 20 February 2023].

Metaphor.icsi.berkeley.edu.2022. EN MetaNet Wiki, (n.d.). https://metanet.icsi.berkeley.edu/metanet/node/76 [accessed 20 February 2023]; https://metaphor.icsi.berkeley.edu/pub/en/index.php/Frame:Game [accessed 26 June 2023].

CHAPTER 9

Metaphors and political arguments in environmental debates: 'Our house is still on fire'

Anaïs Augé

1 Introduction

In 2002, during the fourth Earth Summit, the then French President Jacques Chirac famously pronounced a statement inviting political world leaders to act upon the environmental crisis: 'Our house is burning, and we are looking the other way' (author's translation).[1] In 2020, during the World Economic Forum, the Swedish climate activist Greta Thunberg relied on a similar metaphorical statement to convince world economists of the urgency to tackle climate change: 'Our house is still on fire. Your inaction is fuelling the flames by the hour.' The use of the metaphor THE EARTH AS A HOUSE ON FIRE by a right-wing politician in 2002 and by a climate activist in 2020 is particularly intriguing. In these two speeches, the metaphor users relied on the metaphor in order to promote similar environmental arguments. The fact that the metaphorical expression previously used by Jacques Chirac occurred again in 2020 gives rise to additional implications linked to the activist's statement, although the French version of the metaphor may only be acknowledged by French speakers. The exploitation of the metaphor emphasises how this time could have been used to EXTINGUISH THE FIRE. Greta Thunberg, thus implicitly (and perhaps unwittingly) confirmed Jacques Chirac's claims which suggest that we have looked the other way and LET THE FIRE SPREAD. Yet she never made any reference to the French political statement. However, in different contexts, it is possible to see that the metaphor THE EARTH AS A HOUSE (ON FIRE) resonates and responds to prior political arguments regarding climate change. This argumentative use of the metaphor in environmental debates is of particular interest.

This chapter aims to uncover the implications of the metaphor THE EARTH AS A HOUSE (ON FIRE) in environmental debates. It presents metaphorical

---

[1] The original expression, in French: 'Notre maison brûle et nous regardons ailleurs' (Jacques Chirac).

occurrences retrieved from political speeches and the discourse produced by climate activists which convey different arguments regarding the climate crisis. These texts exploit the metaphorical mapping in different ways: these may refer to a CLEAN HOUSE, a GLOBAL (GREEN)HOUSE and a HOUSE ON FIRE. The various occurrences shed light on a prevalent metaphor scenario in climate change discourse: THE EARTH AS A HOUSE (ON FIRE). The discussion of the various metaphorical occurrences associated with different environmental arguments can answer the main research question addressed in this chapter: How is the scenario exploited and questioned in discourse to convey different environmental arguments?

The study starts with a brief account of the relevant approaches to metaphor which are used in this study. The methodological steps to select environmental texts, identify metaphorical occurrences and analyse their argumentative function in discourse are then explained. This leads to a discussion about the use of the scenario THE EARTH AS A HOUSE (ON FIRE) in the selected extracts. This chapter ends with a discussion which compares the implications of the scenario in political discourse and in activists' discourse.

2 The use of metaphors to convey environmental arguments

Metaphors are prevalent in political (Hanne 2014) and environmental (Van der Hel et al. 2018) communications. Indeed, these can effectively be used to convince an audience about particular political decisions (Charteris-Black 2011), and they can describe complex topics in familiar terms (Nerlich and Hellsten 2014). The present contribution draws on these two aspects to investigate the implications of metaphors used in argumentative environmental discourse.

Metaphors are required in order to communicate about crises. Following the claims of the conceptual metaphor theory (Lakoff 1993), a metaphor involves a conceptual mapping of a complex, scientific target domain, such as THE EARTH, with a more concrete, familiar source domain, such as HOUSE, which leads to the mapping referred to as THE EARTH AS A HOUSE. Such a mapping can be observed in linguistic occurrences of related metaphorical expressions, such as Greta Thunberg's claim: 'our house is on fire'. The additional qualification of the source domain HOUSE as a HOUSE ON FIRE suggests a communicative strategy which indicates that the conceptual mapping THE EARTH AS A HOUSE has been adapted to the particular context of production, namely an international debate about the climate crisis. The characteristics of the context – although ignored in conceptual metaphor theory (Lakoff 1993) – thus have a significant impact on the linguistic production of a conceptual metaphor (Charteris-Black 2011, 2019). For instance, the context of production has led Greta Thunberg to exploit the metaphor to insist on the danger of the crisis, which consequently transforms the HOUSE into a DANGEROUS HOUSE, in other words, a HOUSE ON FIRE. The activist adds more elements to the mapping by involving the recipients and blames them for their inaction: 'Your inaction is fuelling the flames by the hour.' Hence, the mapping THE EARTH AS A HOUSE is adapted to the context of production. On the one hand, Greta Thunberg describes the danger pertaining to the topic of discourse – climate change. On the other hand, she adapts the mapping to describe the reason why the danger still prevails – recipients' inaction. This is also notable in Jacques Chirac's statement, where the HOUSE is not only ON FIRE, but its INHABITANTS ('we') are assigned a role within the conceptual mapping. By exploiting the metaphor in such a way, the former French president explicitly insists on human responsibility, through the use of presuppositions (Wilson and Sperber 1979) according to which 'we' are expected to pay attention to the danger. Through metaphors, the politician underlines the danger and asks recipients to 'look' at this danger, presumably to convince them to take effective action. The association between metaphorical statements and the contexts of production has been extensively analysed by Steen (2008, 2011) who adjusted conceptual metaphor theory to introduce the 'communication model'. This model takes into account the metaphor user's intentions and the metaphor recipient's understanding of the metaphorical statement in a particular context of production: for example, public discourse, conversation and educational context. This model has been thoroughly analysed in studies investigating metaphors in discourse following Critical Metaphor Analysis (Charteris-Black 2011), as we have aimed to illustrate briefly with reference to Greta Thunberg's and Jacques Chirac's respective statements.

Previous research has uncovered the prevalence of metaphors in communications grounded in science, such as climate change discourse, including THE ECOSYSTEM AS A SICK BODY (Augé 2021, 2022a) and THE EARTH AS A GREENHOUSE (Augé 2022b). Scientists have produced theoretical and pedagogical metaphors (Boyd 1993) to name their environmental discoveries, such as the 'greenhouse effect' (Augé 2022b), and to explain their findings to the largest number, for instance the 'carbon footprint' (Nerlich and Hellsten 2014). Boyd takes the example of catachresis, namely a lexical gap where new concepts are not yet named (1993: 481), in scientific theories. In making new discoveries, scientists adapt the linguistic categories so that the language corresponds to real-world experiences. In order to name the discovered element, they rely on an analogical process which describes their experience of the discovery in terms of an existing element: for example, the greenhouse effect and carbon footprint. Boyd calls this process the 'accommodation' of language (1993: 483). For example, Deignan (2005: 16) notes the use of the metaphor CONNECTED COMPUTERS ARE NODES IN A WEB to understand computer processing through metaphorical expressions such as the '(worldwide) web' and the '(inter)net'.

However, crisis discourse is not restricted to scientific findings. Descriptions of the climate crisis tend to be associated with different viewpoints and approaches to controlling this danger such as climate activism as opposed to climate scepticism. Along these lines, the metaphorical statements produced within such a discourse can be exploited to promote conflicting arguments. For instance, the transition to greener energy may be described as being 'painless' or 'aggressive' depending on the metaphor user's opinion on the topic (Shaw and Nerlich 2015: 38).

In order to examine the specific nature of the context of production consistent with Boyd (1993), Steen (2008, 2011) and Charteris-Black (2011), and the various opinions emerging from the descriptions of the topic consistent with Shaw and Nerlich (2015), this chapter adopts a particular approach to metaphor: it analyses the occurrences of a metaphor scenario (Musolff 2016, 2019) to investigate its implications in climate crisis discourse. Metaphor scenarios are defined as involving assumptions about the source domain (for example: HOUSE) which become part of a metaphorical script, with participants, storyline and outcome. This script advertises a certain evaluation of the topic: successful, unsuccessful, permissible, illegitimate, among others (Musolff 2016: 30–1). To illustrate this, in a corpus of metaphors used in the press coverage of European politics (2016: 14), the source domain FAMILY (MEMBERS) has been identified. Its exploitation in discourse conveys different views on the relationships between Britain and the European Union such as PARENT–CHILD relationships, MARRIED LIFE of the EU couple and LOVE–MARRIAGE relationships. This exploitation provides grounds for evaluative descriptions: the EU family has an egalitarian structure, the EU family has a hierarchical structure, and the EU as a homogeneous entity with which Britain is engaged in a bilateral but asymmetric love relationship (Musolff 2016: 31–3).

The scientific grounding of climate crisis discourse may be assumed to prevent such ideological exploitations of a metaphor scenario, as scenarios have mainly been analysed in political discourse (Musolff 2016, 2019). Yet the actions required to mitigate the environmental crisis also involve political considerations. Climate change can thus be identified as a political issue, and climate change metaphors can promote different political arguments. For instance, Lakoff (2010) suggests that the politicians who favour the enactment of climate policies do not show a good mastery of argumentation through metaphors (Charteris-Black 2011; Fairclough and Fairclough 2012). He claims that this may be the reason behind the fact that not enough climate policies have been voted in the United States of America (henceforth US) (Lakoff 2010: 73). Politicians may promote certain metaphorical conceptualisations in order to advertise the environmentally friendly aspects involved or not in their decisions. For example, Lakoff (2004: 22) refers to the legislation named the 'Clear Skies Act' whose outcome would increase pollution rates, while the metaphor 'clear' suggests an absence of polluting gases. The political implications involved in climate change metaphors have, however, triggered limited interest in existing literature. The present contribution therefore proposes to provide an insight into the argumentative function of metaphors (Charteris-Black 2011) occurring in climate crisis discourse.

Metaphors and political arguments in environmental debates   191

In this chapter, the focus is on the argumentative exploitation of the scenario THE EARTH AS A HOUSE (ON FIRE). We demonstrate how the source domain HOUSE can be attributed different metaphorical characteristics to convince recipients about the need for or the ineffectiveness of climate actions. For this purpose, we analyse different statements produced by politicians and climate activists who share different views on the climate crisis. We explain our methodology in the following section.

3 Methodology

This study draws on a larger corpus-based project (Tognini-Bonelli 2001) which investigates the wide range of scenarios in climate crisis discourse (Augé 2023). As part of this project, we have collected a large number of texts retrieved from political speeches, newspaper articles, activists' discourse, scientific discourse, and messages posted on social media. This resulted in a corpus of 12,212 texts produced in English and in French. Among the different scenarios observed within this corpus, particular attention has been paid to the opposing arguments conveyed through the metaphorical expressions used by politicians and climate activists. Notably, it has been observed that the scenario THE EARTH AS A HOUSE (ON FIRE) can either advertise the environmental aspects of political decisions or blame politicians for their inaction (for instance, Greta Thunberg's use of the expression 'our house is still on fire').

For this study, the original corpus has been reduced in order to focus on texts produced by politicians and climate activists, and this reduced version of the corpus is referred to as the 'dataset' in the remainder of this chapter. In order to discuss THE EARTH AS HOUSE (ON FIRE) scenario, we have selected occurrences produced by the non-governmental organisations (NGOs) Friends of the Earth and Fridays for Future, British political leaders' speeches, international activists and politicians in statements published on their official Twitter accounts. We have concentrated our search on data produced between 1980 and 2020. Within this dataset, we have looked for metaphorical expressions related to the source domain HOUSE, in particular. We have conducted a semi-automated search within this dataset using the words 'house', 'home', and the French equivalent '*maison*' as search terms to observe their occurrences in the entirety of the corpus. Each occurrence has then been analysed qualitatively to determine the metaphorical or literal meaning of the occurrence (see below) and to observe its use in context.

An analysis of each occurrence has been conducted following the Metaphor Identification Procedure (MIPVU) (Steen et al. 2010) to determine if the occurrences are used metaphorically or literally. The Procedure establishes the following methodological steps: reading texts and identifying an 'alien' word (specifically, a word which seems to be semantically unrelated to the topic of discourse); searching for a more 'basic' meaning of this word; if this 'basic' meaning differs from the contextual meaning (the meaning of the word in the text), the metaphorical mapping is identified (Steen et al. 2010). The contextual information provided with each occurrence has been analysed to identify the main arguments and to observe varying extrapolations of this source domain, for example: a 'green-house'. This semi-automated search in the dataset has then resulted in the identification of 45 metaphorical occurrences.

It should be noted that the scope of this chapter is qualitative and does not aim at making any claims regarding systematic findings observed in the dataset. For instance, occurrences related to the scenario THE EARTH AS HOUSE (ON FIRE) were also observed in different texts collected as part of the larger corpus (in newspapers and scientific articles). The present study focuses on a more limited range of occurrences which explicitly promote opposing environmental arguments. The selected occurrences which are discussed below can thus illustrate how the source domain HOUSE can be exploited by activists and politicians who make contradictory claims about climate change. The following section illustrates the argumentative use of the scenario THE EARTH AS A HOUSE (ON FIRE) as it has been observed in the dataset.

4 A CLEAN HOME or a HOUSE ON FIRE: Environmental arguments in metaphorical statements

4.1 The EARTH AS A SHARED (CLEAN) HOME

The analysis starts with the statements produced by politicians and climate activists which promote the image of THE EARTH AS A SHARED CLEAN HOME. The metaphor characterises the Earth according to its unique capacity to host life. Therefore, related occurrences emphasise the responsibility of humans to keep the HOME suited for human life. Alternatively, activists' arguments suggest that climate change threatens to damage this SHARED HOME: it is inferred that its potential destruction would make its INHABITANTS HOMELESS. This is exemplified in the statement produced by Friends of the Earth:

(1) We are bitterly angry that the OPEC countries, Japan and the United States have combined in this way to help wreck the world's environment and endanger the security of our common home. (Kate Hampton, Climate Campaigner for Friends of the Earth, 2 September 2002)

Friends of the Earth link environmental threats to the SECURITY OF THE HOME. The focus is on the necessity for every human being to live within a HOME to survive. However, the positive implications conveyed by the conceptualisation of THE EARTH AS A HOME are questioned by the differentiation of the

INHABITANTS OF THE HOME. The characterisation of the HOME as COMMUNAL helps the metaphor user, Kate Hampton, to emphasise the negative effects of the 'Action Plan' deal which does not involve any target for the use of renewable energy. The description of the planet as a SHARED HOME is a way for the activist to metaphorically reduce the distance between different populations: she implicitly identifies the BAD INHABITANTS OF THE SHARED HOME (in other words, Organisation of the Petroleum Exporting Countries – OPEC) whose decisions have negative consequences for ALL INHABITANTS. In other words, the metaphorical shrinkage of the planet into a HOME emphasises the non-environmentally-friendly effects of the Action Plan approved by the OPEC countries. The conceptualisation of THE EARTH AS A HOME highlights a link between humans and the place they live in. This establishes a relation of possession between humans and their HOME. This link can be questioned by politicians who rely on a different aspect of the source domain HOUSE, as in:

(2) The core of Tory philosophy and the case for protecting the environment are the same. No generation has a freehold on this earth. All we have is a life tenancy with a full repairing lease. And this Government intends to meet the terms of that lease in full. (Margaret Thatcher, 14 October 1988)

The characterisation of THE EARTH-HOME AS A TENANCY involves a wider range of implications in the context of climate change mitigation. According to the then British prime minister, Margaret Thatcher, the Earth should be perceived as A HOME WHICH NEEDS TO BE KEPT CLEAN AND IN GOOD REPAIR. The characterisation of the INHABITANTS having to share a space is extended to include FUTURE INHABITANTS. Human lifetime is perceived as the duration of the TENANCY CONTRACT which includes 'full repairing lease': the HOME is presented as a commodity which the current generation will hand over to the next one. The British politician aims to highlight the DUTIES comprised within the concept of a SHARED TENANCY: these involve REPARATION AND CLEANING DUTIES so that FUTURE INHABITANTS can enjoy the resources provided by the environment. This argument is emphasised in the last sentence describing the goal of the government to 'meet the terms of that lease in full'. On the one hand, this shows the extent of the actions the government wants to perform (especially leaving the place intact) and, on the other hand, it acknowledges that humans can damage the place (with a 'full repairing lease'). This exploitation of the source domain HOUSE also insists on the negative aspects of pollution which is implicitly perceived as DIRT OR BROKEN OBJECTS. The argument derived from this conceptualisation presents climate actions as a DUTY: the audience is called to CLEAN THE HOME not because their aim is to live in a pleasant place, but because they are under the terms of a CONTRACT. This extrapolation, observed within a political speech produced by the former British prime minister, is a way for the discourse producer to insist on her authority as a political leader. Indeed, this CONTRACT represents 'evidence' of a signed agreement which forces the protagonists to respect its content: TAKING CARE OF THE EARTH-HOUSE. Accordingly, in her position as a political leader, Margaret Thatcher presents herself as the individual who has authority over the TENANTS to ensure that this CONTRACT is respected by the population.

In these two examples, the British politician and the climate activist rely on the conceptualisation of the SHARED CLEAN HOME to shed light on the BAD INHABITANTS. In Friends of the Earth's statement, these are represented by the OPEC countries, and in Margaret Thatcher's speech these are implicitly represented by the people living during the 1980s who are called upon to 'meet the terms of that lease'. However, it is possible to see how arguments differ in the two examples: the description of a TENANCY AGREEMENT in the political speech promotes an optimistic view of the future and presents climate mitigation as a moral obligation. This optimism does not appear in the activist's statement, which insists on the damage caused by the decisions taken by the OPEC countries.

In the following section, we discuss the use of the scenario THE EARTH AS A (GREEN)HOUSE in texts arguing about the effective damage caused by pollution.

4.2 THE EARTH AS A GLOBAL GREENHOUSE

The conceptualisation of THE EARTH AS A HOUSE (ON FIRE) can be associated with the more common metaphorical expression 'the greenhouse effect' in climate crisis discourse. Specifically, this expression has been established as a theoretical metaphor in existing literature (Nerlich and Hellsten 2014). It names an environmental concept which cannot be named literally (Boyd 1993). The source domain GREENHOUSE refers to a container which is characterised by the temperatures associated with its content. In view of the warming experienced as a result of the environmental crisis, the temperatures provided by the EARTH-GREENHOUSE metaphor comprise a dangerous feature: the GREENHOUSE provides excessively warm temperatures. The association between temperatures and greenhouse gases (as a form of pollution) is exploited in the texts from the dataset. Gas emissions are explicitly described as a component of the EARTH-GREENHOUSE which can alter the life of its CONTENT (namely humanity). This is exemplified in the extract provided below:

> (3) George W. Bush spoke of emerging technologies and said that 'all nations, including the developing countries can advance economically, while slowing the growth in the global greenhouse and avoid pollutants that undermine public health'. (Friends of the Earth, 21 February 2005)

The former president of the United States, George W. Bush, advertises a global perspective on climate change mitigation: 'all nations, including the developing countries'. He refers to the Earth as a GLOBAL GREENHOUSE in order to insist on the global consequences of the environmental crisis. This focus subsequently leads him to promote shared responsibilities regarding the reduction of emissions to 'avoid pollutants'. He relies on another metaphor – the JOURNEY metaphor – to advertise the need for such reduction: he first describes an ECONOMIC ADVANCEMENT which is presented as a desirable goal for all nations ('can'). This description is intended to address existing disputes which pit environmental mitigation against economic prosperity (Nerlich and Koteyko 2010). The first instance of the JOURNEY metaphor provides a concrete, figurative image of a future global economy which takes into account environmental risks: according to the US politician, this possible type of economy would not limit the JOURNEY embarked upon by nations. This is, however, immediately questioned in the following proposition, 'while slowing the growth in the global greenhouse', which relies again on the JOURNEY metaphor to mention the need to SLOW the growth. Consequently, George W. Bush's argument uses metaphors to depict the complex topic of global economy and its role in controlling the climate crisis. While the JOURNEY undertaken by nations is not to be impacted by environmental considerations, the living conditions in the GLOBAL GREENHOUSE make it necessary to SLOW THE PACE OF THE JOURNEY UNDERTAKEN BY NATIONS. In other words, the uncontrolled SPEED of the global growth is said to impact 'public health' and therefore needs to be limited.

It is possible to see the argumentative use of the GREENHOUSE and JOURNEY metaphors: by relying on figurative language, George W. Bush significantly simplifies the main topics addressed in his speech. These include 'global economy-growth', 'sustainable economy-growth', 'pollutants' and 'global climate'. This oversimplification results in a very vague claim about global sustainability which does not present any explicit political decision regarding emission reductions. This has also been criticised by Friends of the Earth in the remainder of their communication:

(4) Friends of the Earth International said that the US – the world's biggest polluter – must accept that we need to do far more than 'slowing the growth' of greenhouse gases, and called on the US to commit itself to join the rest of the world in tackling global warming by pledging itself to a significant reduction in carbon dioxide levels. (Friends of the Earth, 21 February 2005)

Accordingly, the NGO highlights the vagueness resulting from George W. Bush's JOURNEY metaphor 'we need to do far more', since this political consideration does not even explicitly mention the cause of the danger (carbon dioxide) which is, in contrast, described in the NGO's statement (a 'significant reduction in carbon dioxide levels'). The activists also rephrase the politician's GREENHOUSE metaphor: while the former US president refers to a 'greenhouse world' which implies shared global responsibilities, the NGO favours the expression 'greenhouse gases' which thereby insists on the different and differing origins of harmful emissions. Friends of the Earth also sheds light on George W. Bush's own responsibility as the then leader of the 'world's biggest polluter'.

This political quotation also shows the conceptual limits of the (GREEN) HOUSE metaphor: in the context of environmental mitigation, the 'global' aspect contained within this metaphorical conceptualisation can be disputed. Moreover, George W. Bush refers to pollution, the economy and growth as concepts which do not have any specific national or regional characteristics. The global feature of the GREENHOUSE metaphor thus explicitly attributes the same responsibilities to developed and developing nations and discards the national-regional differences pertaining to pollution rates, environmental consequences, health consequences and economic consequences (see Augé 2023; Scandrett 2016).

This use of the GREENHOUSE metaphor by the former US president – quoted after Friends of the Earth – highlights the way such a conceptualisation can effectively facilitate our understanding of complex concepts. However, it also shows how metaphors can oversimplify the problem and generate misguided beliefs regarding global responsibilities (Augé 2022b).

In the following section, we analyse the occurrences of the metaphor THE EARTH AS A HOUSE ON FIRE, which offers a hyperbolic view on the temperature increase caused by climate change.

4.3 THE HOUSE ON FIRE: A real emergency?

We now focus on the occurrences of the scenario which inspired this chapter: the HOUSE ON FIRE metaphor. This occurrence may effectively derive from the metaphors previously discussed: THE EARTH AS A SHARED HOUSE and THE EARTH AS A GREENHOUSE. While the former insists on the need to KEEP THE HOUSE CLEAN, the latter comprises a notion of danger which needs to be controlled, that is to say the temperatures of the GREENHOUSE. In the case of the HOUSE ON FIRE metaphor, this danger is conceptually expanded. Not only does the FIRE reflect the dangerous consequences of the 'warming' resulting from the environmental crisis, but it also represents a tangible experience of threats. The descriptions of tangible threats can help us to identify solutions to control such threats, which means EXTINGUISHING THE FIRE.

The conceptual association between THE FIRE and ways to EXTINGUISH THE FIRE is at the heart of the arguments promoted in the video[2] produced by the NGO Fridays For Future (retrieved from Greta Thunberg's official Twitter account). This video shows the daily life of a 'typical' family (consisting of white, heterosexual parents with two kids) within the family's HOUSE.

---

[2] Video available at https://www.youtube.com/watch?v=eT32UFzA7E8 [accessed 12 June 2022].

We can see them perform daily tasks such as waking up, preparing dinner and doing homework. These tasks are performed by the family members while a FIRE is spreading within the HOUSE, to the extent that it consumes the entire building. Yet while the FLAMES are easily visible, none of the characters notice the danger and each of them continues to perform their tasks in a 'business as usual' manner. The video ends with a white screen where we can read 'Our house is on fire. React'. The argument derived from this video heavily relies on the conceptual association between the FIRE representing a tangible danger and the actions which can be taken to EXTINGUISH it. By contradicting the viewers' expectations, Fridays for Future produces an effective depiction of the absurd behaviour of humanity and, in particular, the conduct of developed nations. The implicit reference to the environmental crisis is derived from prior knowledge about Fridays for Future's main fight which in turn results from Greta Thunberg's school strike. In this visual occurrence of the scenario, climate change is identified as a SPREADING FIRE WHICH NOBODY NOTICES. The HOUSE is a metaphorical, visual shrinkage of the EARTH AFFECTED BY CLIMATE CHANGE. This shrinkage also involves an immediate danger because the HOUSE represents a typical human habitat. It draws heavily on the viewers' affect. As the concept of HOUSE is associated with the concept of FAMILY, this makes it easier for viewers to create an affective connection with the characters, which means that they can be conceptually associated with each viewer's own family or house. This association is further enhanced by the representation of the characters' actions which represent typical, daily actions performed by most individuals living in developed countries. Therefore, this visual occurrence of the scenario draws on the affective meaning comprised in the HOUSE concept while the FIRE represents a controllable, tangible, danger which is not yet controlled. This results in an absurd image which blames humans for 'looking the other way'. The metaphor of the HOUSE ON FIRE can also effectively cause alarm about 'literal' fires. This metaphorical reference to literal fires can be observed in the political statement provided below:

(5) Our house is burning. Literally. The Amazon, the lung of our planet which produces 20% of our oxygen, is on fire. This is an international crisis. G7 members, see you in two days to talk about this emergency. #ActForTheAmazon (Emmanuel Macron, Twitter, 8 August 2019, author's translation)[3]

In this tweet published by the President of France, Emmanuel Macron, the metaphor of the HOUSE ON FIRE implicitly refers to the former version produced by Jacques Chirac, as it is assumed that Emmanuel Macron is

---

[3] 'Notre maison brûle. Littéralement. L'Amazonie, le poumon de notre planète qui produit 20% de notre oxygène, est en feu. C'est une crise internationale. Membres du G7, rendez-vous dans deux jours pour parler de cette urgence.'

familiar with this 2002 speech and its popularity among French citizens and climate activists.

Yet this metaphorical statement is not only a mere repetition of a well-known speech. As is explicitly mentioned by the adverb 'literally', Emmanuel Macron highlights additional implications conveyed through the metaphor which are at work in the context of the fires which damaged the Amazon in 2019. The metaphor functions as a topic-triggering device: 'an aspect of the topic under discussion inspires the choice of the metaphorical source domain which is evoked via the metaphorical expressions used in the text' (Semino 2008: 27). For example, the *Guardian* refers to the conflict between South Africa and Morocco over control of Western Sahara as a' diplomatic desert', where 'desert' applies to both the lack of diplomatic relationships, and to the literal desert of Sahara (Semino 2008: 27). In this political tweet, the French president 'revitalises' (Goatly 1997: 31–5, 289) Jacques Chirac's metaphor by drawing a link between the metaphorical FIRE described in 2002 and the literal fire occurring in 2019. This 'revitalisation' serves several functions, as outlined below.

First, the reference to Jacques Chirac's metaphor insists on Emmanuel Macron's stance on climate change. This represents thinly veiled criticism of previous French political leaders (such as Nicolas Sarkozy and François Hollande) and Amazonian political leaders (such as Jair Bolsonaro) who did not EXTINGUISH THE FIRE previously identified by Jacques Chirac. This political reference from 2019 is thus ideologically oriented. It endorses the 2002 conceptualisation and, by referring to a 'literal' fire, implies that this fire has, in effect, spread without control. This tweet has generated major political disagreements. The then Brazilian President publicly contested this viewpoint:

(6) I regret that President Macron seeks to use an internal issue surrounding Brazil and other Amazonian countries for personal political gain. The sensationalist tone with which he refers to the Amazon (even using fake photos) does nothing to solve the problem. The Brazilian government remains open to dialogue, based on objective data and mutual respect. The French President's suggestion that Amazonian issues be discussed at the G7 without the participation of the countries of the region evokes a misplaced colonialist mindset in the 21st century. (Jair Bolsonaro, Twitter, 23 August 2019; translation generated automatically by Twitter)[4]

---

[4] 'Lamento que o presidente Macron busque instrumentalizar uma questão interna do Brasil e de outros países amazônicos p/ ganhos políticos pessoais. O tom sensacionalista com que se refere à Amazônia (apelando até p/ fotos falsas) não contribui em nada para a solução do problema. O Governo brasileiro segue aberto ao diálogo, com base em dados objetivos e no respeito mútuo. A sugestão do presidente francês, de que assuntos amazônicos sejam discutidos no G7 sem a participação dos países da região, evoca mentalidade colonialista descabida no século XXI.'

According to the Brazilian politician, the 'sensationalist tone' adopted by Emmanuel Macron reflects a political self-interest which overlooks prevalent environmental concerns among Amazonian leaders. Jair Bolsonaro refers to the topic-triggering metaphor used in the tweet in French and deconstructs its grounding by informing recipients that the picture of the fire is 'fake'. He insists on the 'fake' characteristic of the photograph to then apply this particular characteristic to the remainder of the French message. His argument shows that 'dialogue' between the two leaders is only possible with reliance on 'objective data'. It follows that the lack of objectivity involved in the use of a 'fake' photograph prevents such a dialogue.

Second, in (5), Emmanuel Macron refers to the forthcoming G7 meeting. The revitalised metaphor sheds light on Macron's participation at the meeting and advertises the position which he is to adopt during this event. The reuse of a popular French metaphor to mention the G7 meeting is an effective way to attract attention to the French President's stance as opposed to other politicians' environmental stances. In (6), Jair Bolsonaro also refers to the G7 meeting. He stresses that Amazonian leaders cannot take part in this event, which similarly prevents effective dialogue. The impossibility for Amazonian leaders to attend political discussions is compared with colonialist practices (especially in French Guiana, which is a former French colony located in the Amazon). This political meeting gives G7 leaders authority over former Amazonian colonies. However, the leaders of these former colonies are not invited to share their viewpoints on environmental policies.

Third, in (5), the topic-triggering function of the metaphor promotes a global perspective on the environmental crisis, coherent with the context of the G7 meeting. The fire which damaged the Amazon is presented as damage to 'our house'. The source domain HOUSE suggests that for Emmanuel Macron, the literal fire has consequences on every nation, and this is enhanced by the metaphor of the LUNG. It implicitly contradicts possible beliefs related to the different climatic effects in Europe as opposed to South America (Scandrett 2016). The source domain HOUSE insists on Macron's stance towards climate change, which is presented as a concern for every world nation, and for France, in particular. In contrast, in (6), Jair Bolsonaro insists on the fake photograph of the fire to dispute Emmanuel Macron's metaphorical mapping: the visual reference to 'literal' fire is fake. Therefore, the use of the FIRE source domain and arguments conveyed through the metaphor is, to some extent, unjustified. This enables him to promote national capacities to avert the climatic threat at the local level as opposed to the international level.

Yet Emmanuel Macron and Jair Bolsonaro do not expand on the metaphorical conceptualisation to mention the need to EXTINGUISH THE FIRE or PROTECT THE LUNG OF OUR PLANET in (5). These arguments may well be indirectly derived from the political statements. However, the image of a HOUSE ON FIRE, enhanced by the photograph of a literal fire damaging the Amazon, produces a feeling of emergency. This feeling is contradicted, however, by the announcement of the G7 meeting scheduled to take place two days later. Emmanuel Macron effectively demonstrates the emergency to tackle the crisis and the delay caused by supposed political inaction at the beginning of his tweet. This is, however, followed by the description of another delay of 'two days' to take an allegedly 'colonialist' political decision about the 'literal' fire which damages 'our house'.

Overall, Emmanuel Macron effectively draws on Jacques Chirac's argument by displaying images of a literal fire showing that he is not 'looking the other way', but the lack of advertised solution, political disagreements over data, and the chronological incoherence help to explain why our house is still on fire.

5 Discussion and concluding remarks

This study was inspired by the observed reoccurrence of the metaphor THE EARTH AS A HOUSE ON FIRE in Jacques Chirac's speech from 2002 and in Greta Thunberg's speech from 2020, and the chapter has compared the reliance on the scenario THE EARTH AS HOUSE (ON FIRE) by politicians and by climate activists. This comparison establishes the different implications conveyed by different metaphor users who have exploited the source concept HOUSE to promote and legitimise their own stance on the environmental crisis.

First, activists and politicians used the source concept HOUSE to characterise it as a SHARED-CLEAN HOME (namely Margaret Thatcher and Friends of the Earth). Yet the analysis of the two metaphorical declarations has highlighted significant conceptual differences: while the politician referred to pollution as a form of DIRT OR BROKEN OBJECTS WITHIN THE HOME – which can then be easily removed or replaced to 'meet the terms of the lease' – the activists became alarmed about the security within the HOME, which is increasingly questioned by international decisions. The optimism implied in the former British prime minister's speech (which may be explained by the period during which this speech was produced) fulfils argumentative functions: it promotes the Conservative Party's environmental considerations. This optimism is absent from the activists' statement, which aims to warn people about the consequences of non-environmentally-friendly international agreements. In other words, in Margaret Thatcher's statement, the HOME is to be taken care of so that it remains intact, whereas in Friends of the Earth's statement, the HOME is increasingly being damaged by decisions taken by world nations.

Second, activists and politicians also relied on the metaphor THE EARTH AS A (GREEN)HOUSE (specifically, George W. Bush and Friends of the Earth). In the extracts under discussion, the global aspect involved in this conceptualisation was heavily relied upon by the former president. He oversimplified the nations' responsibilities for climate change and the multiple consequences of the crisis. He effectively insisted on the 'global' aspect of the GREENHOUSE to call on every nation to act upon the climatic threat. Yet this led him to hide the greater responsibility of developed countries, such as the United States, compared with the limited contributions of developing countries. This 'global' perspective has been criticised by activists, whose main argument can be related to the notion of 'climate justice' (Scandrett 2016; Augé 2023). This notion points to the uneven consequences of the environmental crisis and demonstrates the unequal means available for facing climatic threats in different countries.

Third, it has been demonstrated that the metaphor THE EARTH AS A HOUSE ON FIRE can be related to other versions of the scenario (CLEAN HOUSE; GLOBAL GREENHOUSE). The other versions of the scenario all involved unpleasant or dangerous living conditions within the HOUSE, which include a lease to be respected or increasing temperatures. The HOUSE ON FIRE version expands on these arguments to refer to a more tangible and immediate danger which may typically occur within one's own house. This common knowledge and experience of FIRE has been at the heart of activists' arguments, particularly those made by Fridays for Future. They used the metaphor to contradict people's expectations associated with this common knowledge. Their video displayed an absurd image of the human response to climate change. Alternatively, the political version of the metaphor, given by Emmanuel Macron, focused on political inaction. The topic-triggering function of the metaphor, in other words, with its references to the literal fire (Semino 2008: 27), represents a political argument responding to Jacques Chirac's blame: by posting a 'fake' picture of the Amazon fires on his Twitter account, Emmanuel Macron argues that he is not 'looking the other way'. Nonetheless, the impact of colonialism in the Amazon and the chronological descriptions contradicted the emergency involved in the metaphorical image of the HOUSE ON FIRE, and this eventually confirmed Greta Thunberg's claim: our house is still on fire.

This chapter has demonstrated that similar exploitations of a particular source domain, HOUSE, do not necessarily result in similar environmental arguments. This finding is coherent with existing literature looking at the use of scenarios in political debates (Musolff 2016, 2019). For instance, Charteris-Black (2019) and Musolff (2019) convincingly established how the proverb 'having your cake and eating it' could promote opposite arguments in the context of Brexit debates. We have demonstrated that a similar process is at work in environmental debates opposing politicians to climate activists. The scenario THE EARTH AS HOUSE (ON FIRE) seems to be relevant to these two communities in order to promote their own views on climate change mitigation. The popularity of the scenario may be explained by the feeling of emergency which it effectively helps to convey to recipients. However, as the conceptual mapping relies heavily on our common knowledge, experience and affect, we conclude that such a scenario may be used with caution by politicians who do not yet have any established plan to EXTINGUISH THE FIRE. The political misuse of the scenario may then only confirm the activists' stance, and especially Fridays for Future's stance, which argues that we keep on living in a 'business as-usual' manner while there is a fire in the house.

References

Augé, A. (2021). COVID-19 as a framing device for environmental protest: the ECOSYSTEM HEALTH metaphor. *Environmental Communication*, online first. doi: 10.1080/17524032.2021.1890174.

Augé, A. (2022a). COVID-19 is the Earth's vaccine: Controversial metaphors in environmental discourse. *Interface: Journal of European Languages and Literatures*, 17, pp. 5–33. doi: 10.6667/interface.17.2022.158.

Augé, A. (2022b). From scientific arguments to scepticism: Humans' place in the GREENHOUSE. *Public Understanding of Science*, 31 (2), pp. 179–94. doi: 10.1177/09636625211035624.

Augé, A. (2023). *Metaphor and Argumentation in Climate Crisis Discourse*. New York: Routledge.

Boyd, R. (1993). Metaphor and theory change: What is 'metaphor' a metaphor for? In: Ortony, A., ed., *Metaphor and Thought*. 2nd edn. Cambridge: Cambridge University Press, pp. 481–532.

Charteris-Black, J. (2011). *Politicians and Rhetoric: The Persuasive Power of Metaphor*. London: Palgrave Macmillan.

Charteris-Black, J. (2019). *Metaphors of Brexit: No Cherries on the Cake?* London: Palgrave Macmillan.

Deignan, A. (2005). *Metaphor and Corpus Linguistics*. Amsterdam: John Benjamins.

Fairclough, I. and Fairclough, N. (2012). *Political Discourse Analysis*. New York: Routledge.

Goatly, A. (1997). *The Language of Metaphors*. New York: Routledge.

Hanne, M. (2014). An introduction to the 'warring with word' project. In: Hanne, M., Crano, W. D. and Mio, J. S., eds, *Warring with Words: Narrative and Metaphor in Politics*. New York: Psychology Press, pp. 1–57.

Lakoff, G. (1993). The contemporary theory of metaphor. In: Ortony, A., ed., *Metaphor and Thought*. 2nd edn. Cambridge: Cambridge University Press, pp. 202–52.

Lakoff, G. (2004). *Don't Think of an Elephant! Know Your Values and Frame the Debate: The Essential Guide for Progressives*. White River Junction, VT: Chelsea Green.

Lakoff, G. (2010). Why it matters how we frame the environment. *Environmental Communication*, 4 (1), pp. 70–81. doi: 10.1080/17524030903529749.

Musolff, A. (2016). *Political Metaphor Analysis: Discourse and Scenarios*. London: Bloomsbury Academic.

Musolff, A. (2019). How (not?) to quote a proverb: The role of figurative quotations and allusions in political discourse. *Journal of Pragmatics*, 155, pp. 135–44. doi: 10.1016/j.pragma.2019.10.011.

Nerlich, B. and Hellsten, I. (2014). The greenhouse metaphor and the footprint metaphor: Climate change risk assessment and risk management seen through the lens of two prominent metaphors. *Technikfolgenabschatzung: Theorie und Praxis*, 23 (2), pp. 27–33. doi: 10.14512/tatup.23.2.27.

Nerlich, B. and Koteyko, N. (2010). Carbon gold rush and carbon cowboys: A new chapter in green mythology? *Environmental Communication*, 4 (1), pp. 37–53. doi: 10.1080/17524030903522389.

Scandrett, E. (2016). Climate justice: Contested discourse and social transformation. *International Journal of Climate Change Strategies and Management*, 8 (4), pp. 477–87. doi: 10.1108/IJCCSM-05-2015-0060.

Semino, E. (2008). *Metaphor in Discourse*. Cambridge: Cambridge University Press.

Shaw, C. and Nerlich, B. (2015). Metaphor as a mechanism of global climate change governance: A study of international policies, 1992–2012. *Ecological Economics*, 109, pp. 34–40. doi: 10.1016/j.ecolecon.2014.11.001/

Steen, G. J. (2008). The paradox of metaphor: Why we need a three-dimensional model of metaphor. *Metaphor and Symbol*, 23 (4), pp. 213–41. doi: 10.1080/10926480802426753/.

Steen, G. J. (2011). The contemporary theory of metaphor – now new and improved! *Review of Cognitive Linguistics*, 9 (1), pp. 26–64. doi: 10.1075/rcl.9.1.03ste.

Steen, G. J., Dorst, A. G., Berenike Herrmann, J., Kaal, A. A., Krennmayr, T. and Pasma, T. (2010). *A Method for Linguistic Metaphor Identification*. Amsterdam: John Benjamins.

Tognini-Bonelli, E. (2001). *Corpus Linguistics at Work*. Amsterdam: John Benjamins.

van der Hel, S., Hellsten, I. and Steen, G. (2018). Tipping points and climate change: Metaphor between science and the media. *Environmental Communication*, 12 (5), pp. 605–20. doi: 10.1080/17524032.2017.1410198.

Wilson, D. and Sperber, D. (1979). Ordered entailments: An alternative to presuppositional theories. In: Oh, C. K. and Dineen, D. A., eds, *Syntax and Semantics 11: Presuppositions*. New York: Academic Press, pp. 299–323.

Details of the corpus

British Political Speeches Database: https://www.britishpoliticalspeech.org.

Emmanuel Macron's official Twitter account: https://www.twitter.com/Emmanuel Macron.

Fridays For Future *Our House Is on Fire* video: https://www.youtube.com/watch?v=eT32UFzA7E8 [accessed 12 June 2022].

Friends of the Earth official website: https://www.foe.org.

Greta Thunberg's official Twitter account: https://www.twitter.com/GretaThunberg.

Greta Thunberg's speech at the World Economic Forum, 2020: https://www.democracynow.org/2020/1/21/our_house_is_still_on_fire#:~:text=Our%20house%20is%20still%20on%20fire.,your%20children%20above%20all%20else [accessed 26 June 2023].

Jacques Chirac's speech at the Earth Summit, 2002: https://www.francetvinfo.fr/meteo/climat/video-notre-maison-brule-et-nous-regardons-ailleurs-le-discours-visionnaire-de-jacques-chirac-a-johannesbourg_4382153.html [accessed 26 June 2023].

CONCLUDING REMARKS

Towards Legitimisation Studies in contemporary crises

Robert Butler and Anaïs Augé

1 Introduction

The study of discourse cannot avoid the analysis of discourse production and discourse reception. This volume has sought to explore the gap between public expectations and political commitment. Contexts of crisis reveal certain significant features of political discourse. Legitimisation shows that despite attempts to bridge the gap between expectation and delivery, legitimisation strategies have certain limits. Further research is needed to show why these tools have varying degrees of success. In this final discussion, cases where these strategies may expose their limits will be examined. Can discursive strategies be enhanced or improved to make legitimisation strategies more effective for political actors and thereby reduce the gap between expectation and performance? In times of crisis, it becomes even more important for political actors to appear to be legitimate while relying on discourse to support their positions and actions.

2 Legitimisation through didactic discourse

In times of crisis, politicians are required to communicate efficiently in order to guide the public. In particular, they need to enforce specific measures aimed at controlling the crisis and avoid a runaway stage where the crisis cannot be controlled anymore.[1] For these measures to be effective, they need to be implemented collectively, at the national or international level. The combined impact of political measures can also involve enforcement and authority. In such cases, political authority can be perceived as a legitimate process through which the politicians make use of their legislative power to reach a prospective stage of public safety. This process is best

---

[1] See the discussion of 'runaway' climate crisis in van der Hel et al. (2018).

illustrated by the measures taken against the COVID-19 virus during which politicians across the world enforced national lockdowns, mask-wearing measures and social-distancing measures to protect their populations.

Yet, as widely reported in the existing literature, the reliance on political authority was heavily criticised and mocked by the public and the media (Hanne 2022; Musolff 2022). There was also a significant spread of conspiracy theories which assigned mischievous or problematic characteristics to governments and likened politicians to dictators or gurus (Jolley and Paterson 2020; Bierwiaczonek et al. 2022).

As a result, there may be a perception held by the media and the public in which legitimate policies are seen as illegitimate. This perception may reside in the collective enforcement of such policies, which can eventually undermine individual circumstances. It may also reside in the flaws of political discourse which aim to legitimise political authority over the public. For instance, a large body of research has demonstrated the questionable use of WAR-like imageries in existing political discourse about COVID-19. To illustrate this point: 'The fight to slow the spread of COVID-19 is "our big war," [US President] Trump said Thursday. "It's a medical war. We have to win this war. It's very important"' (Bennett and Berenson 2020, quoted after Musolff 2022: 77). The significant exploitation of this kind of imagery in political and public discourse (Charteris-Black 2021; Olza et al. 2021) has ultimately shed light on the controversial connotations involved in the conceptualisation of COVID-19 AS WAR. Accordingly, sick individuals have been perceived as PUBLIC ENEMIES and health workers as FIGHTERS bearing the brunt of the management of the pandemic (Semino 2020).

It has been argued that political discourse which addresses crisis may promote legitimacy by adopting didactic strategies (Augé 2022a, 2023: 164–79). Since legitimisation also involves the public reception of political discourse, it is all the more necessary for politicians to adapt their discourse to the particularity of the audience: for example, the different ages of recipients, experiences, cultures, knowledge, genres, professions and ethnicities, among many other factors (see Charteris-Black 2011, 2014, 2021). Their discourse must also adapt to the specific nature of the socio-political context in which the discourse is taking place – the context of crisis.

Crises like the COVID-19 pandemic and the climate crisis still represent abstract concepts: these crises are related to an 'invisible' virus (Augé 2022a) and long-term, uneven climatic phenomena (van der Hel et al. 2018). This means that the risks associated with crises need to be thoroughly explained – and in concrete terms – to the public so that collective enforcement of safety measures like mask-wearing or sustainable behaviour are perceived as legitimate by the recipients.

Climate crisis discourse represents a pertinent illustration of didactic discourse about crisis. The significant reliance on 'pedagogical' metaphorical expressions has already been investigated (Boyd 1993), including the metaphors of the 'carbon footprint' (Nerlich and Hellsten 2014), the 'tipping point' (van der Hel et al. 2018) and the 'greenhouse effect' (Augé 2022b; see also Chapter 9 in this volume) in discourse aiming to explain to recipients the urgency of tackling the crisis. By conceptually mapping a concrete source domain with a complex target domain associated with public fear and misunderstanding, discourse producers (notably scientists and activists) have promoted a didactic depiction of the crisis scenario with the use of familiar terms which can appeal to the public.

This type of didactic discourse is yet to be adopted by politicians who, instead, have been reported to favour highly conventional metaphorical expressions (Ly 2013) such as the JOURNEY-PATH-MOVEMENT metaphor, as in 'Now is the time to . . . set off on a journey to a cleaner, greener future' (Boris Johnson, 26th Conference of the Parties, 2021; quoted after Augé 2023: 65). The reliance on didactic discursive strategies, as applied, for example, to activists' discourse (Rapport 1995; Ross et al. 1997) has been shown to have an impact on recipients' reasoning about the crisis (Thibodeau and Boroditsky 2011, 2013; Nay and Brunson 2013).

Consequently, the didactic discourse about crisis situations forms a significant dimension of political legitimisation. The numerous contestations related to political illegitimacy in the context of crisis could possibly be explained by the focus on political authority and collectivism, while didactic political discursive strategies have yet to be documented.

3 The impact of new forms of media

The opportunity to address public comments and questions in political discourse and decision-making could form the first step towards more didactic discursive strategies to be adopted by politicians. Importantly, the political exchanges with citizens which are facilitated by the new media present significant discursive patterns. The development of new media formats in recent years is the result of technological progress in the digital domain. These formats include video platforms like YouTube and Twitch and social media platforms such as Facebook and Twitter. The rise of social media has enabled the public to share information, opinions and experiences (Roxburgh et al. 2019). Although these different websites may appeal to different audiences for different reasons, they all share a facility for disseminating news, documents or ideas quickly. This brings into question to what extent new media, understood in terms of their formats, should be analysed as the new media and as part of a journalistic enterprise. In contexts of crisis and conflict, this technological phenomenon gives rise to a number of observations and challenges for future research in respect of discourse legitimisation through the new media.

Firstly, new media formats are not incompatible with the dissemination of legitimised discourse through moral evaluation, where the message may not only be superficial, but also transmissible in different contexts through the accessible nature of simplified notions. Although transferable, these simplifications of reality have far-reaching and complex political ramifications. One study analyses the spread of misinformation on the online social media platform Twitter with respect to the alleged health benefits of nicotine in the face of COVID-19 (Silver et al. 2022). The authors draw on observations made by Papacharissi (2015): the democratisation of journalism means that the publishing of purposeful public discourse finds itself cohabiting with misinformation and comments made incoherently or in bad faith (Silver et al. 2022). The cohabitation of misleading and accurate public information can be seen through the ease with which detailed and accurate news reports can be redistributed online in the form of short, succinct pieces which can reach out to a large audience with minimal effort. The size of an audience may depend on the composition of the social group and whether the issue transcends international boundaries. For example, Froio and Ganesh (2019) conducted a study of far-right movements and political groups on Twitter in a transnational context and concluded that the retweeting of messages between members in different countries depends on the subject at stake, with the economy and immigration being retweeted the most at the transnational level.

Secondly, the relative ease with which a news item can be redistributed leads to another challenge for the legitimisation of political discourse, and discourse in general. The emphasis on dissemination and the reaching out by new sources of information can lead to misleading interpretations of expert sources of authority. There is some evidence that the transmission of information and ideas is organised differently between Twitter and YouTube, according to a study by Park et al. (2015) into the social networks of the 'Occupy Wall Street' movement. In this study, networks on Twitter were found to be organised around a hierarchical structure with a relatively small number of powerful users involved in republishing information, while YouTube was more conducive to the sharing of ideas, interconnection and solidarity between users (Park et al. 2015). The question of expertise is not an issue only for online social media platforms, but also for the mainstream terrestrial television channels. The problem is illustrated by the rise in the United Kingdom of the 'presentician', whose status lies ambiguously between news presenter or journalist, and political campaigner or politician (Boulton 2023). This may lead to scenarios in which political and social actors self-legitimise their discourse with the help of their own expertise, or become recognised as experts because of their ability to disseminate information.

Finally, the new media may have a polarising effect on public opinion (Sun et al. 2023). The risk is greater where the subjects to which participants are exposed are more diverse (Lee et al. 2014: 706). Conflicts are therefore at risk of being exacerbated rather than leading to discourse smoothing processes. Questions remain, for example, over the use of the expression 'nuclear card'[2] or 'nuclear cards'[3] with respect to the options allegedly open to the leader of Russia at the time of the Russia–Ukraine conflict. As demonstrated by Tomoshige (Chapter 8), the CARD metaphor is extendable to new contexts. Its implications have the potential to go well beyond the level of interaction between individuals. In some of the replies given at a press conference given by Hua Chunying, Assistant Minister of Foreign Affairs in China, on 4 August 2022, Chunying claims that 'The US has sought to play the "Taiwan card" to contain China' in order to de-legitimise the US's position in relation to China. However, the Assistant Minister appears to legitimise any response by China by stating that 'We will not sit by and watch the US play the "Taiwan card" to serve the US's domestic politics and the selfish interests of some politicians.'[4] More research is needed into the transmission of such short but powerful evaluative messages and how these messages can be transmitted widely and quickly, but at what cost to the legitimisation of a political position and to the resolution of a crisis situation.

4 The impact on the public: Over-legitimisation?

As discussed in the above section, the new media form part of a particular context of discourse where political legitimisation is brought into question. Political discourse is spread and exploited not only by journalists who can be perceived as professional communicators, but also by political opponents and the public. These media represent a platform for displaying various opinions and arguments about political decisions and scandals (Edwards 2013). As a result, political legitimacy can be tested through the exploitation of political discourse in the new media.

The challenge to political legitimacy is particularly relevant in cases where the political discourse has already been established as legitimate: for example, following scientific experiments and findings or contextual evidence. In contexts of crisis, the recurrence of political quotes across diverse media can ultimately generate overwhelming fear among the public, which in turn can prevent effective measures from being implemented. The need to surrender to political authority, and possible feelings of powerlessness due to the impact of the crisis, may cause resignation from within the public (Augé 2023: 62–103). This negative impact of legitimisation in times

---

[2] Jake Sullivan (White House national security adviser), interviewed by CBS, is reported as saying that the United States told Russia that it will face 'catastrophic consequences' if tactical nuclear weapons are used in Ukraine. Quoted in Epstein and Haltiwanger (2022).

[3] The expression is used by John R. Bolton, a former national security adviser in the United States of America (Bolton 2023).

[4] The expression is used by Hua Chunying (Embassy of the People's Republic of China in the United States of America 2022, original source in English).

of crisis can be illustrated in the case of the climate crisis, where environmental activists have been criticised for relying on 'alarmism' (Risbey 2008; Küppers 2022) – for example, by depicting the climate crisis as a 'time bomb' (Doyle 2007). While such an 'alarmist' stance could be required in order to inform the public about the risk of environmental inaction, the global relevance of the topic and the ease with which the discourse can be accessed and exploited may ultimately favour a predominant impression of fear. The 'retweet' and 'quoted tweet' options available on the social media platform Twitter may be significant tools giving rise to predominant emotions experienced by the public. In the context of the climate crisis, the emotion of fear is best encapsulated by the notion of 'ecoanxiety' (Hickman 2020; Coffey et al. 2021) through which recipients are surrounded by various pieces of information regarding a wide range of safety measures. These measures are all perceived as being legitimate, to the extent that individual actions taken in order to control the crisis become an obsession preventing recipients from imagining a life in a society free of crisis. The example of 'ecoanxiety' thus represents a case where legitimate discourse has been misused because it may have not have taken into account the specific features and popularity of the new media. This example also shows that discourse can be established as legitimate and subsequently be perceived as illegitimate following the public (mis)use of the new media (Abrams et al. 2021).

This process will tentatively be referred to as cases of over-legitimisation, whereby access to mainly online information significantly impacts the legitimisation strategies adopted by politicians. This impact is due not only to the documented spread of 'rumors' and 'fake news' brought about by the new media (Naeem et al. 2020; Apuke and Omar 2021; Gür-Şeker et al. 2022), but also the particularities of the context of crisis which is characterised by political authority, public fear, and collectivism. Therefore, extended access to crisis discourse may prevent adequate practices as authorised in such discourse, and can result in providing grounds for de-legitimisation.

If the significant use of the new media by the public is considered, the above observation leads to the hypothesis that political debates and oppositions, as well as humorous or sarcastic 'deconstructions' (Musolff 2022) of political discourse in times of crisis, might actually serve to reinforce legitimisation strategies. While didactic discourse helps politicians to communicate the risks and legitimise associated policies, the discourse of the new media represents a platform where individuals' arguments and emotions regarding these policies can be easily expressed, debated or deconstructed. However, the importance of gatekeeping on the discourse produced in the new media must be considered (Liu et al. 2021). As such, the producers of discourse in the new media may not resort to legitimisation strategies in the same way that political discourse requires legitimisation. Legitimisation in discourses of crisis produced in the new media may be excessively exploited to the extent that the public reception overly adapts to such discourse, which might result in generalised fear and resignation.

The dialogue permitted by the new media between individuals (primarily politicians and the public) is a significant asset in the arsenal of legitimisation strategies and still requires thorough analysis by linguists and political scientists. By sharing personal or local experiences of the crisis, questioning the scopes of particular policies and expressing emotions generated by crisis discourse, discourse producers can legitimise their stances, specifically through didactic discursive strategies. These strategies can help to limit the adverse impacts on political authority and manage the public's fear, both of which characterise legitimate political discourse on matters of crisis.

5 Conclusion

The exploration of Legitimisation Studies points to the need for Critical Discourse Studies to reappraise how political actors justify their actions in contexts where threat, uncertainty and urgency lead to crisis, and through the medium of conflict between actors. Further research is needed on the techniques used to legitimise political action, and this must take into account the multifarious de-legitimisation strategies also used to spread myths and mistruths and deflect blame and accountability on to political counterparts. It seems easier than ever for actors in society to become experts, to self-impose their own forms of authority and influence others.

Legitimisation signals the need for actors in the political sphere to develop and improve their dialogue with the public and in all areas of the political system. This dialogue should not obfuscate the essential illocutionary forces expressed in speech acts, such as apologising to the electorate (Butler 2016), or compromise other speech acts where a political position must be justified. Legitimisation strategies require a greater awareness not only of the psycho-social forces between social and political actors, but also of the cognitive linguistic interactive forces which can guide a political management strategy (Butler 2018).

In addition to the need for developing new legitimisation strategies, a more prominent place should be reserved for Proximisation Theory (Cap 2008, 2010, 2014) in which a spatial-temporal-axiological (STA) model is used for the justification of the controversial policy. Its main goal is to legitimise the policies and actions of the speaker and also to 'neutralize the growing impact of the negative, "foreign", "alien", "antagonistic", entities' (Cap 2014: 17). Proximisation Theory has already been used in a number of key studies, such as interventionist political discourse during the invasion of Iraq by the United States, and makes it possible to observe the multiplicity of rhetorical patterns reflected in legitimisation (Cap 2008, 2010). Whichever forms of legitimisation are identified by researchers, it is likely that future research in Legitimisation Studies may follow so long as crises remain and conflicts cannot be solved.

References

Abrams, N., Augé, A., Nowakowsky, M. and Tenbrink, T. (2021). Mask-wearing was not disputed in previous crises – so why is it so hotly contested today? *The Conversation*. Available from: https://theconversation.com/mask-wearing-wasnt-disputed-in-previous-crises-so-why-is-it-so-hotly-contested-today-171536 [accessed 26 June 2023].

Apuke, O. D. and Omar, B. (2021). Fake news and COVID-19: Modelling the predictors of fake news sharing among social media users. *Telematics and Informatics*, 56 (101475). doi: 10.1016%2Fj.tele.2020.101475.

Augé, A. (2022a). Ideological and explanatory uses of the COVID-19 as a war metaphor in science. *Review of Cognitive Linguistics*, 20 (2), pp. 412–37, https://doi.org/10.1075/rcl.00117.aug.

Augé, A. (2022b). 'From scientific arguments to scepticism: humans' place in the Greenhouse.' *Public Understanding of Science*, 31 (2), pp. 179–94. doi: 10.1177/09636625211035624.

Augé, A. (2023). *Metaphor and Argumentation in Climate Crisis Discourse*. New York: Routledge.

Bennett, B. and Berenson, T. (2020). 'Our big war.' As coronavirus spreads, Trump refashions himself as a wartime president. *Time*, 19 March. https://time.com/5806657/donald-trump-coronavirus-war-china/ [accessed 26 June 2023].

Bierwiaczonek, K., Gundersen, A. and Kunst, J. (2022). The role of conspiracy beliefs for COVID-19 health responses: A meta-analysis. *Current Opinion in Psychology*, 46 (101346). doi: 10.1016/j.copsyc.2022.101346.

Bolton, J. R. Putin did the world a favor by suspending Russia's participation in New START. *The Washington Post*, 6 March 2023. Available from: https://www.washingtonpost.com/opinions/2023/03/06/russia-china-united-states-tripolar-nuclear-powers/ [accessed 26 June 2023].

Boulton, A. (2023). The growing list of 'presenticians' as lines blur between broadcast news and campaigning politicians. *Sky News*, 10 March 2023. Available from: https://news.sky.com/story/adam-boulton-the-growing-list-of-presenticians-as-lines-blur-between-broadcast-news-and-campaigning-politicians-12829885 [accessed 26 June 2023].

Boyd, R. (1993). Metaphor and theory change: What is 'metaphor' a metaphor for? In: Ortony, A., ed., *Metaphor and Thought*. 2nd edn. Cambridge: Cambridge University Press, pp. 481–532.

Butler, R. (2016). Gérer la déconvenue: les frais de scolarité, le manifeste des *Liberal Democrats* et la coalition Britannique. In: Albrespit, J., François, N. and Thión Soriano-Mollá, L., eds, *Fabriques de vérité(s): Communication et imaginaires*. Vol. 1. Paris: L'Harmattan, pp. 149–66.

Butler, R. (2018). Approche multimodale de l'analyse du discours politique: l'exemple des *Liberal Democrats*. PhD thesis. Université de Pau et des Pays de l'Adour, Pau.

Cap, P. (2008). Towards the proximization model of the analysis of legitimization in political discourse. *Journal of Pragmatics*, 40 (1), pp. 17–40. doi: 10.1016/j.pragma.2007.10.002.

Cap, P. (2010). Axiological aspects of proximization. *Journal of Pragmatics*, 42 (2), pp. 392–407. doi: 10.1016/j.pragma.2009.06.008.

Cap, P. (2014). Applying cognitive pragmatics to Critical Discourse Studies: A proximization analysis of three public space discourses. *Journal of Pragmatics*, 70 (1), pp. 16–30. doi: 10.1016/j.pragma.2014.05.008.

Charteris-Black, J. (2011). *Politicians and Rhetoric: The Persuasive Power of Metaphor*. London: Palgrave Macmillan.

Charteris-Black, J. (2014). *Analysing Political Speeches: Rhetoric, Discourse and Metaphors*. London: Palgrave Macmillan.

Charteris-Black, J. (2021). *Metaphors of Coronavirus: Invisible Enemy or Zombie Apocalypse?* Cham: Springer Nature.

Coffey, Y., Bhullar, N., Durkin, J., Islam, S. and Usher, K. (2021). Understanding eco-anxiety: A systematic scoping review of current literature and identified knowledge gap. *The Journal of Climate Change and Health*, 3 (100047). doi: 10.1016/j.joclim.2021.100047.

Doyle, J. (2007). Picturing the clima(c)tic: Greenpeace and the representational politics of climate change communication. *Science as Culture*, 16 (2), pp. 129–50. doi: 10.1080/09505430701368938.

Edwards, A. (2013). (How) do participants in online discussion forums create eco chambers? The inclusion and exclusion of dissenting voices in an online forum about climate change. *Journal of Argumentation in Context*, 2 (1), pp. 127–50. doi: 10.1075/jaic.2.1.06edw.

Embassy of the People's Republic of China in the United States of America (2022). Foreign Ministry spokesperson Hua Chunying's regular press conference on August 4, 2022. 4 August 2022. Available from: http://us.china-embassy.gov.cn/eng/lcbt/wjbfyrbt/202208/t20220805_10734891.htm [accessed 5 August 2022].

Epstein, J. and Haltiwanger, J. (2022). US says it told the Kremlin that Russia will face 'catastrophic consequences' if it uses tactical nuclear weapons in Ukraine. *Business Insider*, 26 September. Available from: https://www.businessinsider.com/us-russia-catastrophic-consequences-firing-nuclear-weapons-ukraine-war-2022-9?r=US&IR=T [accessed 26 June 2023].

Froio, C. and Ganesh, B. (2019) The transnationalisation of far right discourse on Twitter. *European Societies*, 21 (4), pp. 513–39. doi: 10.1080/14616696.2018.1494295.

Gür-Şeker, D., Boonen, U. and Wentker, M. (2022). #conspiracymemes: A framework-based analysis of conspiracy memes as digital multimodal units and ensuing user reactions on Instagram. In: Demata, M., Zorzi, V. and Zottola, A., eds, *Conspiracy Theory Discourses*. Amsterdam: John Benjamins, pp. 267–94.

Hanne, M. (2022). How we escape capture by the 'war' metaphor for Covid-19. *Metaphor and Symbol*, 37 (2), pp. 88–100. doi: 10.1080/10926488.2021.1935261.

Hickman, C. (2020). We need to (find a way to) talk about ... ecoanxiety. *Journal of Social Work Practice*, 34 (4), pp. 411–24. doi: 10.1080/02650533.2020.1844166.

Jolley, D. and Paterson, J. (2020). Pylons ablazed: Examining the role of 5G COVID-19 conspiracy beliefs and support for violence. *British Journal of Social Psychology*, 59 (3), pp. 628–40. doi: 10.1111/bjso.12394.

Küppers, A. (2022). Climate soviets, alarmism, and eco-dictatorship: The framing of climate change scepticism by the populist radical right Alternatives for Germany. *German Politics*, online first. doi: 10.1080/09644008.2022.2056596.

Lee, J. K., Choi, J., Kim, C. and Kim, Y. (2014). Social media, network heterogeneity, and opinion polarization. *Journal of Communication*, 64 (4), pp. 702–22. doi: 10.1111/jcom.12077.

Liu, Y., Augé, A. and Yan, W. (2021). Does social media expand the traditional role of Chinese TV journalists as Gatekeeper on Weibo and WeChat J-accounts? *The Frontiers of Society, Science and Technology*, 3 (6), pp. 29–37. doi: 10.25236/FSST.2021.030605.

Ly, A. (2013). Images and roles of the European Union in the climate change debate: A cognitive approach to metaphors in the European parliament. In: Fløttum, K., ed., *Speaking of Europe: Approaches to Complexity in European Political Discourse*. Amsterdam: John Benjamins, pp. 151–71.

Musolff, A. (2022). 'World-beating' pandemic responses: Ironical, sarcastic, and satirical use of war and competition metaphors in the context of COVID-19 pandemic. *Metaphor and Symbol*, 37 (2), pp. 76–87. doi: 10.1080/10926488.2021.1932505.

Naeem, S. B., Bhatti, R. and Khan, A. (2020). An exploration of how fake news is taking over social media and putting public health at risk. *Health Information and Libraries Journal*, 38 (2), pp. 143–9. doi: 10.1111/hir.12320.

Nay, C. and Brunson, M. (2013). A war of words: Do conflict metaphors affect beliefs about managing 'unwanted' plants? *Societies*, 3, 158–69. doi: 10.3390/soc3020158.

Nerlich, B. and Hellsten, I. (2014). The greenhouse metaphor and the footprint metaphor: Climate change risk assessment and risk management seen through the lens of two prominent metaphors. *Technikfolgenabschatzung: Theorie und Praxis*, 23 (2), pp. 27–33. doi: 10.14512/tatup.23.2.27.

Olza, I., Koller, V., Ibarrexte-Antunano, I., Pérez-Sobrino, P. and Semino, E. (2021). The #ReframeCovid initiative: From Twitter to society via metaphor. *Metaphor and the Social World*, 11 (1), pp. 98–120. doi: 10.1075/msw.00013.olz.

Papacharissi Z. (2015) *Affective Publics: Sentiment, Technology, and Politics*. Oxford: Oxford University Press.

Park, S. J., Lim, Y. S. and Park, H. W. (2015). Comparing Twitter and YouTube networks in information diffusion: The case of the 'Occupy Wall Street' movement. *Technological Forecasting & Social Change*, 95, pp. 208–17. doi: 10.1016/j.techfore.2015.02.003.

Rapport, D. (1995). Ecosystem health: More than a metaphor? *Environmental Values*, 4 (4), 287–309. doi: 10.3197/096327195776679439.

Risbey, J. (2008). The new climate discourse: Alarmist or alarming? *Global Environmental Change*, 18 (1), pp. 26–37. doi: 10.1016/j.gloenvcha.2007.06.003.

Ross, N., Eyles, J., Cole, D. and Iannantuono, A. (1997). The ecosystem health metaphor in science and policy. *The Canadian Geographer*, 41 (2), pp. 114–27. doi: 10.1111/j.1541-0064.1997.tb01152.x.

Roxburgh, N., Guan, D., Shin, K. J., Rand, W., Managi, S., Lovelace, R. and Meng, J. (2019). Characterising climate change discourse on social media during extreme weather events. *Global Environmental Change*, 54, pp. 50–60. doi: 10.1016/j.gloenvcha.2018.11.004.

Semino, E. (2020). 'Not soldiers but firefighters' – Metaphors and Covid-19. *Health Communication*, 36 (1), pp. 50–8. doi: 10.1080/10410236.2020.1844989.

Silver, N., Kierstead, E., Kostygina, G., Tran, H., Briggs, J., Emery, S. and Schillo, B. (2022). The influence of provaping "gatewatchers" on the dissemination of COVID-19 misinformation on Twitter: Analysis of Twitter discourse regarding nicotine and the COVID-19 pandemic. *Journal of Medical Internet Research*, 24 (9). doi: 10.2196%2F40331.

Sun, R., Zhu, H. and Guo, F. (2023). Impact of content ideology on social media opinion polarization: The moderating role of functional affordances and symbolic expressions. *Decision Support Systems*, 164 (113845). doi: 10.1016/j.dss.2022.113845.

Thibodeau, P. and Boroditsky, L. (2011). Metaphors we think with: The role of metaphor in reasoning. *PLoS ONE*, 6 (2), (e16782). doi: 10.1371/journal.pone.0016782.

Thibodeau, P. and Boroditsky, L. (2013). Natural language metaphors covertly influence reasoning. *PLoS ONE* 8 (1), (e52961). doi: 10.1371/journal.pone.0052961.

van der Hel, S., Hellsten, I. and Steen, G. (2018). Tipping points and climate change: Metaphor between science and the media. *Environmental Communication*, 12 (5), pp. 605–20. doi: 10.1080/17524032.2017.1410198.

Index

action verbs, 130
agitprop, 113
allegory, 159–60, 162
altruism, 15, 106
   benefit, 157
anaphora, 159, 163
argumentation, 8, 187–8, 190–1
   argumentation process, 5
argumentative *see* argumentation
Aristotle, 6
audience, 2, 9, 42, 48, 96, 106, 108–9, 113–15, 119, 124, 126–8, 132, 140, 163
authorisation, 13, 106; *see also* legitimisation
authority, 3, 13, 17–19, 54–6, 161, 172, 176–8, 180, 193–4, 199, 204–5, 207–8
   charismatic, 4
   legal-rational, 3–4

Bateman, J., 134
Biden, J., 18, 124–6, 129, 132, 136–7, 140–1
blended space, 134
body movements, 124, 126, 128, 131, 141
Bolsonaro, J., 198–9
Borisov, B., 107, 110–14
Boyd, R., 189–90
Bozizé, F., 154
Brandt, P. A., 124
Brexit, 7, 17, 78–9, 84, 86, 88–90, 93 97, 201
Britain *see* United Kingdom
Brown, P., 44

Bucholtz, M., 78, 80
Bulgaria, 105–6
Burkina Faso, 148, 156
Bush, G. W., 194–6, 200

camera angles, 131–2
   close-up, 131, 141
   Dutch angles, 132, 134
   middle-up, 131, 135–7, 141
   point-of-view, 132
   side angle, 137
camera movements, 124
Cao, Q., 26
Cap, P., 12, 14–16; *see also* Proximization Theory
CAR *see* Central African Republic
card game metaphor (CGM), 173–5, 181–3
CARD metaphor, 19, 167–8, 170–3, 176–83, 208
   ace card, 175
   cancer card, 177
   celebrity card, 177
   emotion (sympathy) card, 178–9
   friend card, 178
   gender card, 169, 182
   kids card, 177–8
   nationalism card, 177
   nuclear card, 208
   orange card, 168–9
   race card, 168–9, 179, 181–2
   sure card, 168
   Taiwan card, 208

CARD metaphor (*cont.*)
   trump card, 169, 175
   winning card, 175
   woman card, 179, 181
   X card, 19, 167, 172–3, 180, 182–3
   see also metaphor
cartoons, 36
catachresis, 189
Catalan, 71–2
Catalonia, 62, 70–1, 75
CDA *see* Critical Discourse Analysis
CDS *see* Critical Discourse Studies
Central African Republic (CAR), 148–9, 154
CGM *see* card game metaphor
Chad, 148–9, 157
Charteris-Black, J., 9, 190, 201
checks and balances, 114, 116
Chi Square Calculator, 92
   Chi-square test, 92–5
Chilton, P., 4–5, 16, 61, 106, 150–1, 153, 155
China, 17, 25–9, 33–7, 177, 208
Ching, M. K., 170–2
Chirac, J., 187, 189, 198, 200
cinematography, 125
   cinematic, 125–9, 131, 134–6, 139, 141
citizen journalism, 104, 118
Ciudadanos (Cs), 66, 70
climate change, 190, 192–4, 196–7
climate scepticism, 190
Clinton, H., 175, 179–83
COCA *see* Corpus of Contemporary American English
coercion, 3–5, 13, 17, 79, 106
cognition
   cognitive-pragmatic, 18, 123–4, 127, 141
   cognitive-semiotic, 18, 123–4, 134, 141
   see also semiotics
cognitive linguistics, 163, 170
commercial, 18, 125–34, 136–7, 139–41
Communist Party of China (CPC), 26–30, 34, 37
conceptual integration, 134–5, 141
conceptualiser, 78, 80–2, 95–6
conflict
   causes, 160
   collocations, 158

   contexts of conflict, 8
   definition, 6–7
   disorder, 10
   instability, 148
   interrelationship with crisis, 9–10
   military, 18, 148, 161
   multidimensional, 149, 161
   non-violent, 11–13
   opinions, 147
   pity card, 178
   solutions, 162
   terrorism, 148
   violent, 11–13, 149
   see also face
Congo, 53
Conservative Party, 79, 89–90, 92–5, 200
Conservatives *see* Conservative Party
conspiracy theories, 104, 205
context, 1, 7, 9, 13, 16, 25–6, 28–31, 34, 37, 43, 45–6, 50, 53, 55, 62–3, 67–73, 75, 105, 108, 110–11, 130, 148, 151–2, 160, 167, 173–5, 178, 188, 191, 193, 204–8
context-based, 123
context-bound, 176
contextual void, 110
control, 2, 5, 17, 26, 31, 34, 78, 81–2, 86, 96–7, 104, 118–19, 130, 177, 198, 209
   effective control, 78, 81, 93, 97
   epistemic control, 78, 81, 93, 97
   state control, 25, 85
corpus, 26, 29–33, 35, 43–6, 48, 50–2, 61, 63–4, 72, 74, 90–1, 94, 97, 125, 148, 151–4, 161–2, 183, 190–2; *see also* Xi Jinping Corpus
Corpus-Assisted Discourse Studies, 43
corpus-based, 18, 61, 97, 147, 162, 167, 191
Corpus Frequency Test Wizard, 92
Corpus linguistics, 9, 17, 30
Corpus of Contemporary American English (COCA), 167, 169, 172–5, 177–9, 181–2
Corpus of Historical American English (COHA), 181
correspondence analysis, 45–7
corruption, 161
COVID-19, 1, 9, 111–12, 205, 207
crisis
   causes, 147, 158, 162

Index 217

climate, 1–2, 18–19, 188–91, 194, 209
conceptualisation, 19
consequences, 201
constitutive elements, 10
contexts of crisis, 7, 204–5, 208
crisis and conflict, 9–10
crisis scenario, 13, 15–16
crisis situation, 12, 208
definition, 6–7, 11
diplomacy, 53, 56
disorder, 10
environmental, 187, 195–6, 199
state of crisis, 1–2
threat, 4, 8–12, 14, 16, 18, 44, 55, 67–71, 74, 192, 196, 199, 201, 210
uncertainty, 10–12, 16, 210
urgency, 10–12, 16, 51, 187, 206, 210
Critical Discourse Analysis (CDA), 5n, 28, 30, 149; *see also* Critical Discourse Studies (CDS)
Critical Discourse Studies (CDS), 3, 5–6, 9–10, 17–18, 149; *see also* Critical Discourse Analysis (CDA)
Critical Metaphor Analysis (CMA), 6, 9, 18, 189
cross-modal mapping, 131
Cs *see* Ciudadanos
curriculum, 27

dataset, 17, 45, 62–7, 70–2, 74–5, 106–8, 116–17, 151–2, 162, 191–2; *see also* corpus
De Cleen, B., 67, 107
Déby Itno, I., 157
Deely, J., 123
deictic, 111
Deignan, A., 189
de-legitimisation, 5, 7–8, 10, 12–14, 16–19, 61, 64, 71–2, 74–5, 106, 183, 208–10
de-legitimise *see* de-legitimisation
Demjén, Z., 171–3
democracy, 4, 67–9, 73–4, 103–4, 107, 162
deonticity *see* effective stance
Devitt, A., 29
diachronic approach, 17, 43, 63
diachronic study *see* diachronic approach
Díez Velasco, O., 150

digital communication channels, 103
digital platforms, 105
discourse
  consensus, 27
  defined, 43
  didactic, 205–6, 210
  Discourse Theory, 60
  discursive functions, 150
  fiction, 2
  fragmentation, 118
  identity, 78
  infotainment, 2
  institutional, 29
  keywords, 61–2
  see also Critical Discourse Studies (CDS), smoothing
Discourse-Historical Approach (DHA), 6, 17, 28, 45
Discourse-Society-Cognition model, 6; *see also* van Dijk
domain
  domain reduction, 150
  source domain, 9, 149, 159, 188, 190–4, 198–9, 201, 206
  target domain, 188, 206
Dowty, D., 150–1, 153
Du Bois, J. W., 78–80, 89

echo chamber, 103–4, 114
education, 25–8, 30, 32–7
EF *see* effective stance
effective stance, 17, 78–83, 85, 89–91, 93–4, 97
  deonticity (DM), 86, 91, 95
  directivity (DIR), 86, 91, 95–6
  inclination (INC), 87, 91, 95–6
  intentionality (INT), 87, 91, 95–6
  normativity (NRM), 87, 91, 95–6
  potentiality (POT), 88, 91, 95–6
  see also modality
emotion, 15, 18, 106, 127–31
  extreme emotional elicitation, 15
EP *see* epistemic stance
epistemic bubble, 104, 117, 119
epistemic stance, 17, 78–83, 85, 89–91, 93–4, 97
  cognitive attitude (CGA), 84, 91, 94, 97
  epistemic modality (EM), 84, 91, 94, 97

epistemic stance (*cont.*)
    impersonal factives (IFV), 83, 91, 94
    indirect-inferential evidentiality (IIE), 84, 91, 94
    indirect interpretation/reformulation (IIR), 85, 91, 94–5
    personal cognitive factives (PFV), 83, 91, 94, 97
    see also modality
epistemic vigilance, 81
epistemicity *see* epistemic stance
epistrophe, 159, 163
ethnography, 6
EU *see* European Union
European Union (EU), 7, 67, 88–90, 190
evidentiality, 83–5
    evidential predicates, 85

face, 8, 44, 54–5
Facebook, 18, 103, 105, 109–10, 114–15, 117, 119, 206
facial expression, 131, 135
factivity, 83
fake news, 2, 73, 104, 209
Fauconnier, G., 134
fear, 4, 15, 18, 126, 130–7, 141, 209
filmmakers, 128–9, 139–40
force, 82
foregrounding, 147, 162
frame, 29–30, 35, 109–14, 119, 172–3
    aggression, 160
    entertainer, 111
    good faith, 160
    ordinary citizen, 112–13
    performer, 114
    politician, 111, 113
France, 62–3, 67–8, 199
    National Assembly, 17, 63
Front national *see* Le Rassemblement national (RN)

Galera-Masegosa, A., 150
Gbagbo, L., 148, 158–60
gender, 19, 176, 179
genre, 29, 42, 44, 48
Germany, 54, 67
globalisation, 1
glorification, 157–8

Goffman, E., 29, 44, 105, 109
government, 51–2, 55–6, 115

Habermas, J., 4, 105–6
Hall, K., 78, 80
Hart, C., 10
Huang, M., 6–7, 10
human rights, 54–5
    Human Rights Commission, 53
    Human Rights Council, 53
hypothetical futures, 13–15

ICM *see* identity card metaphor
identity card metaphor (ICM), 173, 175–6, 181, 183
identity politics (IP), 174, 180–1, 183
ideology, 5, 17, 25–6, 30, 32, 34, 37, 60, 74, 147, 157–8, 162
Iglesias, P., 63
illocutionary act, 108–9, 168, 182; *see also* speech acts
illocutionary force, 86–7, 210; *see also* illocutionary act
Ima Takav Narod (ITN), 105, 107, 111
image schema, 173
inferences, 85
interaction, 80
international organisations, 42
intersubjectivity *see* subjectivity
intertextuality, 29, 32, 36, 45
IP *see* identity politics
Israel, 53
Issoufou, D., 154–7
Istanbul Convention, 54
ITN *see* Ima Takav Narod
Ivory Coast, 148, 158

Johansen, J., 11
Johnson, B., 79, 89–90, 92–6, 155, 170
Johnstone, B., 78, 80

Kaboré, R. M. C., 148, 156
Kelsey, D., 10
Kerbrat-Orecchioni, C., 44
KhosraviNik, M., 10
knowledge, 35, 78, 81–2, 85, 97, 139, 197, 201–2
Koselleck, R., 6–7, 10
Kranert, M., 61

Index

La France insoumise (LFI), 62, 69–70
La République en Marche (LREM), 65–6, 69, 71
Lakoff, G., 128, 150, 155, 170, 190
Lall, M., 25
Lams, L., 26
Langacker, R., 78, 80–2
Le Rassemblement national (RN), 62, 67
legitimacy, 2–5, 44, 53–6, 81, 205
  consent, 3
  crisis, 4
  functions, 3–5
  public image, 53, 55
legitimation *see* legitimisation
legitimisation
  actions, 183
  functions, 3, 79, 106, 167
  kinship, 108
  knowledge, 97
  limits, 204
  online image, 119
  self-legitimisation, 64, 68, 73, 75, 207
  shared values, 116
  strategy, 16, 18–19, 82, 112, 116, 179–80
  techniques, 16, 105–6
  typology, 13
  see also de-legitimisation
Legitimisation Studies, 16, 210
lessons, 35
Levinson, S., 44
lexical bundles, 30–1
lexicalisation, 147
LFI *see* La France insoumise
Libya, 53
Locke, J., 3
log-likelihood test (LL), 93, 94–5
Loi PACTE, 69
LREM *see* La République en Marche

Macron, E., 70, 197–201
Mali, 148, 152, 154, 157
manipulation, 2, 147
Marxism, 33, 35
May, T., 79, 88–90, 92–6
meaning
  meaning-in-context, 18, 124
  meaning-making, 18, 123–31, 134–7, 139–41
  on-screen meanings, 128, 140
media, 2, 7, 9, 29, 31, 37, 113–16, 118–19, 123, 163, 206, 208
  alternative media, 111, 118
  campaign, 116
  consumers, 117
  digital, 9, 18, 104
  discourses, 61
  interviews, 8
  mainstream, 10, 111, 117
  media outlets, 114, 119
  mediatisation, 4, 8–9, 13
  mediatised political discourse, 4
  new media, 2, 17–18, 103, 109, 206–10
  publications, 140
  social media, 4, 9–10, 18, 103–4, 191, 206–7
  state, 27, 29–30, 37
  the media, 1, 9, 11–12, 42, 62, 115–16, 205
Mélenchon, J.-L., 62
mental representations, 160
Merkel, A., 54
Merriam Webster (MW), 168–9
MetaNet Metaphor Wiki (MMW), 167, 172, 176
metaphor, 6, 9–10, 18–19, 66, 68, 74–5, 147, 149–50, 153, 155, 157–60, 162, 167, 170–3, 175, 177, 180, 182, 187–90, 194–201, 206; *see also* Conceptual Metaphor Theory (CMT), Critical Metaphor Analysis (CMA)
  BODY PARTS, 152
  BUILDING, 152
  collocations, 147, 156, 158
  conceptual metaphor, 188
  conceptualisation, 154, 159
  extended metaphor *see* allegory
  FAMILY, 152
  GREENHOUSE, 194–6
  HOMELAND, 153, 158
  HOUSE ON FIRE, 196–7, 199, 201
  JOURNEY, 195
  LIFE IS PLAYING A GAME, 170, 172
  mapping, 149, 152, 188, 192

metaphor (*cont.*)
    metaphor scenario, 6, 188, 190
        NATION-AS-BUILDING, 152–3
        SOCIETY AS A PLAYGROUND, 167, 170, 172–3, 182
        TENANCY, 193, 194
        THE EARTH AS A GREENHOUSE, 189
        THE EARTH AS A HOME, 192, 193
        THE EARTH AS A HOUSE (ON FIRE), 187–8, 191–2, 200–1
        THE EARTH AS A SHARED CLEAN HOME, 192
        THE ECOSYSTEM AS A SICK BODY, 189
        THE NATION IS A MOTHER/FATHER, 154, 157
        THE NATION IS A PERSON, 150
Metaphor Identification Procedure, 151, 191
metonymy, 9, 18, 147, 150, 153, 155, 158–60, 162, 168, 182
    CAUSE FOR EFFECT, 168, 182–3
    conceptualisation, 154–5
    domain, 155
    FAITH FOR PERSON, 160
    GOVERNMENT FOR PRESIDENT/MINISTERS, 154
    matrix domain, 150
    metonymic mappings, 151–2
    REBELLION FOR REBELS, 155
    TERRORISM FOR TERRORISTS, 155
Mexico, 53
Ministry of Education (MOE), 27, 30–1, 35–6
minorities, 176
misinformation, 104, 207
MMW *see* MetaNet Metaphor Wiki
modality, 48, 128
    deontic, 51, 56, 95–7
    epistemic, 83, 108
    modal auxiliaries, 46, 49–53, 55–6, 88
    modals, 78, 80, 82, 86–7, 94
    semi-modals, 88
    sensory modality, 128
    see also epistemic stance
mode, 128–30
Monoconc, 91
moral evaluation, 13–15, 17–18, 106, 206; *see also* legitimisation

moral judgement *see* moral evaluation
moral outrage, 15, 106, 108, 118–19; *see also* legitimisation
moral outrage porn *see* moral outrage
multimodal *see* multimodality
multimodality, 10, 35–6, 123–6, 128–9, 134, 139, 141
    multimodal blend, 139
Musolff, A., 9, 150, 190, 201
MW *see* Merriam Webster
mythopoesis, 13–15, 18, 106; *see also* legitimisation
    cautionary tale, 14–15, 18, 104
    moral tale, 14–15

nation, 42, 44, 152–7, 195
nationalism, 66–7, 71, 74
news, 103
Nguyen, C. T., 12, 15, 106, 108, 119
Niger, 148, 154–7
Nuyts, J., 81

OED *see* Oxford English Dictionary
oppositional futures, 14
order scenario, 82
Oxford English Dictionary (OED), 168–9, 174, 176

parallelism, 159, 163
parliament, 64
Participative Web 2.0, 103, 118
Party-State, 26, 30, 37
patriotism, 35
Patrona, M., 11–12
peace, 42
peacekeeping, 53
People's Education Press, 31
People's Party (PP), 66, 70, 73
People's Republic of China (PRC) *see* China
personal pronoun, 51–2
platforms, 104, 109, 118–19; *see also* media
Podemos, 63, 67, 71–2, 75
politeness, 54
politics
    advertising, 119, 124–5
    identity politics, 182
    political genre, 9

Index

political philosophy, 3
political socialisation, 25–7, 37
populis*, 61–6, 68–70, 72, 74–5
populism, 1, 17, 60, 63, 66–75, 107–8
  populist party, 1, 62–3
  see also populis*
populist *see* populism
power, 3, 5, 7, 27, 108, 110, 161, 177–80, 182; *see also* coercion
PP *see* People's Party
pragmatic function *see* pragmatics
pragmatics, 17, 61, 64, 75, 124, 172
PRC *see* China
presentician, 207
privileged futures, 14
proposition, 82–3
proximisation *see* Proximization Theory
Proximization Theory, 6, 15–16, 210
PSOE *see* Spanish Socialist Workers' Party

race, 19, 176–7, 179
rationalisation, 13–15, 17, 106; *see also* legitimisation
rationality *see* rationalisation
reality, 78, 81–2, 84–5, 97, 151, 158, 207
referendum, 68, 71, 75, 88
Reisigl, M., 28–9, 43
Renmin Ribao, 30
representation, 5, 60
Reyes, A., 12–15
rhetoric, 6, 18, 54, 60, 171
  framing devices, 30
  repetitions, 163
  rhetorical questions, 112
  strategy, 155, 158
RN *see* Le Rassemblement national
Ruiz de Mendoza, F. J., 150

salience, 80
Schmidt, K. H., 134
security, 42
self-branding, 109
Semino, E., 171–3
semiotics, 6, 10, 123
  multisemiotic, 125–8, 134–7, 139, 141
  non-verbal semiotic resource, 131

semiotic resources, 126, 128–9, 134–5, 139, 141
Sketch Engine, 31–2, 64, 151
smoothing, 13, 42–4, 54–6, 207
social actor, 108, 114
social class, 19
social hierarchy, 177–8
social media *see* media
social movements, 180
social position, 179
social practice, 182
social status, 182
socialism
  socialist builders, 33–4, 36
  socialist cause, 33, 37
Sørensen, M. J., 11
sound, 131–2
  diegesis, 132
  non-diegetic music, 134–7, 141
  voice-over, 132, 134–5, 141
sovereign, 107
Spain, 62–3
  Congress of Deputies, 17, 63
  Spanish Socialist Workers' Party (PSOE), 66, 70, 73, 75
speech acts, 6, 86, 210
  speech-act participants, 80
  see also illocutionary act, illocutionary force
stance, 78–9, 81
  affect, 79
  categories, 91
  epistemicity, 79–80, 83
  evaluation, 79
  identity, 90
  moral stance, 108–9
  stancetaking, 89
  see also effective stance, epistemic stance
statistical data, 130
Stavrakakis, Y., 67
strategic interaction, 105–6, 108–9
subjectivity, 80–1
syntax, 130
  dislocation, 159, 163
  sentence structures, 153

teaching materials, 28, 37
textbook, 26, 29, 31, 35–6

textometric approach, 42–3
　specificity scores, 46
　Textometry (TXM), 45–6
Thatcher, M., 193–4, 200
The Republicans (LR), 66
theta-role, 150, 153–4, 162
Thornborrow, J., 11–12, 61
Thunberg, G., 187–9, 191, 196–7, 200–1
Traoré, D., 152, 154, 157
Trifonov, S., 105, 107, 111, 114–18
Trump, D., 18, 124–6, 137, 141, 179–83
TrUMPo, 63–4
Turkey, 54
Turner, M., 134
Twitter, 191, 206–7

UK *see* United Kingdom
UN *see* United Nations
Unger, J. W., 10
United Kingdom (UK), 79, 88–9, 190
United Nations (UN), 17, 42–6, 48, 50–6, 125
United States of America (USA), 18, 53, 175, 195, 201, 208, 210
USA *see* United States of America

values, 25
van Dijk, T. A., 5–6, 149
van Leeuwen, T., 12–15, 106
Vickers, E., 26
voices of expertise, 13, 106; *see also* legitimisation
volition, 87, 151
Vox, 63, 66
vulnerable groups, 176, 179

Weber, M., 3
Williams, B., 12, 15, 106, 108
Wodak, R., 10, 28–9, 43
women
　UN Women, 45, 52
　violence against women, 42–6, 48, 50, 52, 55–6

Xi Jinping, 26–7, 29–30, 33, 36–7
　Xi Jinping Corpus, 30–2, 34, 36
　Xi Jinping Thought, 28, 31, 35
Xinhua, 30, 33

Yellow Vests, 62
Young Pioneers, 36

EU representative:
Easy Access System Europe
Mustamäe tee 50, 10621 Tallinn, Estonia
Gpsr.requests@easproject.com

www.ingramcontent.com/pod-product-compliance
Lightning Source LLC
Chambersburg PA
CBHW051122160426
43195CB00014B/2297